# THE HONOR STUDENT AT Magic High School

Art ◉
**Yu Mori**
Original Story ◉
**Tsutomu Sato**
Character design ●
Kana Ishida

# 5

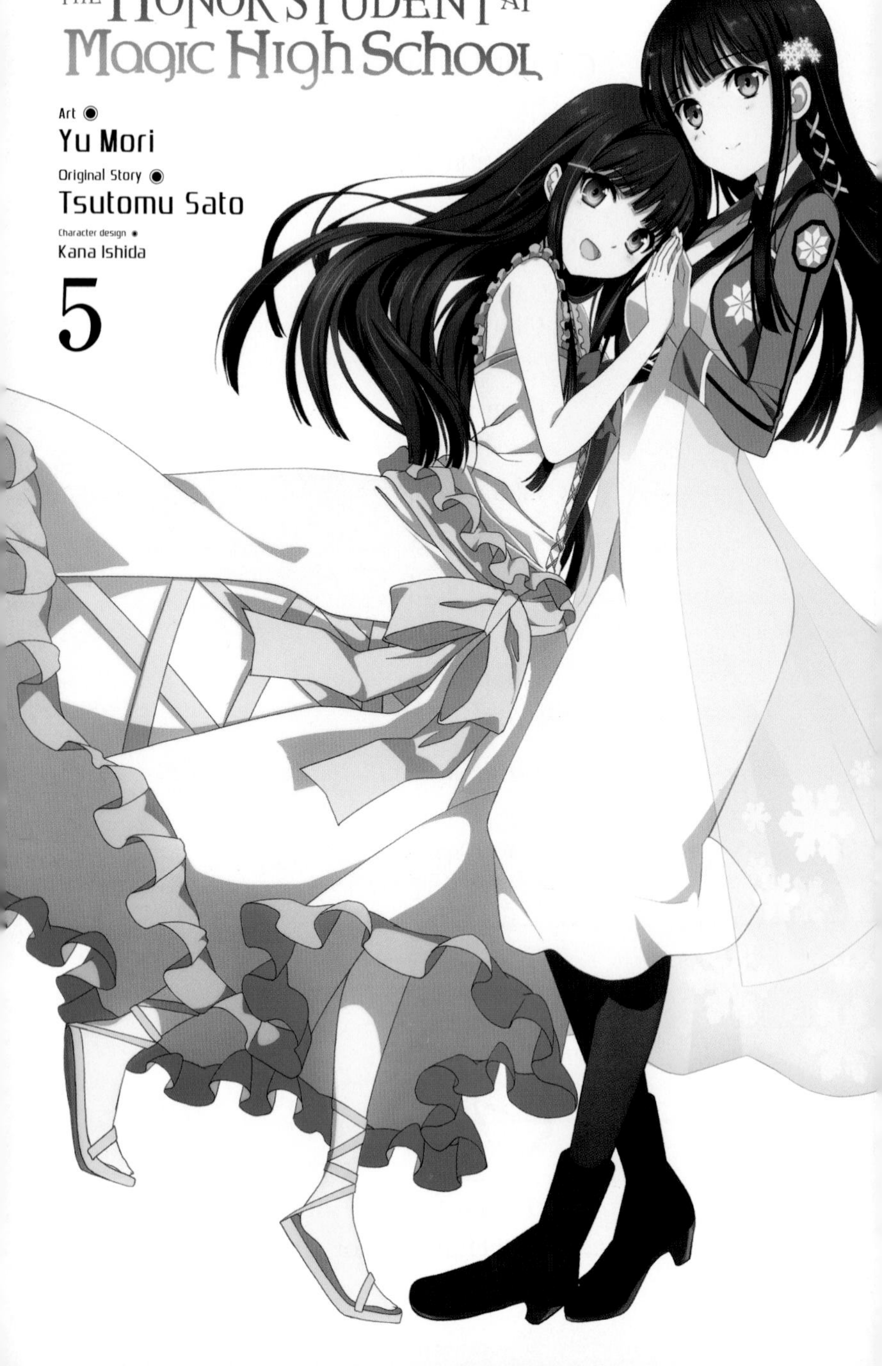

# CONTENTS

The Honor Student
at Magic High School

# CHAPTER 24

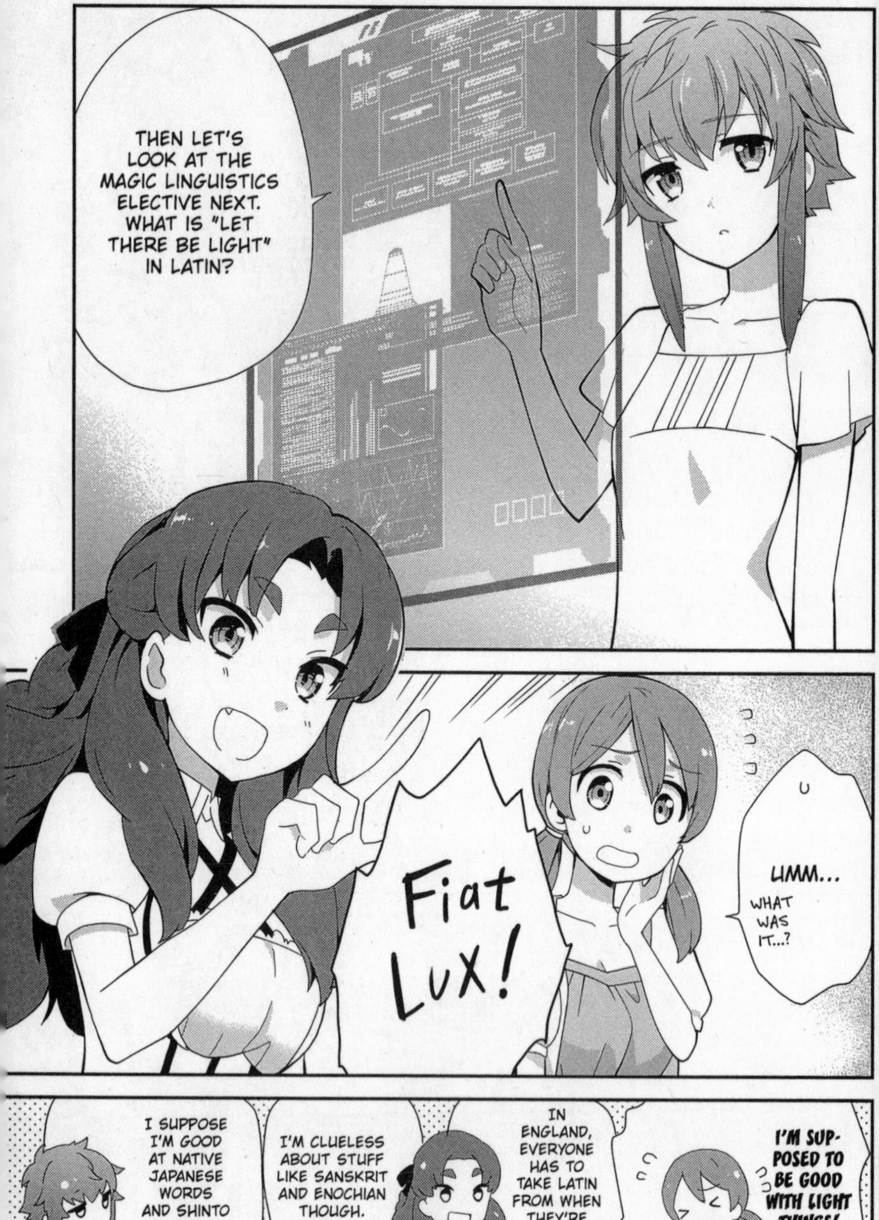
THEN LET'S LOOK AT THE MAGIC LINGUISTICS ELECTIVE NEXT. WHAT IS "LET THERE BE LIGHT" IN LATIN?
UMM... WHAT WAS IT...?
Fiat Lux!
I'M SUP-POSED TO BE GOOD WITH LIGHT THINGS!
IN ENGLAND, EVERYONE HAS TO TAKE LATIN FROM WHEN THEY'RE LITTLE.
I'M CLUELESS ABOUT STUFF LIKE SANSKRIT AND ENOCHIAN THOUGH.
I SUPPOSE I'M GOOD AT NATIVE JAPANESE WORDS AND SHINTO PRAYERS.

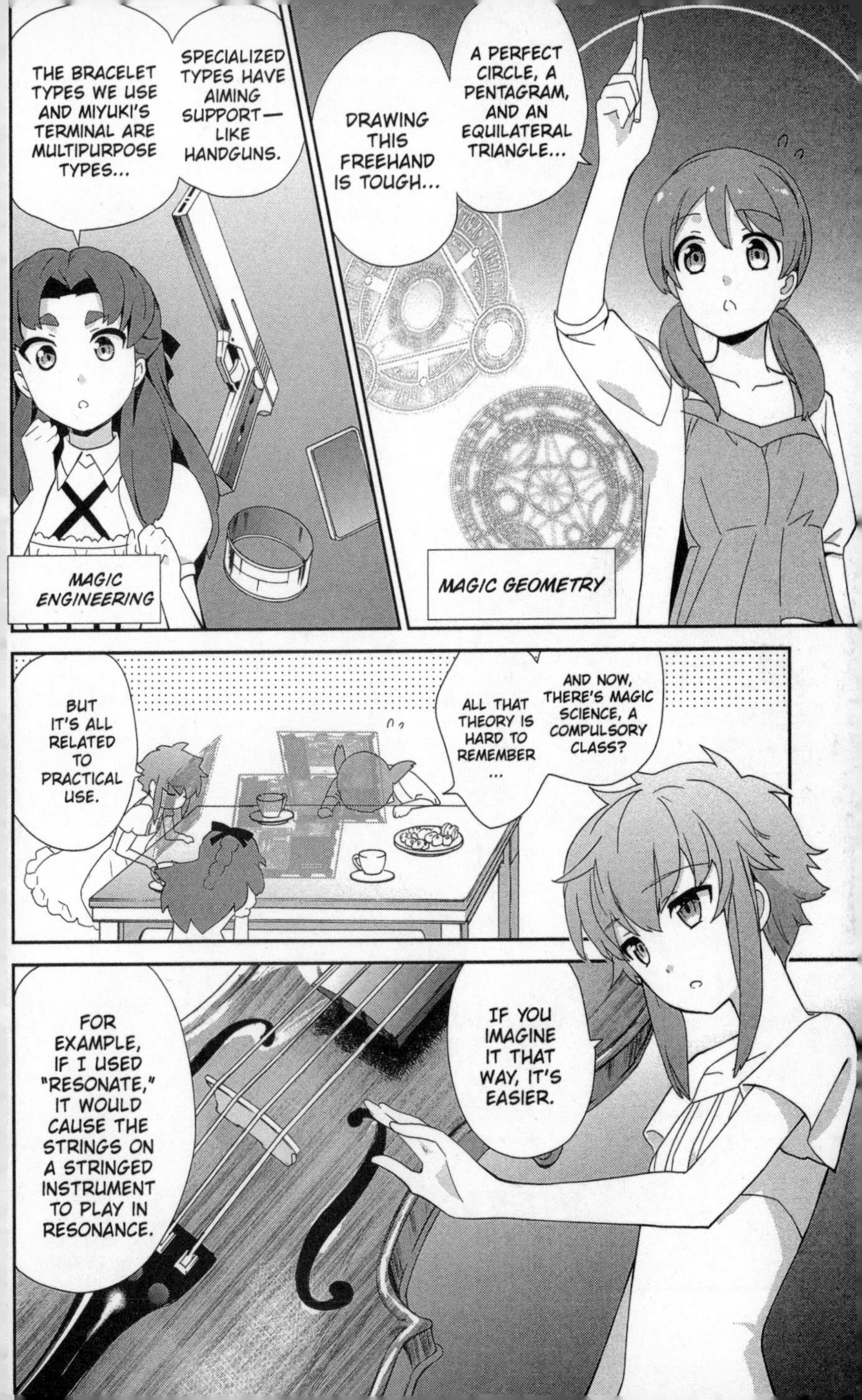
A PERFECT CIRCLE, A PENTAGRAM, AND AN EQUILATERAL TRIANGLE...
DRAWING THIS FREEHAND IS TOUGH...
MAGIC GEOMETRY
SPECIALIZED TYPES HAVE AIMING SUPPORT—LIKE HANDGUNS.
THE BRACELET TYPES WE USE AND MIYUKI'S TERMINAL ARE MULTIPURPOSE TYPES...
MAGIC ENGINEERING
AND NOW, THERE'S MAGIC SCIENCE, A COMPULSORY CLASS?
ALL THAT THEORY IS HARD TO REMEMBER ...
BUT IT'S ALL RELATED TO PRACTICAL USE.
FOR EXAMPLE, IF I USED "RESONATE," IT WOULD CAUSE THE STRINGS ON A STRINGED INSTRUMENT TO PLAY IN RESONANCE.
IF YOU IMAGINE IT THAT WAY, IT'S EASIER.

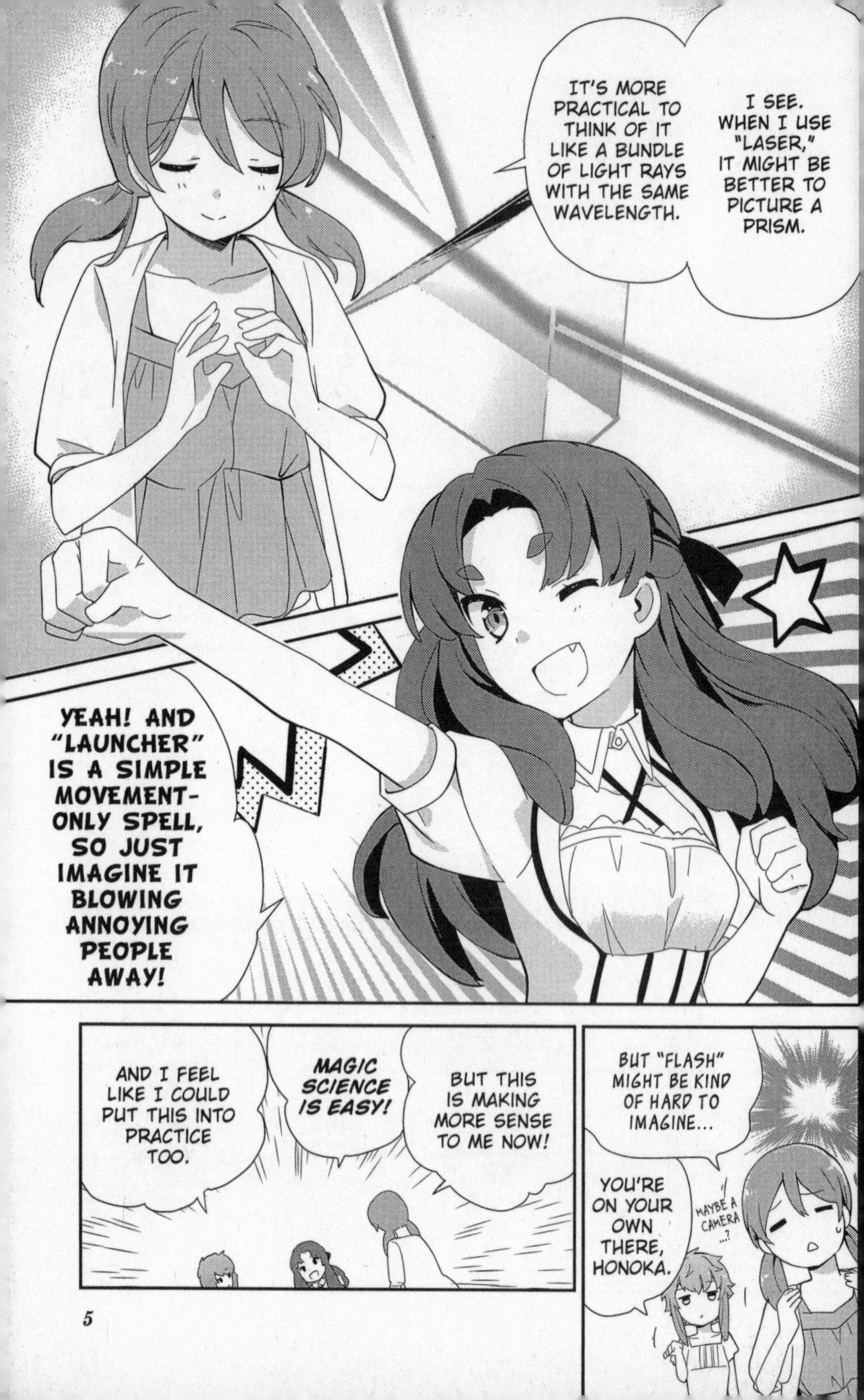
I SEE. WHEN I USE "LASER," IT MIGHT BE BETTER TO PICTURE A PRISM.
IT'S MORE PRACTICAL TO THINK OF IT LIKE A BUNDLE OF LIGHT RAYS WITH THE SAME WAVELENGTH.
YEAH! AND "LAUNCHER" IS A SIMPLE MOVEMENT-ONLY SPELL, SO JUST IMAGINE IT BLOWING ANNOYING PEOPLE AWAY!
BUT "FLASH" MIGHT BE KIND OF HARD TO IMAGINE...
MAYBE A CAMERA ...?
YOU'RE ON YOUR OWN THERE, HONOKA.
BUT THIS IS MAKING MORE SENSE TO ME NOW!
MAGIC SCIENCE IS EASY!
AND I FEEL LIKE I COULD PUT THIS INTO PRACTICE TOO.

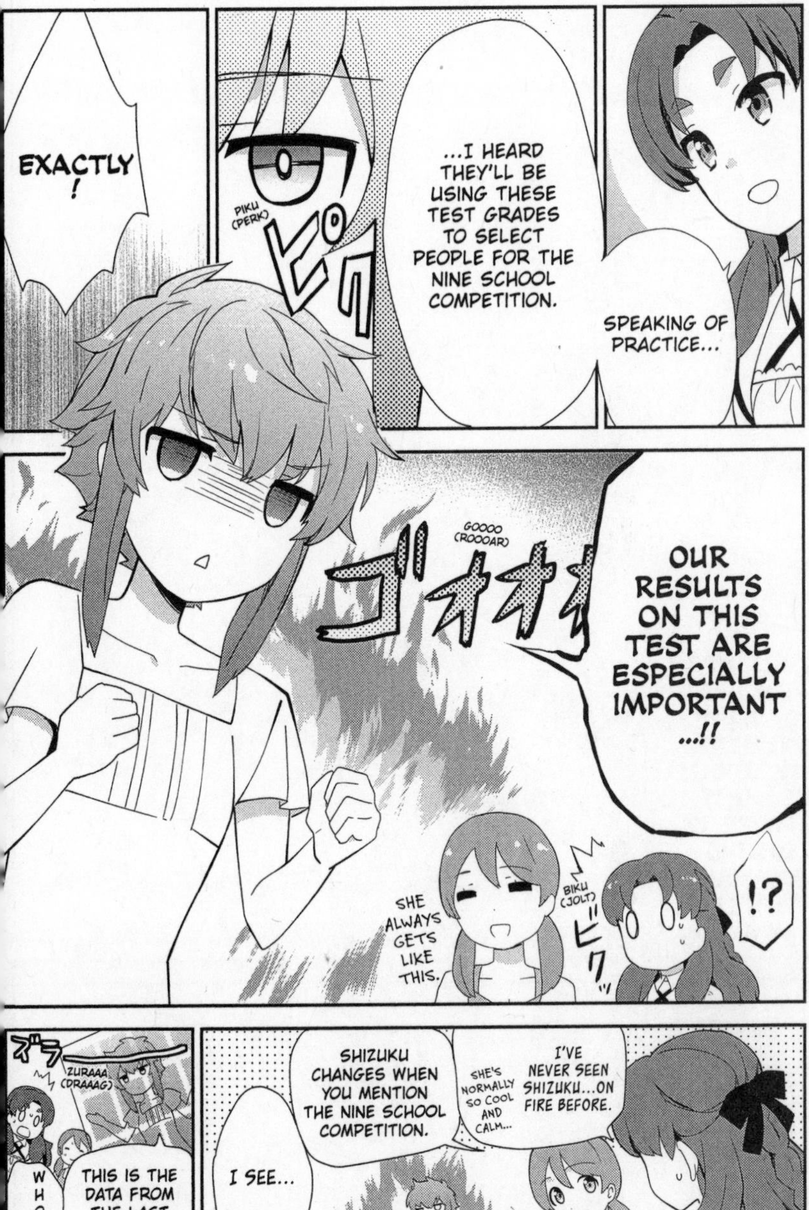
SPEAKING OF PRACTICE...
...I HEARD THEY'LL BE USING THESE TEST GRADES TO SELECT PEOPLE FOR THE NINE SCHOOL COMPETITION.
PIKU (PERK)
EXACTLY!
OUR RESULTS ON THIS TEST ARE ESPECIALLY IMPORTANT ...!!
GOOOO (ROOOAR)
!?
BIKU (JOLT)
SHE ALWAYS GETS LIKE THIS.
I'VE NEVER SEEN SHIZUKU...ON FIRE BEFORE.
SHE'S NORMALLY SO COOL AND CALM...
SHIZUKU CHANGES WHEN YOU MENTION THE NINE SCHOOL COMPETITION.
I SEE...
ZURAAA (DRAAAG)
WHOA!
THIS IS THE DATA FROM THE LAST TEN YEARS.

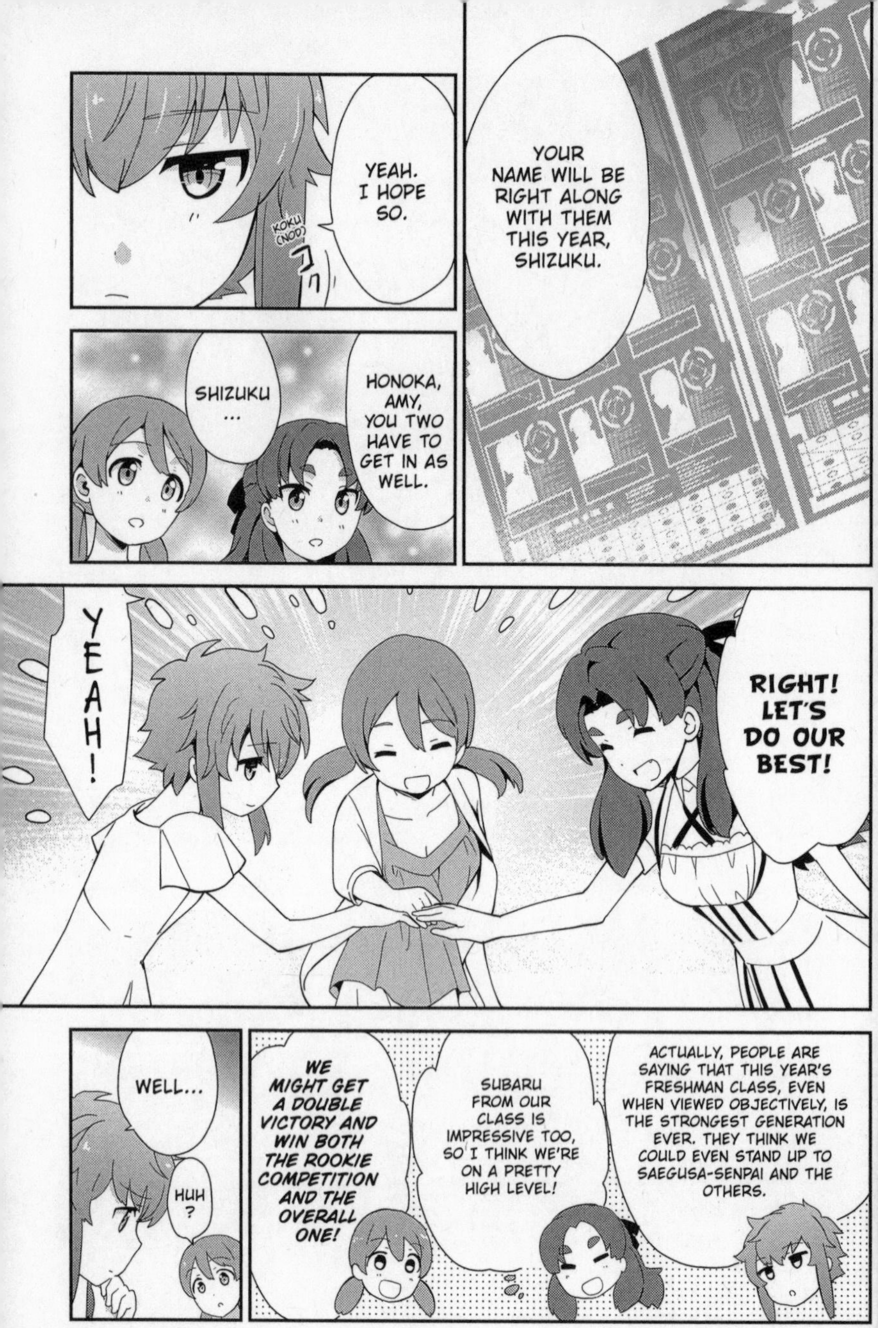
YOUR NAME WILL BE RIGHT ALONG WITH THEM THIS YEAR, SHIZUKU.
YEAH. I HOPE SO.
KOKU (NOD)
HONOKA, AMY, YOU TWO HAVE TO GET IN AS WELL.
SHIZUKU ...
RIGHT! LET'S DO OUR BEST!
YEAH!
ACTUALLY, PEOPLE ARE SAYING THAT THIS YEAR'S FRESHMAN CLASS, EVEN WHEN VIEWED OBJECTIVELY, IS THE STRONGEST GENERATION EVER. THEY THINK WE COULD EVEN STAND UP TO SAEGUSA-SENPAI AND THE OTHERS.
SUBARU FROM OUR CLASS IS IMPRESSIVE TOO, SO I THINK WE'RE ON A PRETTY HIGH LEVEL!
WE MIGHT GET A DOUBLE VICTORY AND WIN BOTH THE ROOKIE COMPETITION AND THE OVERALL ONE!
WELL...
HUH?

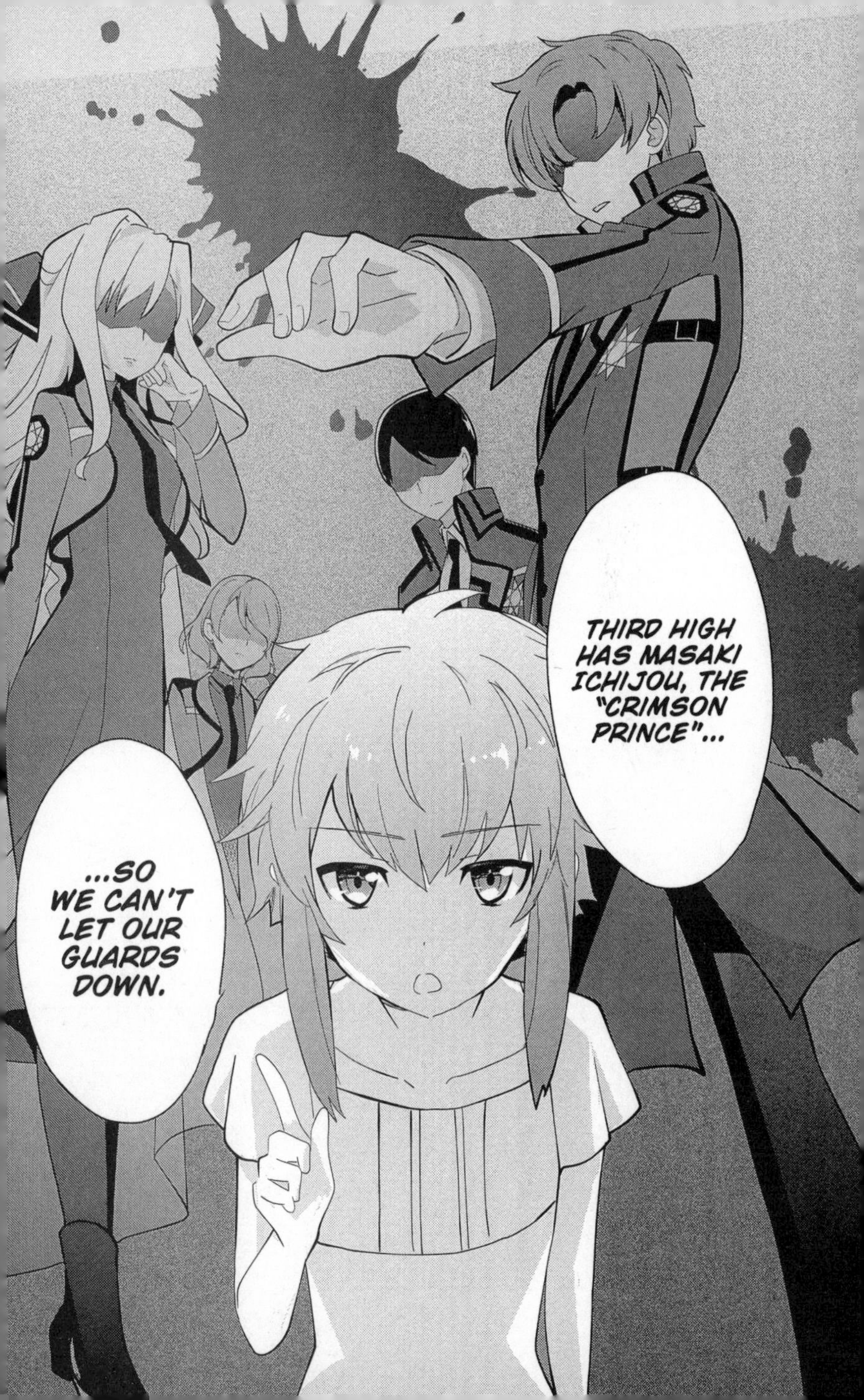
THIRD HIGH HAS MASAKI ICHIJOU, THE "CRIMSON PRINCE"...
...SO WE CAN'T LET OUR GUARDS DOWN.

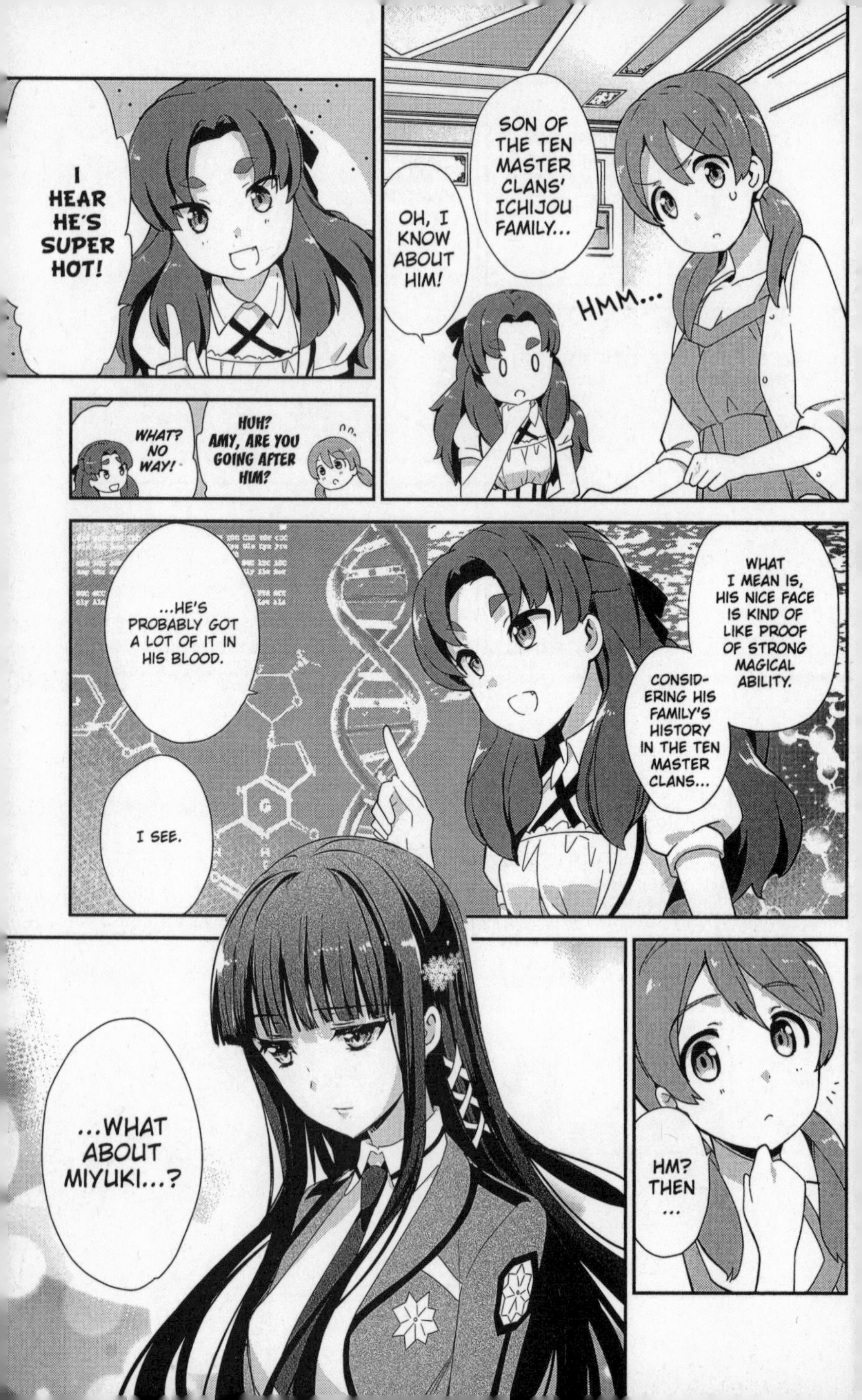
SON OF THE TEN MASTER CLANS' ICHIJOU FAMILY...
OH, I KNOW ABOUT HIM!
HMM...
I HEAR HE'S SUPER HOT!
HUH? AMY, ARE YOU GOING AFTER HIM?
WHAT? NO WAY!
WHAT I MEAN IS, HIS NICE FACE IS KIND OF LIKE PROOF OF STRONG MAGICAL ABILITY.
CONSID-ERING HIS FAMILY'S HISTORY IN THE TEN MASTER CLANS...
...HE'S PROBABLY GOT A LOT OF IT IN HIS BLOOD.
I SEE.
HM? THEN...
...WHAT ABOUT MIYUKI...?

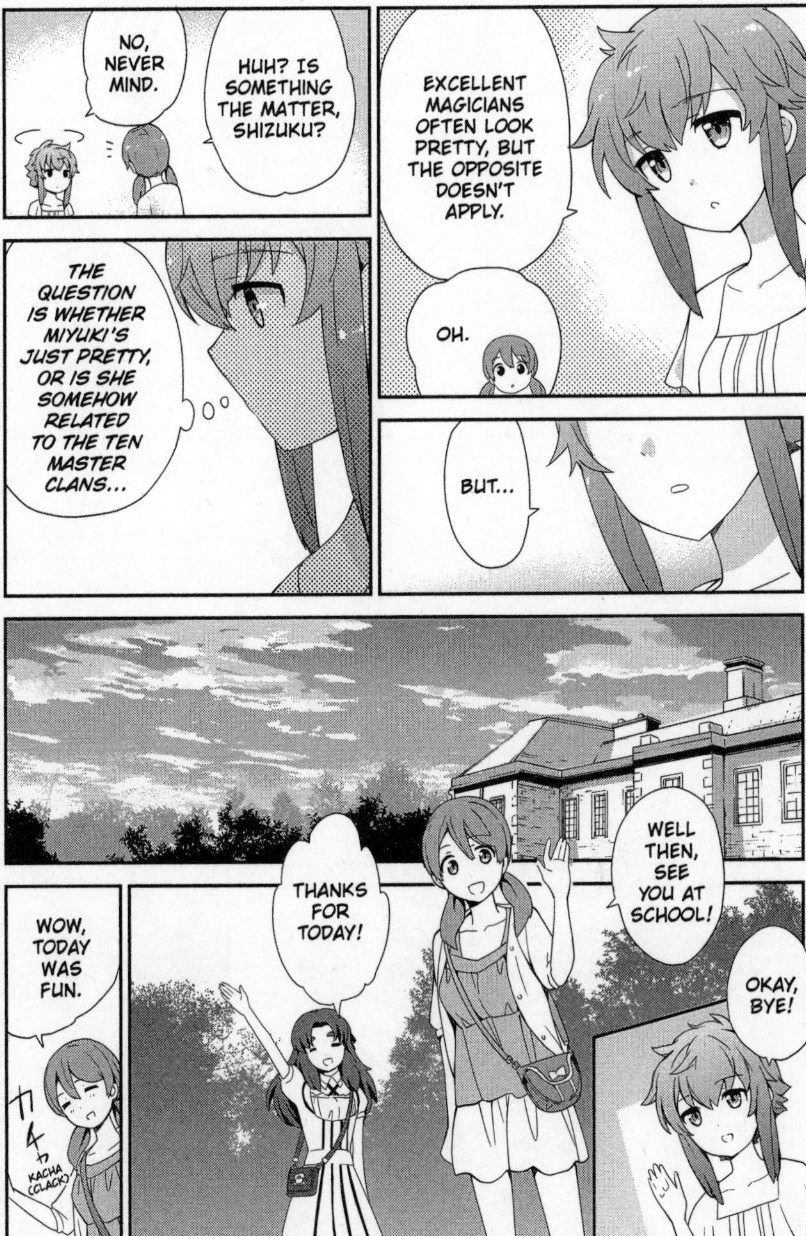
EXCELLENT MAGICIANS OFTEN LOOK PRETTY, BUT THE OPPOSITE DOESN'T APPLY.
OH.
HUH? IS SOMETHING THE MATTER, SHIZUKU?
NO, NEVER MIND.
BUT...
THE QUESTION IS WHETHER MIYUKI'S JUST PRETTY, OR IS SHE SOMEHOW RELATED TO THE TEN MASTER CLANS...
WELL THEN, SEE YOU AT SCHOOL!
THANKS FOR TODAY!
OKAY, BYE!
WOW, TODAY WAS FUN.
カチャ
KACHA (CLACK)

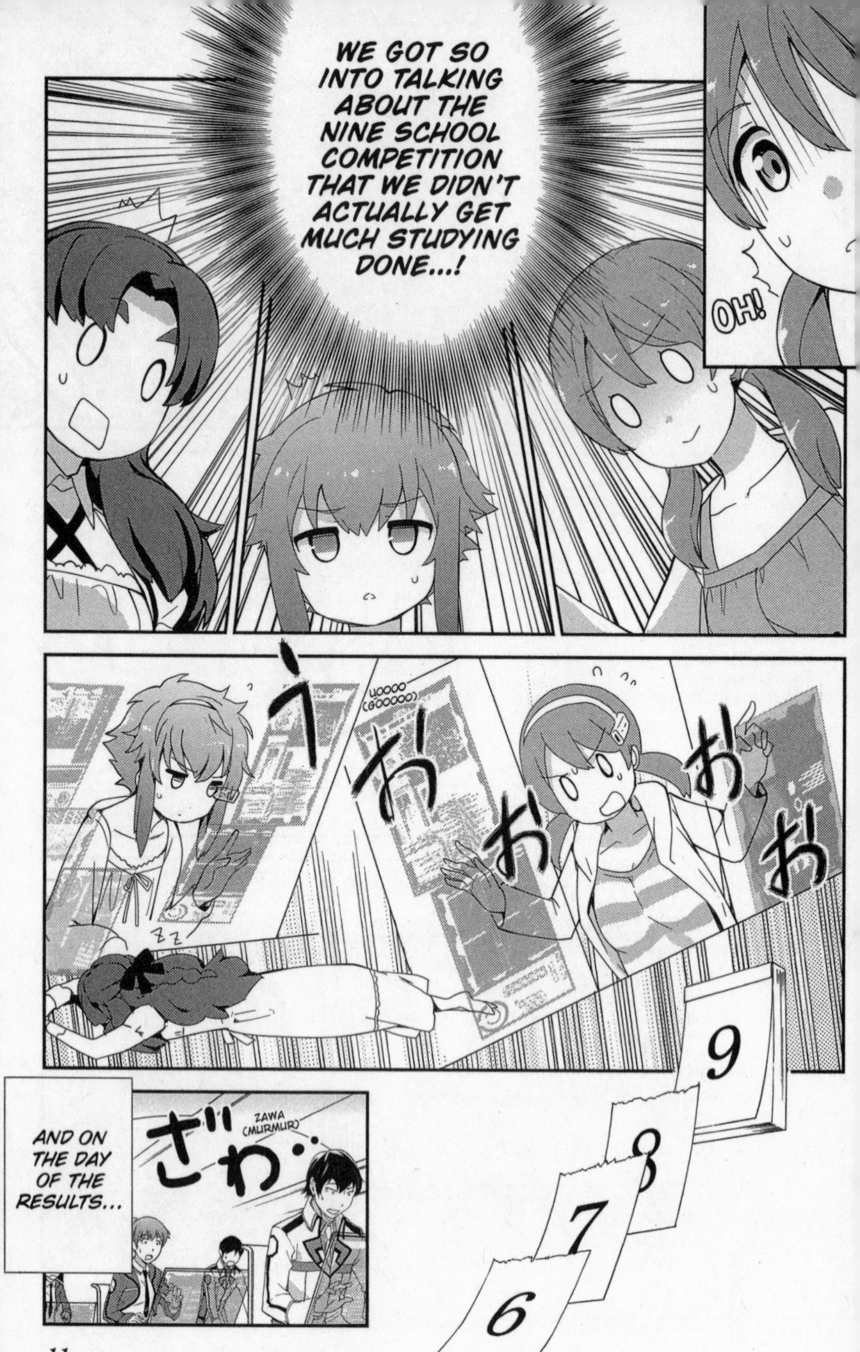
OH!
WE GOT SO INTO TALKING ABOUT THE NINE SCHOOL COMPETITION THAT WE DIDN'T ACTUALLY GET MUCH STUDYING DONE...!
うおおおお
UOOOO (GOOOOO)
9
8
7
6
AND ON THE DAY OF THE RESULTS...
ざわ
ZAWA (MURMUR)

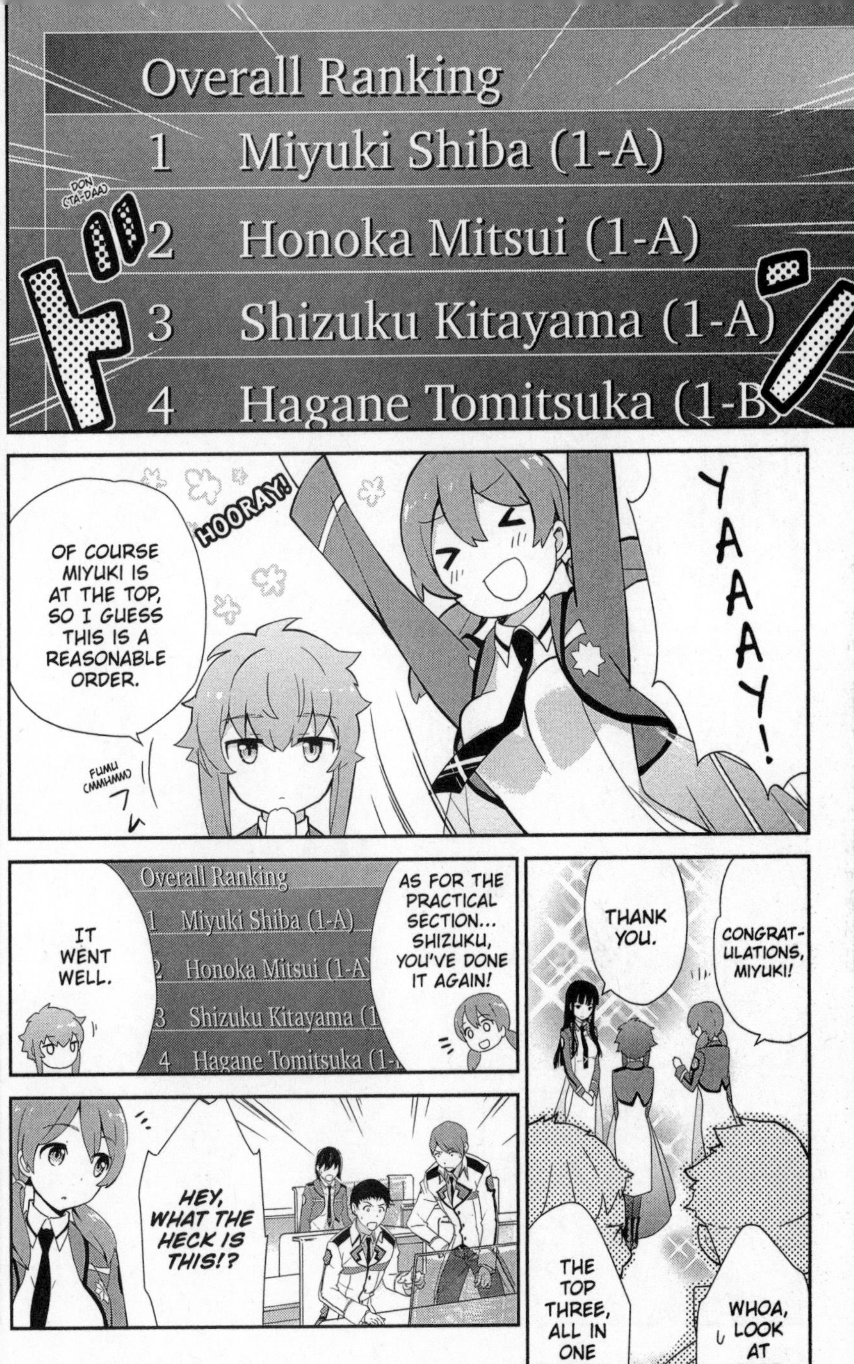
Overall Ranking
1 Miyuki Shiba (1-A)
2 Honoka Mitsui (1-A)
3 Shizuku Kitayama (1-A)
4 Hagane Tomitsuka (1-B)
DON (TA-DAA)
YAAAAY!
HOORAY!
OF COURSE MIYUKI IS AT THE TOP, SO I GUESS THIS IS A REASONABLE ORDER.
FUMU (MMHMM)
CONGRAT-ULATIONS, MIYUKI!
THANK YOU.
WHOA, LOOK AT THAT.
THE TOP THREE, ALL IN ONE PLACE...
AS FOR THE PRACTICAL SECTION... SHIZUKU, YOU'VE DONE IT AGAIN!
IT WENT WELL.
HEY, WHAT THE HECK IS THIS!?

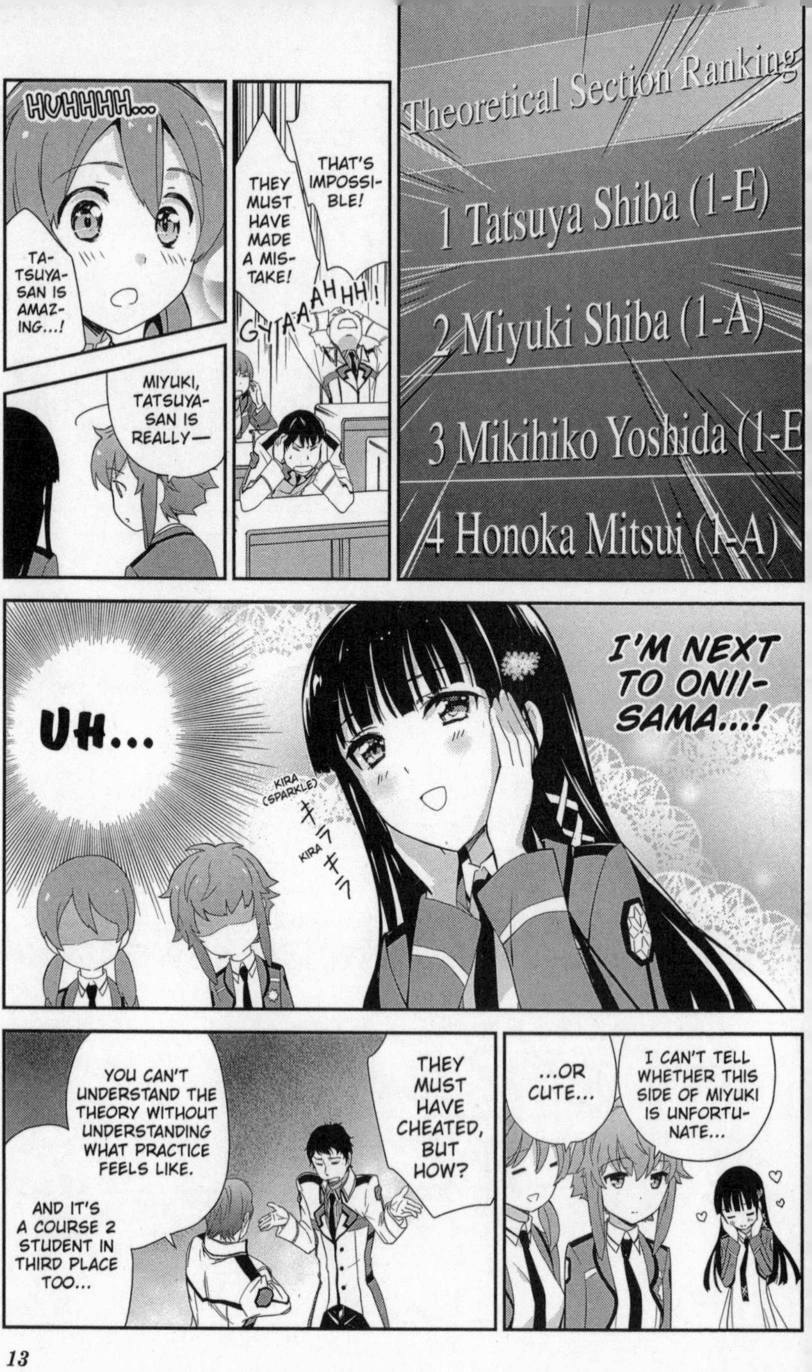
Theoretical Section Ranking
1 Tatsuya Shiba (1-E)
2 Miyuki Shiba (1-A)
3 Mikihiko Yoshida (1-E
4 Honoka Mitsui (1-A)
THAT'S IMPOSSI-BLE!
THEY MUST HAVE MADE A MIS-TAKE!
GYAAAHHH!
HUHHHH...
TA-TSUYA-SAN IS AMAZ-ING...!
MIYUKI, TATSUYA-SAN IS REALLY—
I'M NEXT TO ONII-SAMA...!
KIRA (SPARKLE)
キラ
KIRA
キラ
UH...
I CAN'T TELL WHETHER THIS SIDE OF MIYUKI IS UNFORTU-NATE...
...OR CUTE...
THEY MUST HAVE CHEATED, BUT HOW?
YOU CAN'T UNDERSTAND THE THEORY WITHOUT UNDERSTANDING WHAT PRACTICE FEELS LIKE.
AND IT'S A COURSE 2 STUDENT IN THIRD PLACE TOO...

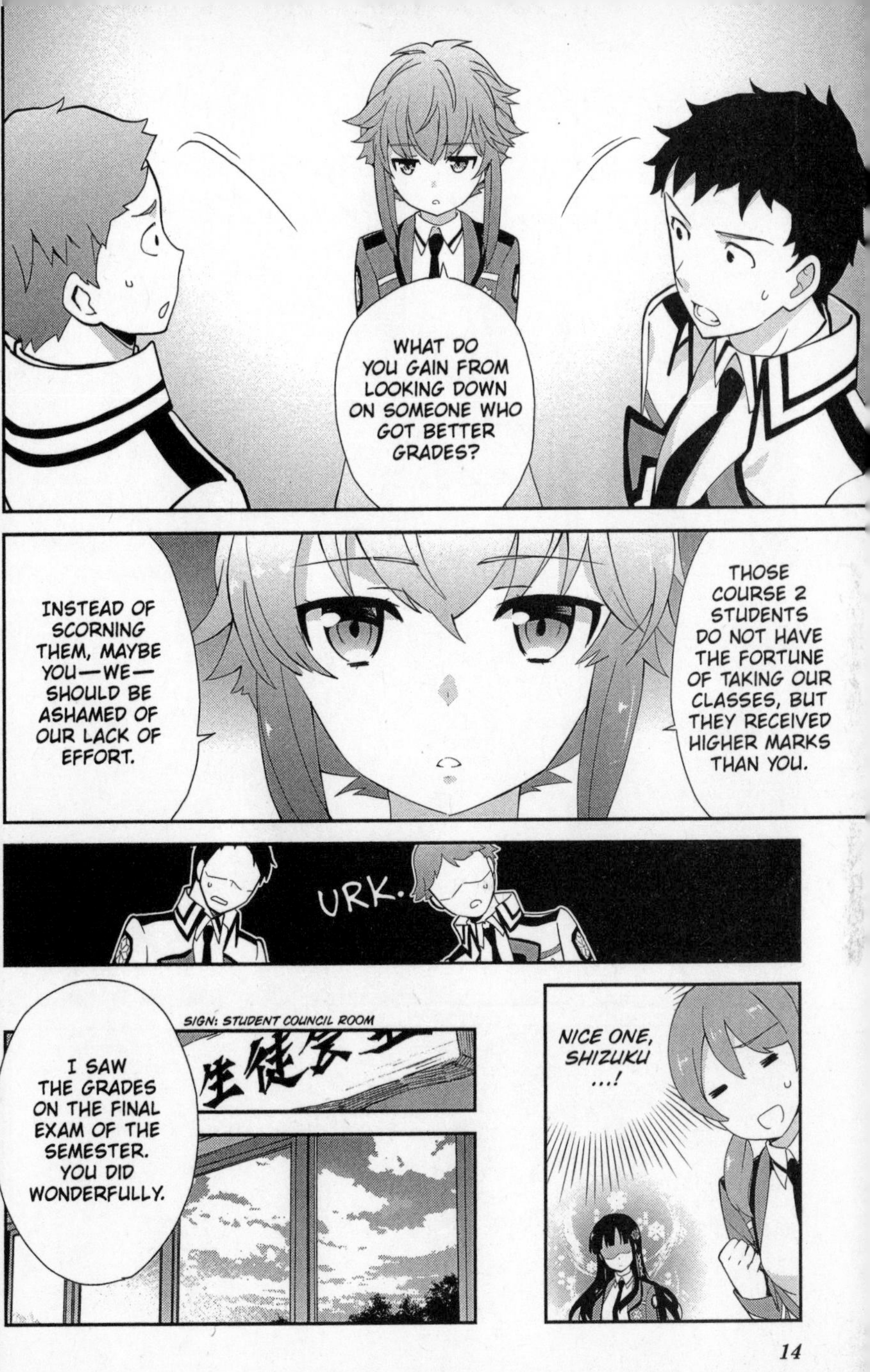
WHAT DO YOU GAIN FROM LOOKING DOWN ON SOMEONE WHO GOT BETTER GRADES?
THOSE COURSE 2 STUDENTS DO NOT HAVE THE FORTUNE OF TAKING OUR CLASSES, BUT THEY RECEIVED HIGHER MARKS THAN YOU.
INSTEAD OF SCORNING THEM, MAYBE YOU—WE—SHOULD BE ASHAMED OF OUR LACK OF EFFORT.
URK.
NICE ONE, SHIZUKU ...!
SIGN: STUDENT COUNCIL ROOM
I SAW THE GRADES ON THE FINAL EXAM OF THE SEMESTER. YOU DID WONDERFULLY.

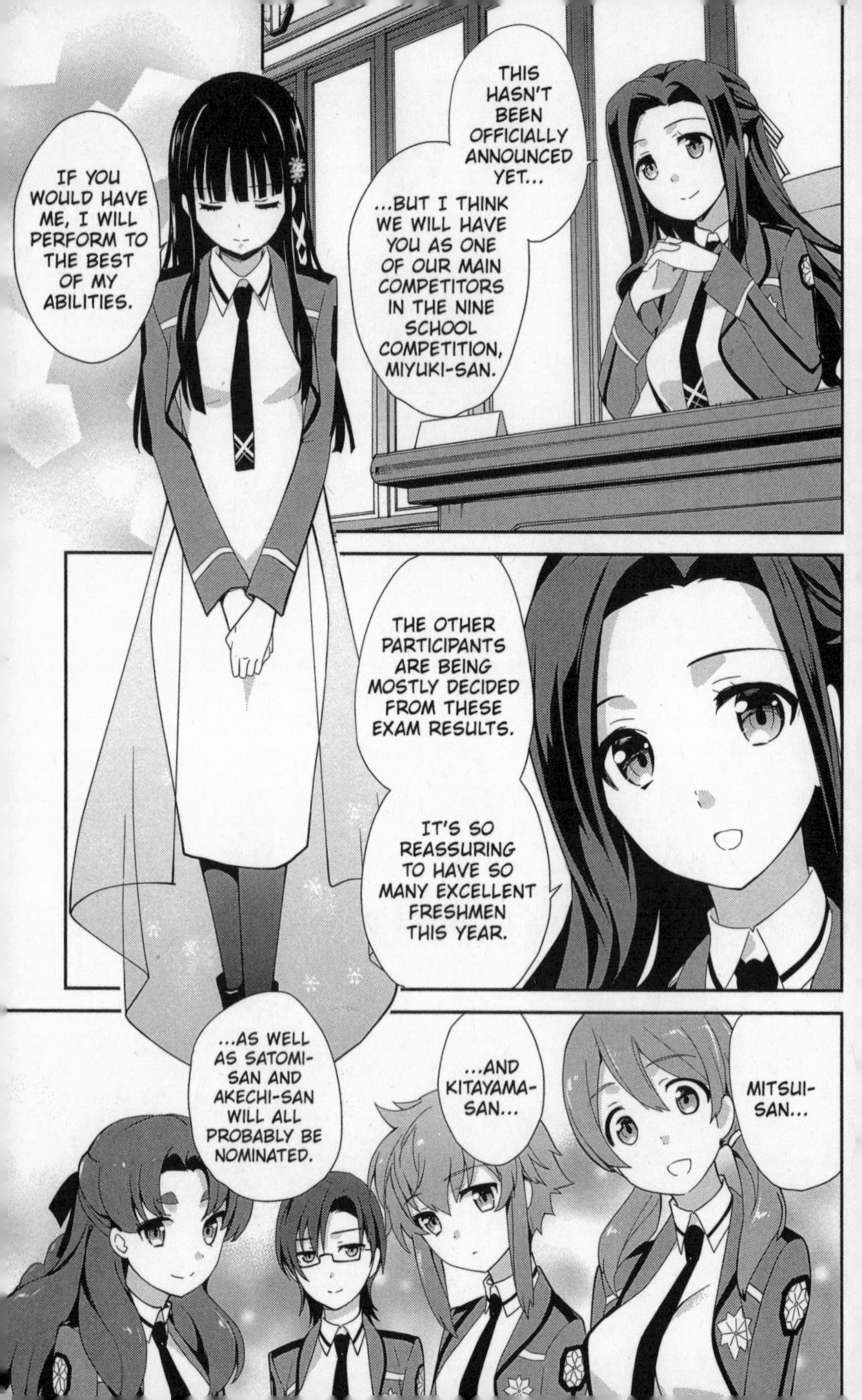
THIS HASN'T BEEN OFFICIALLY ANNOUNCED YET...
...BUT I THINK WE WILL HAVE YOU AS ONE OF OUR MAIN COMPETITORS IN THE NINE SCHOOL COMPETITION, MIYUKI-SAN.
IF YOU WOULD HAVE ME, I WILL PERFORM TO THE BEST OF MY ABILITIES.
THE OTHER PARTICIPANTS ARE BEING MOSTLY DECIDED FROM THESE EXAM RESULTS.
IT'S SO REASSURING TO HAVE SO MANY EXCELLENT FRESHMEN THIS YEAR.
MITSUI-SAN...
...AND KITAYAMA-SAN...
...AS WELL AS SATOMI-SAN AND AKECHI-SAN WILL ALL PROBABLY BE NOMINATED.

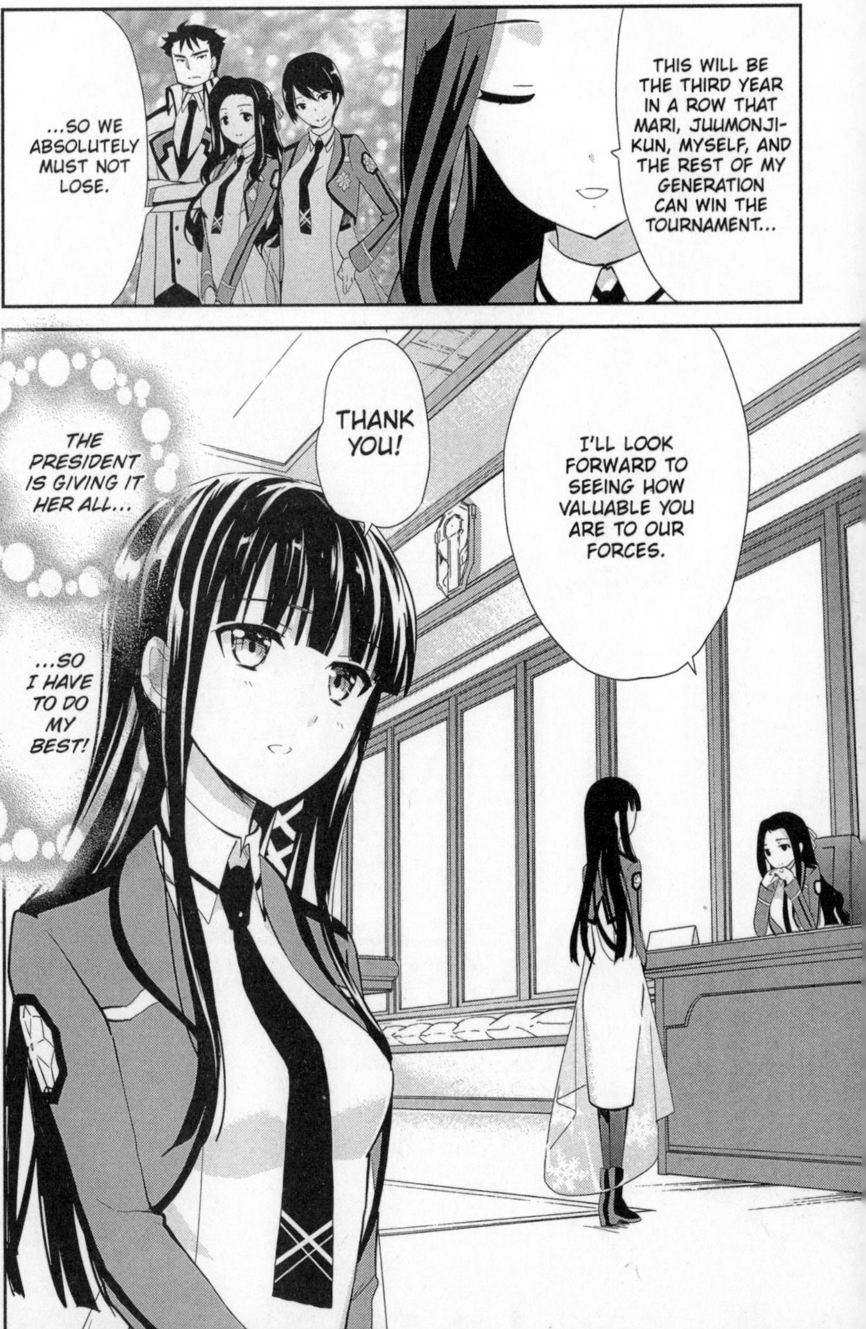
THIS WILL BE THE THIRD YEAR IN A ROW THAT MARI, JUUMONJI-KUN, MYSELF, AND THE REST OF MY GENERATION CAN WIN THE TOURNAMENT...
...SO WE ABSOLUTELY MUST NOT LOSE.
I'LL LOOK FORWARD TO SEEING HOW VALUABLE YOU ARE TO OUR FORCES.
THANK YOU!
THE PRESIDENT IS GIVING IT HER ALL...
...SO I HAVE TO DO MY BEST!

THE HONOR STUDENT AT Magic High School

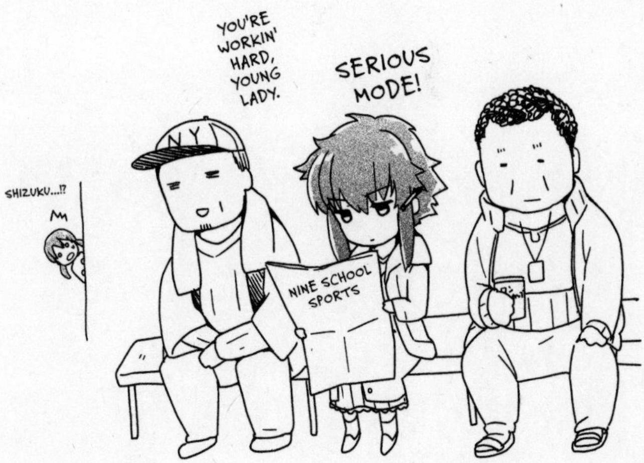
SERIOUS MODE!
YOU'RE WORKIN' HARD, YOUNG LADY.
NINE SCHOOL SPORTS
SHIZUKU...!?

CHAPTER 25

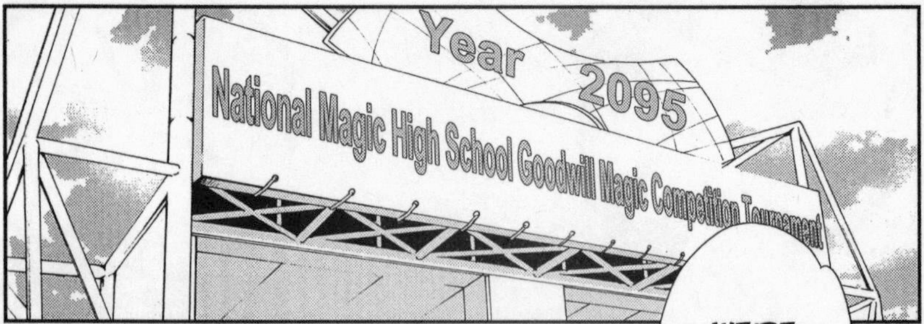
Year 2095
National Magic High School Goodwill Magic Competition Tournament

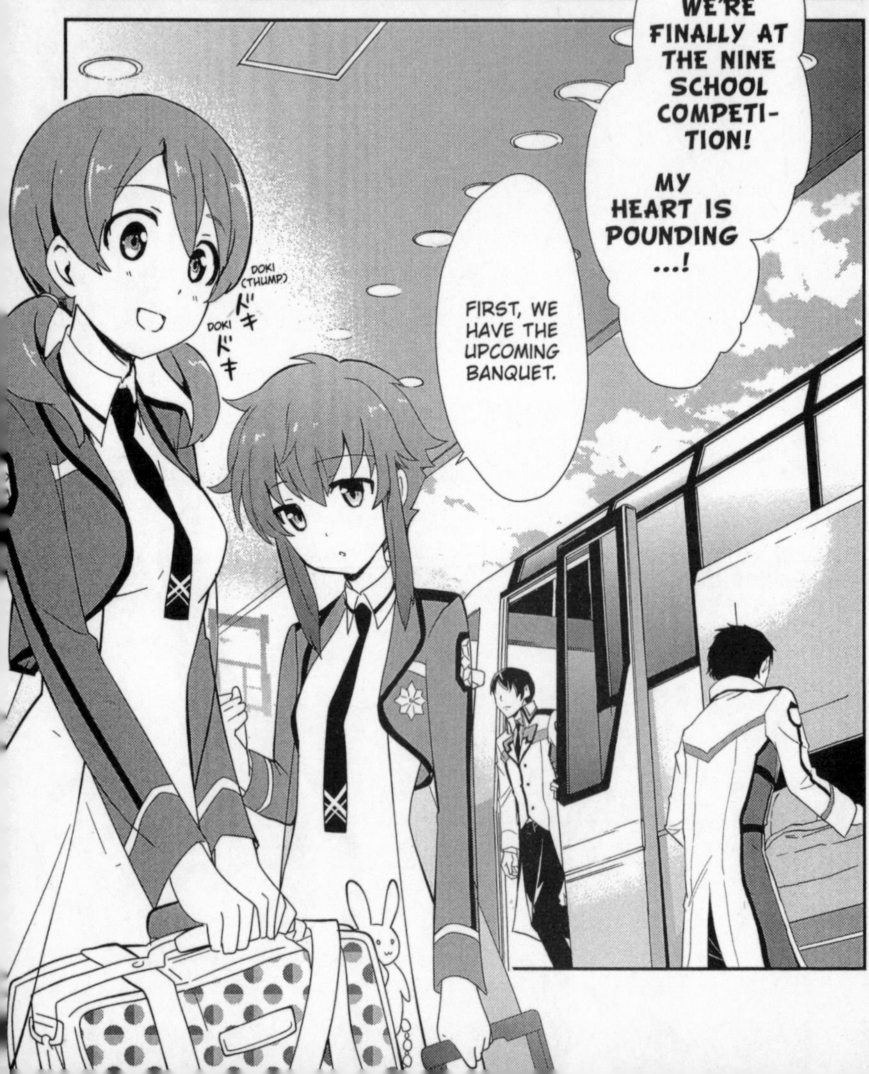
WE'RE FINALLY AT THE NINE SCHOOL COMPETITION!
MY HEART IS POUNDING ...!
FIRST, WE HAVE THE UPCOMING BANQUET.
DOKI (THUMP) ドキ
DOKI ドキ

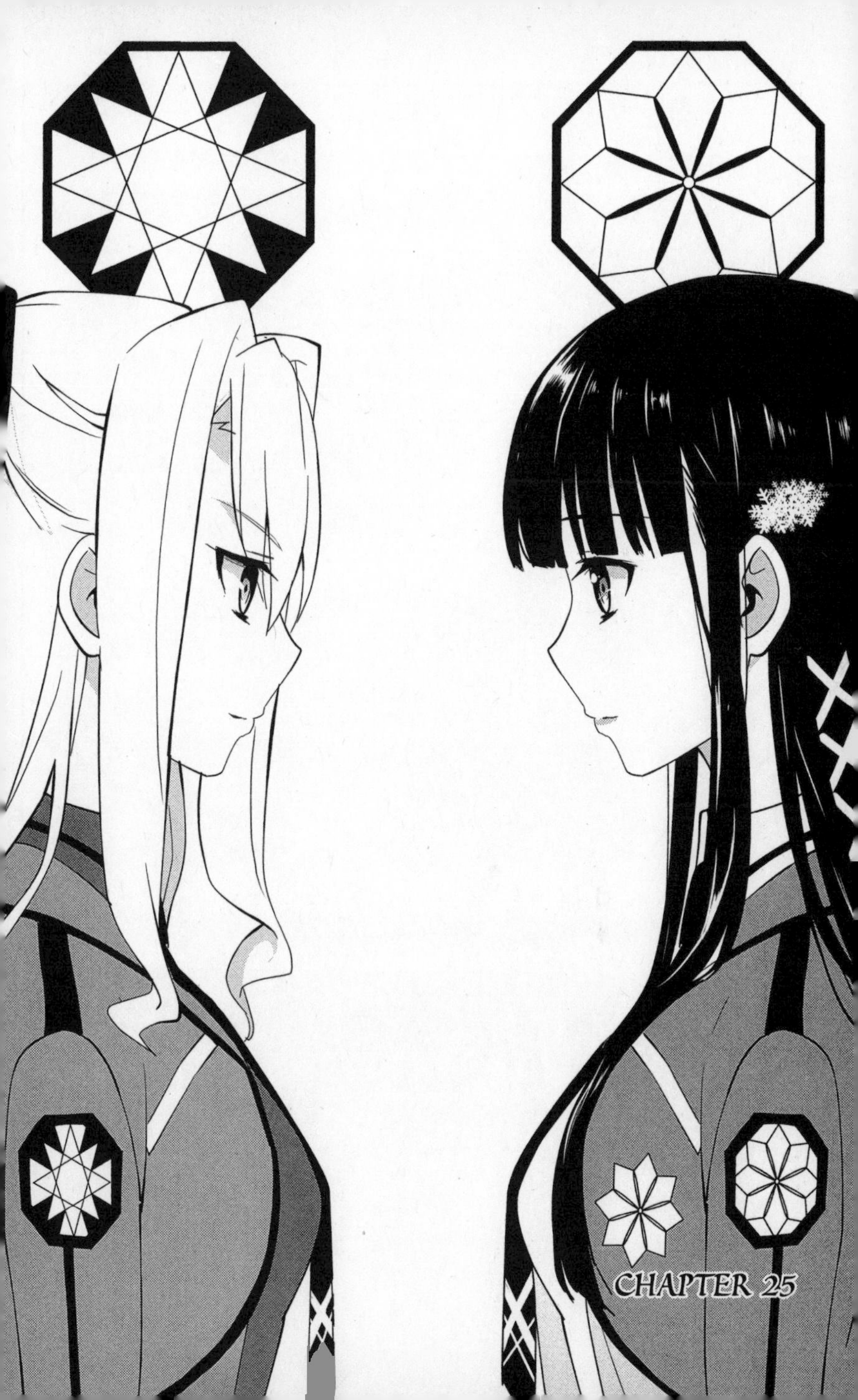
CHAPTER 25

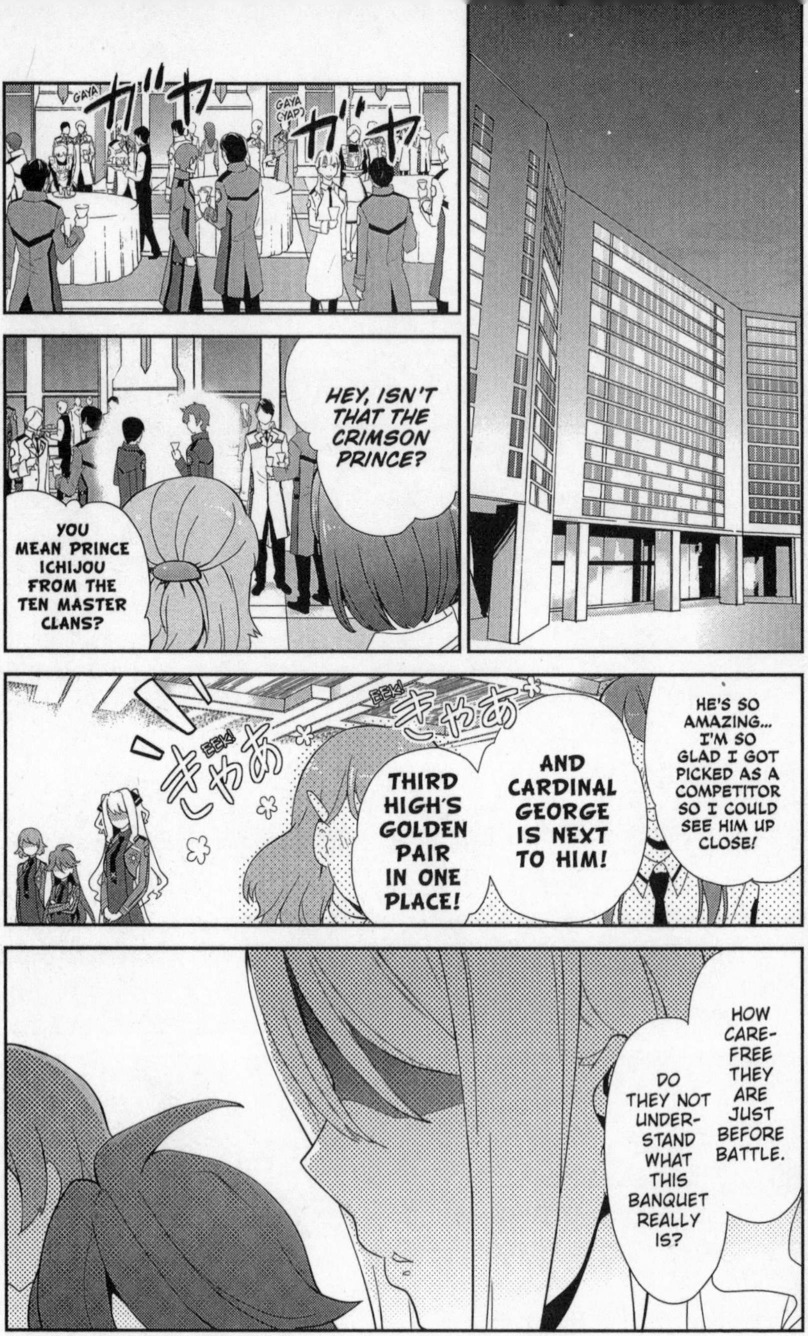
GAYA
ガヤ
GAYA (YAP)
ガヤ
HEY, ISN'T THAT THE CRIMSON PRINCE?
YOU MEAN PRINCE ICHIJOU FROM THE TEN MASTER CLANS?
HE'S SO AMAZING... I'M SO GLAD I GOT PICKED AS A COMPETITOR SO I COULD SEE HIM UP CLOSE!
EEK!
きゃあ
AND CARDINAL GEORGE IS NEXT TO HIM!
THIRD HIGH'S GOLDEN PAIR IN ONE PLACE!
EEK!
きゃあ
HOW CAREFREE THEY ARE JUST BEFORE BATTLE.
DO THEY NOT UNDERSTAND WHAT THIS BANQUET REALLY IS?

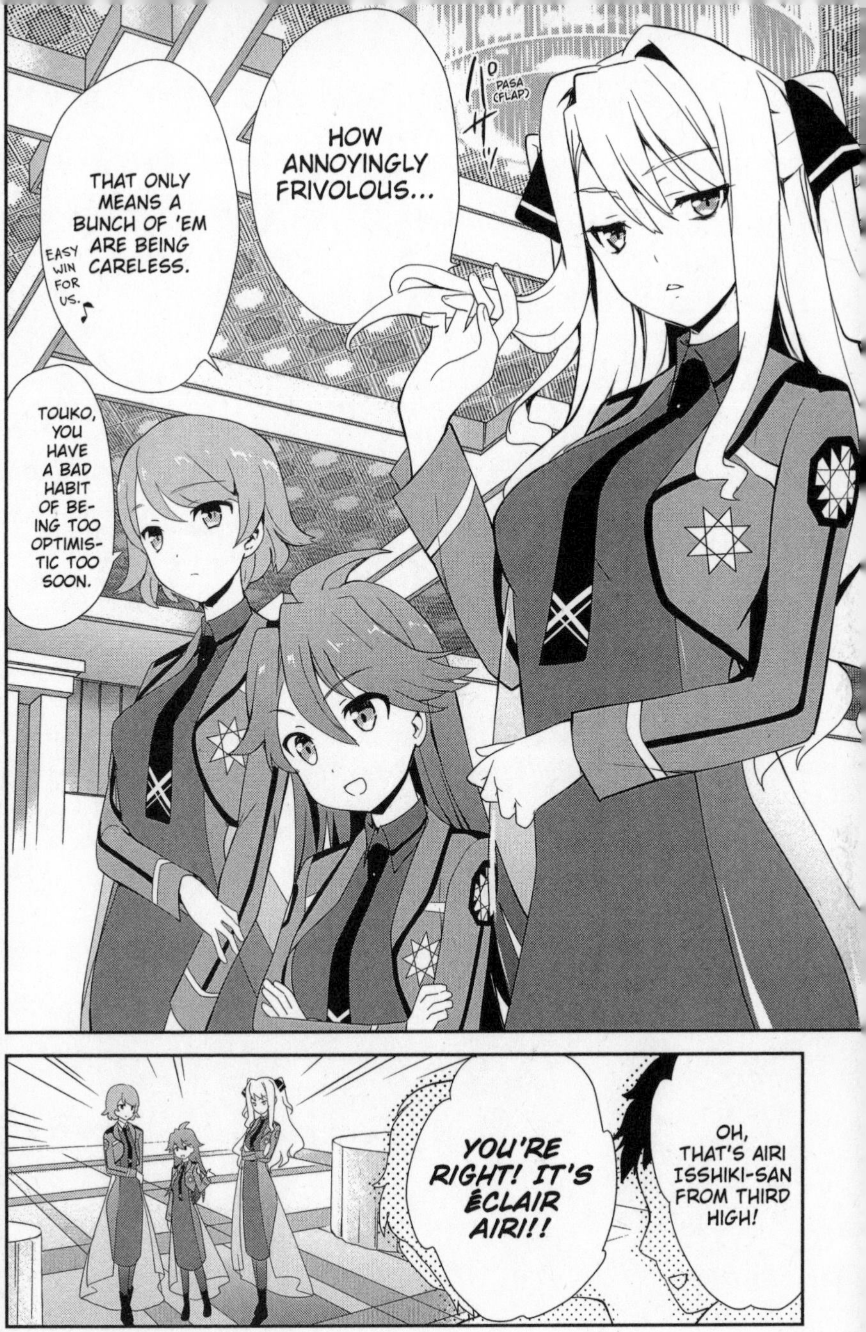
PASA (FLAP)
HOW ANNOYINGLY FRIVOLOUS...
THAT ONLY MEANS A BUNCH OF 'EM ARE BEING CARELESS.
EASY WIN FOR US. ♪
TOUKO, YOU HAVE A BAD HABIT OF BE-ING TOO OPTIMIS-TIC TOO SOON.
OH, THAT'S AIRI ISSHIKI-SAN FROM THIRD HIGH!
YOU'RE RIGHT! IT'S ÉCLAIR AIRI!!

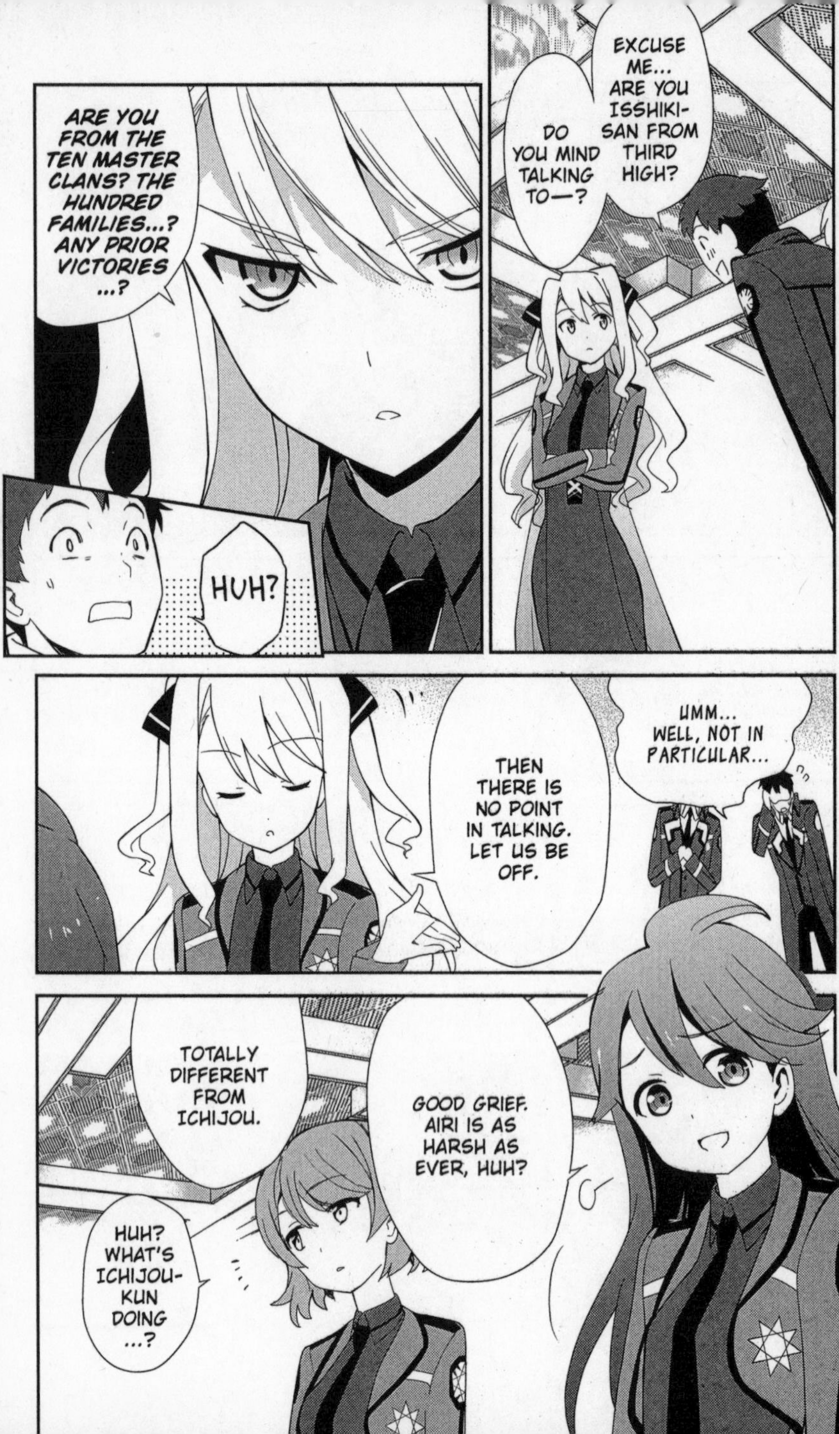
EXCUSE ME... ARE YOU ISSHIKI-SAN FROM THIRD HIGH?
DO YOU MIND TALKING TO—?
ARE YOU FROM THE TEN MASTER CLANS? THE HUNDRED FAMILIES...? ANY PRIOR VICTORIES ...?
HUH?
UMM... WELL, NOT IN PARTICULAR...
THEN THERE IS NO POINT IN TALKING. LET US BE OFF.
GOOD GRIEF. AIRI IS AS HARSH AS EVER, HUH?
TOTALLY DIFFERENT FROM ICHIJOU.
HUH? WHAT'S ICHIJOU-KUN DOING ...?

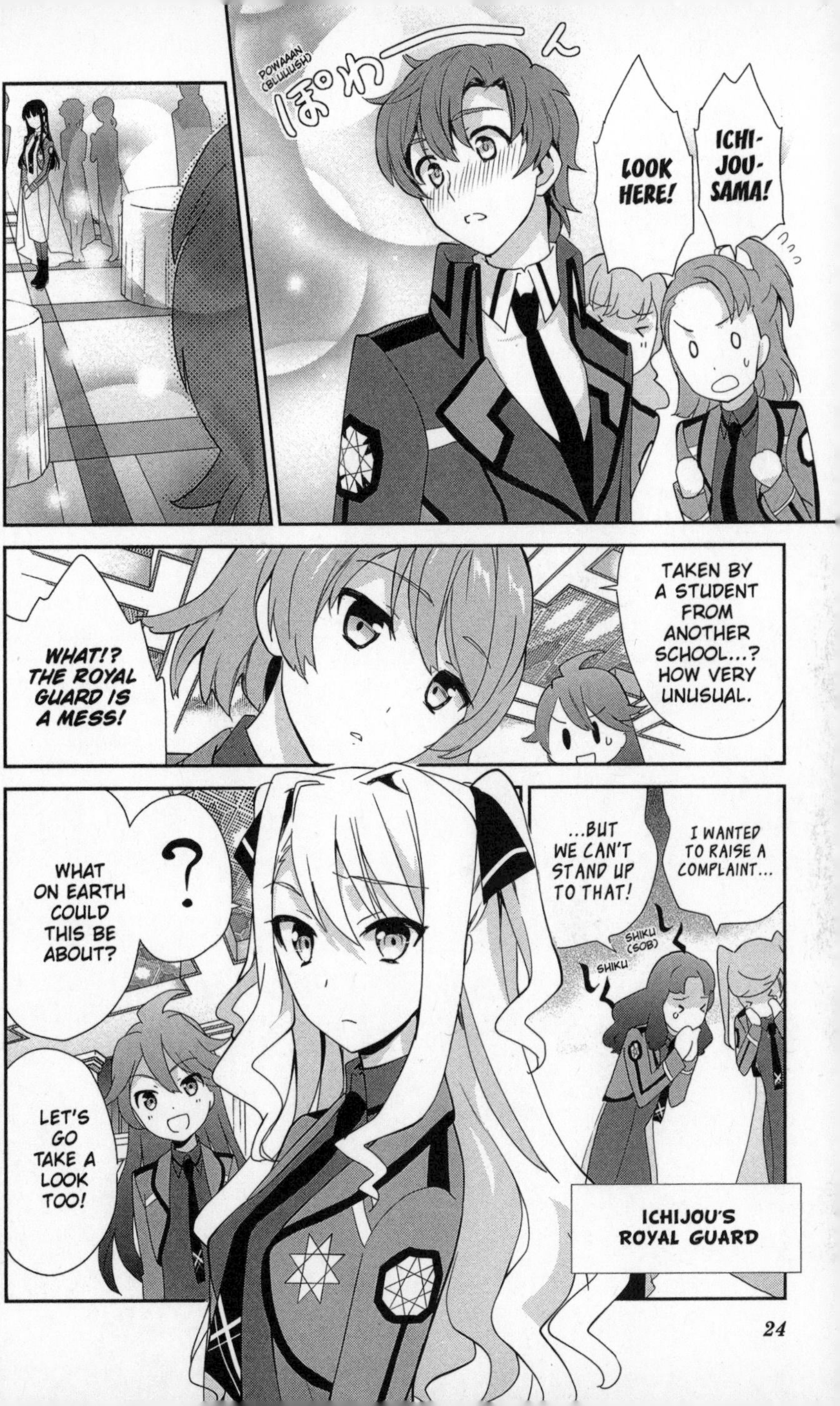
ICHI-JOU-SAMA!
LOOK HERE!
POWAAAN (BLUUUSH)
ぽわーん
TAKEN BY A STUDENT FROM ANOTHER SCHOOL...? HOW VERY UNUSUAL.
WHAT!? THE ROYAL GUARD IS A MESS!
I WANTED TO RAISE A COMPLAINT...
...BUT WE CAN'T STAND UP TO THAT!
SHIKU (SOB)
SHIKU
ICHIJOU'S ROYAL GUARD
?
WHAT ON EARTH COULD THIS BE ABOUT?
LET'S GO TAKE A LOOK TOO!

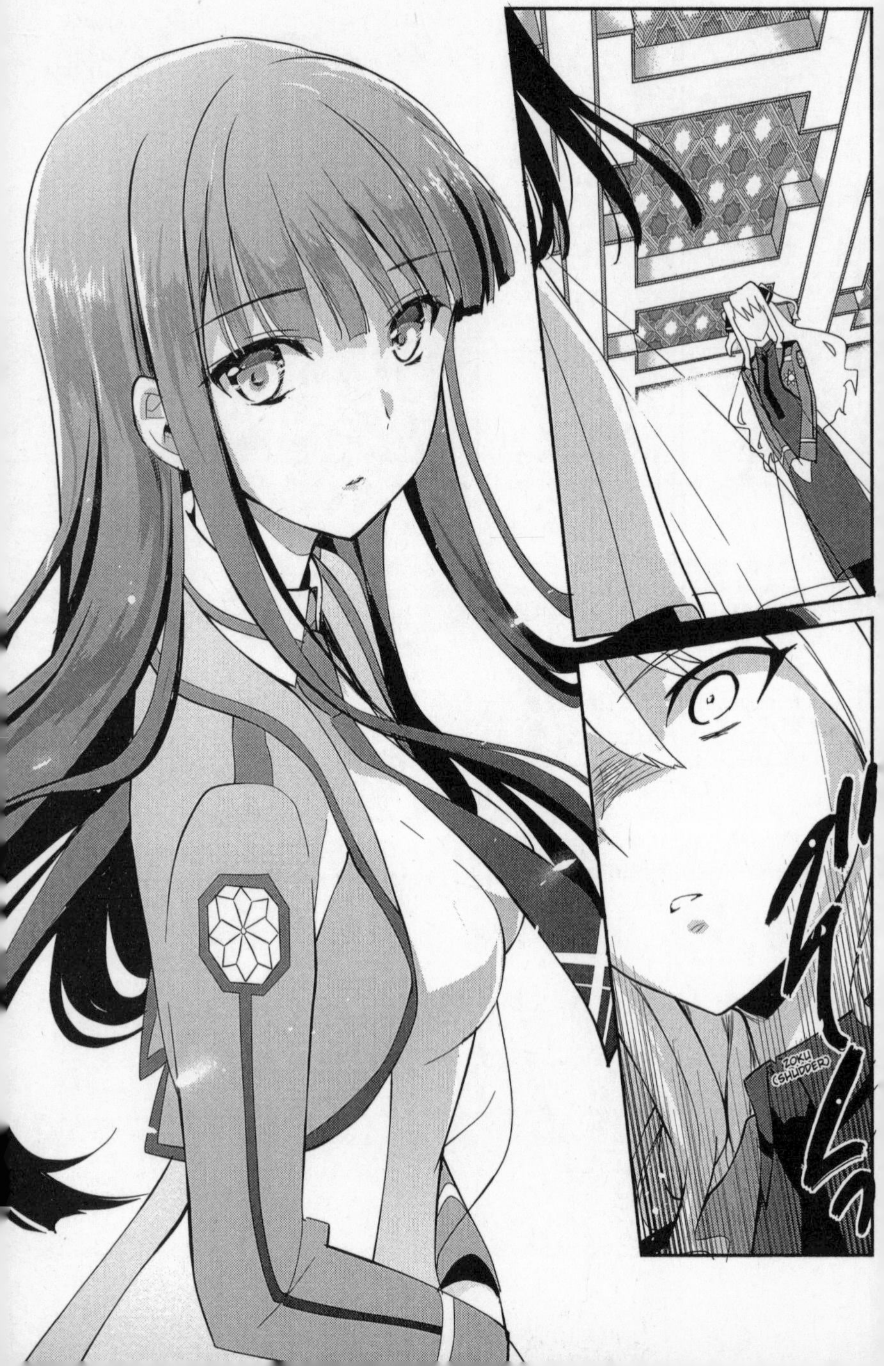
ZOKU (SHUDDER)

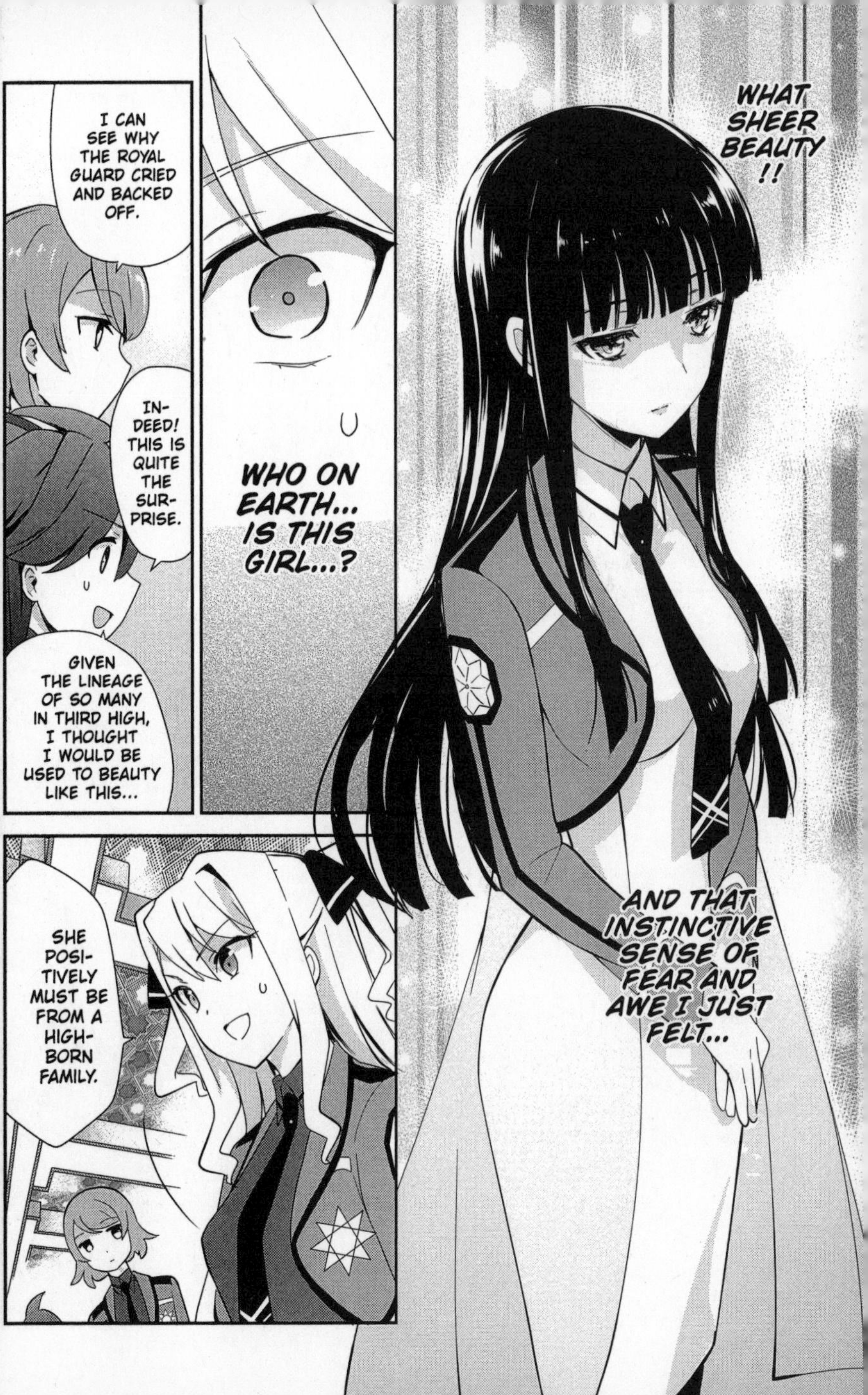
WHAT SHEER BEAUTY!!
AND THAT INSTINCTIVE SENSE OF FEAR AND AWE I JUST FELT...
WHO ON EARTH... IS THIS GIRL...?
I CAN SEE WHY THE ROYAL GUARD CRIED AND BACKED OFF.
INDEED! THIS IS QUITE THE SURPRISE.
GIVEN THE LINEAGE OF SO MANY IN THIRD HIGH, I THOUGHT I WOULD BE USED TO BEAUTY LIKE THIS...
SHE POSITIVELY MUST BE FROM A HIGHBORN FAMILY.

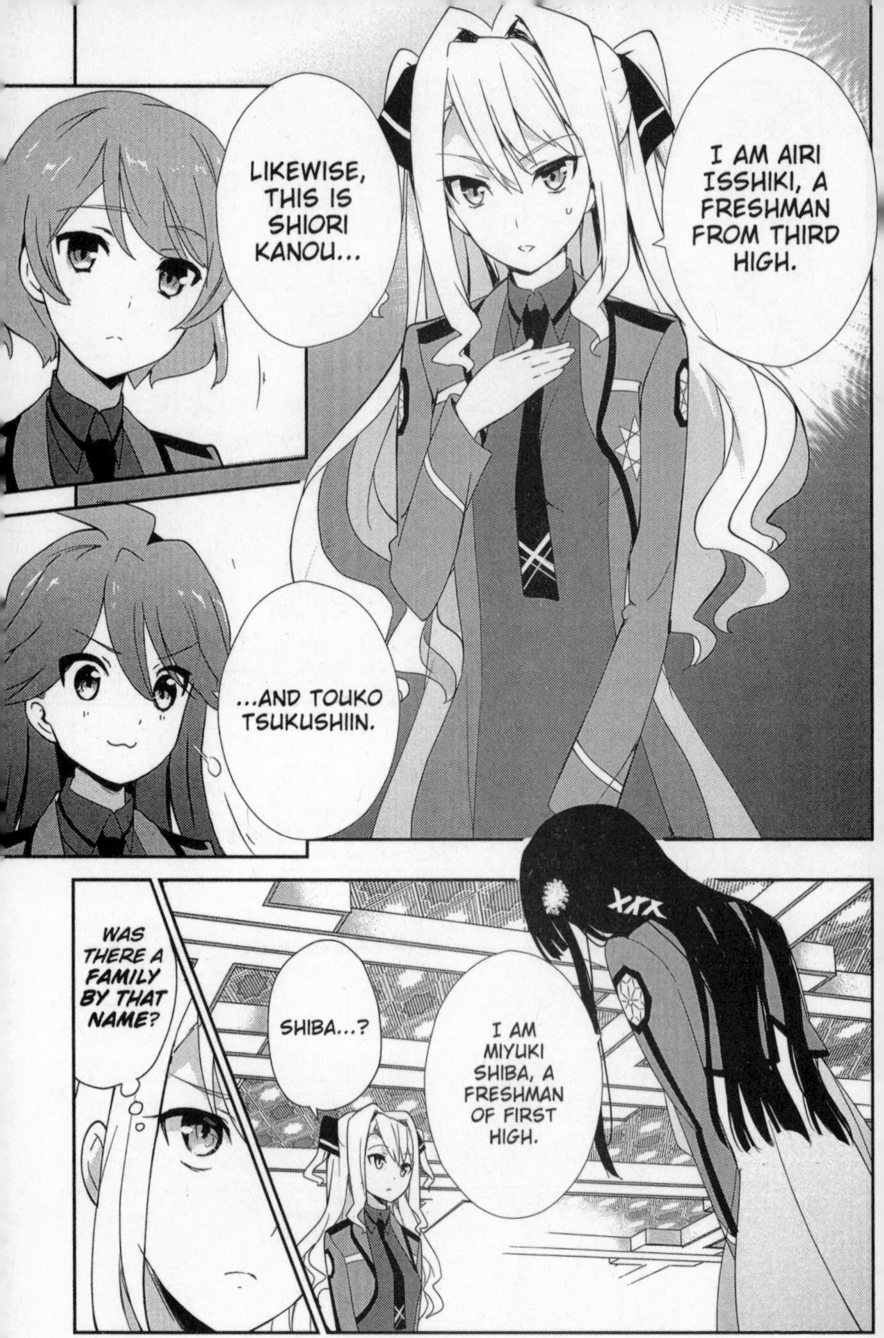
I AM AIRI ISSHIKI, A FRESHMAN FROM THIRD HIGH.
LIKEWISE, THIS IS SHIORI KANOU...
...AND TOUKO TSUKUSHIIN.
I AM MIYUKI SHIBA, A FRESHMAN OF FIRST HIGH.
SHIBA...?
WAS THERE A FAMILY BY THAT NAME?

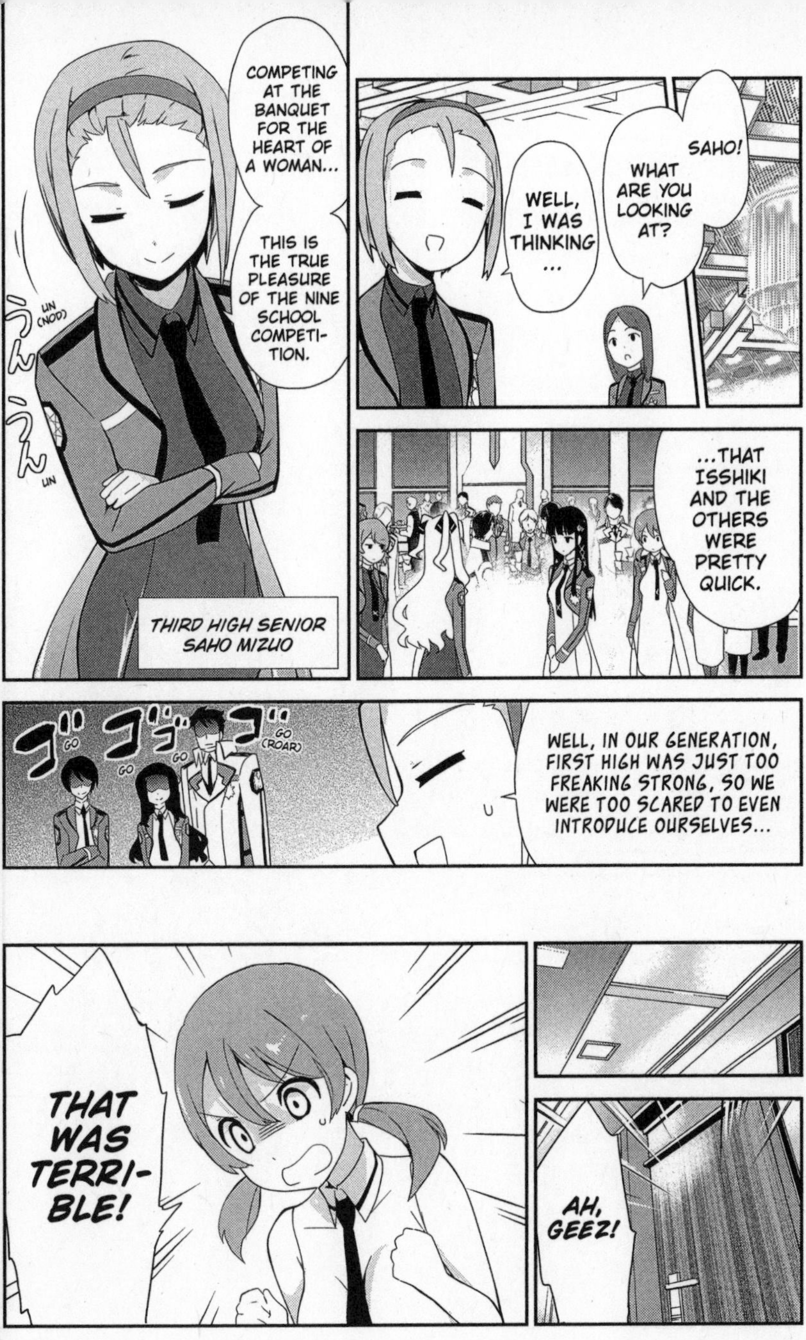
SAHO!
WHAT ARE YOU LOOKING AT?
WELL, I WAS THINKING...
...THAT ISSHIKI AND THE OTHERS WERE PRETTY QUICK.
COMPETING AT THE BANQUET FOR THE HEART OF A WOMAN...
THIS IS THE TRUE PLEASURE OF THE NINE SCHOOL COMPETITION.
うん UN (NOD)
うん UN
THIRD HIGH SENIOR SAHO MIZUO
WELL, IN OUR GENERATION, FIRST HIGH WAS JUST TOO FREAKING STRONG, SO WE WERE TOO SCARED TO EVEN INTRODUCE OURSELVES...
ゴ GO (ROAR)
ゴ GO
ゴ GO
ゴ GO
AH, GEEZ!
THAT WAS TERRIBLE!

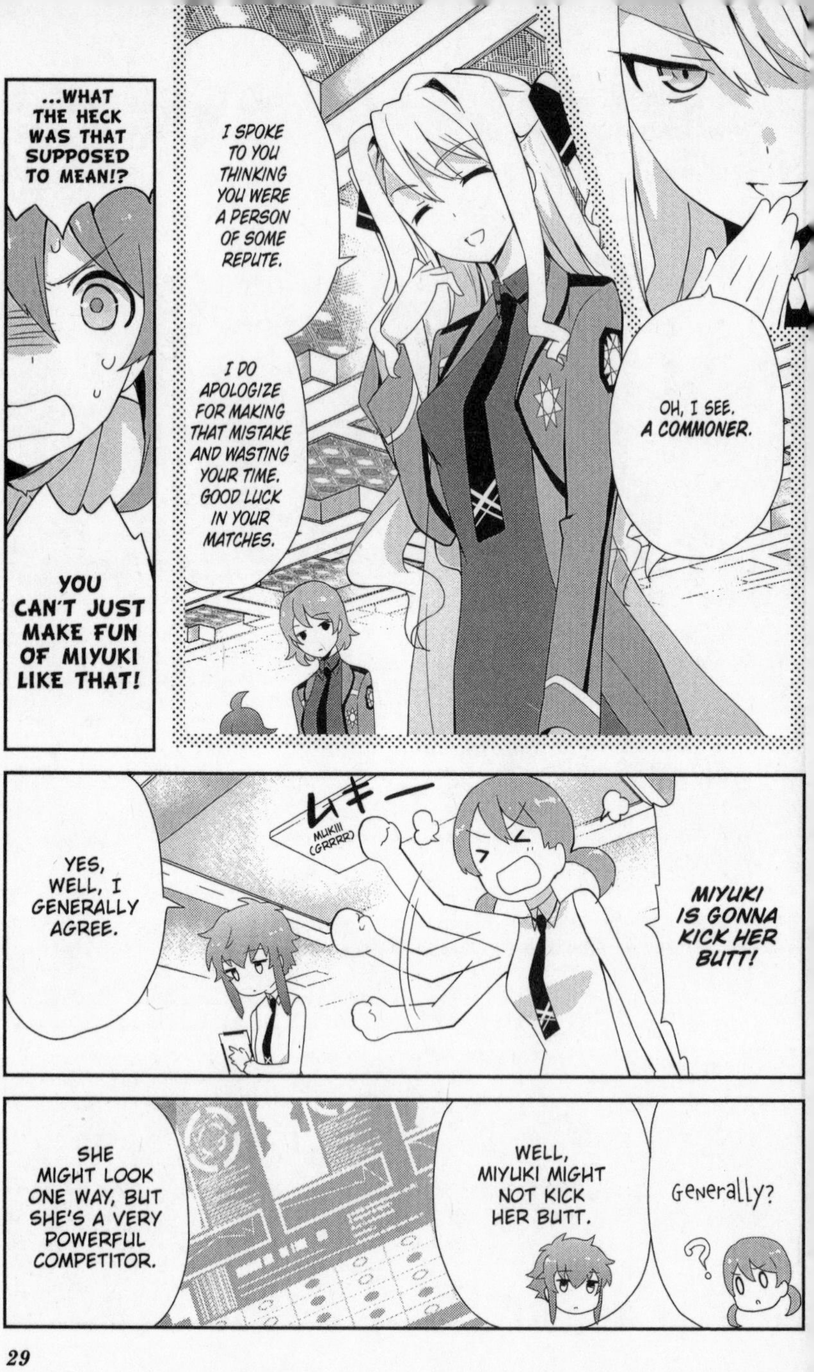
OH, I SEE. A COMMONER.
I SPOKE TO YOU THINKING YOU WERE A PERSON OF SOME REPUTE.
I DO APOLOGIZE FOR MAKING THAT MISTAKE AND WASTING YOUR TIME. GOOD LUCK IN YOUR MATCHES.
...WHAT THE HECK WAS THAT SUPPOSED TO MEAN!?
YOU CAN'T JUST MAKE FUN OF MIYUKI LIKE THAT!
MIYUKI IS GONNA KICK HER BUTT!
ムキー
MUKIII (GRRRR)
YES, WELL, I GENERALLY AGREE.
Generally?
WELL, MIYUKI MIGHT NOT KICK HER BUTT.
SHE MIGHT LOOK ONE WAY, BUT SHE'S A VERY POWERFUL COMPETITOR.

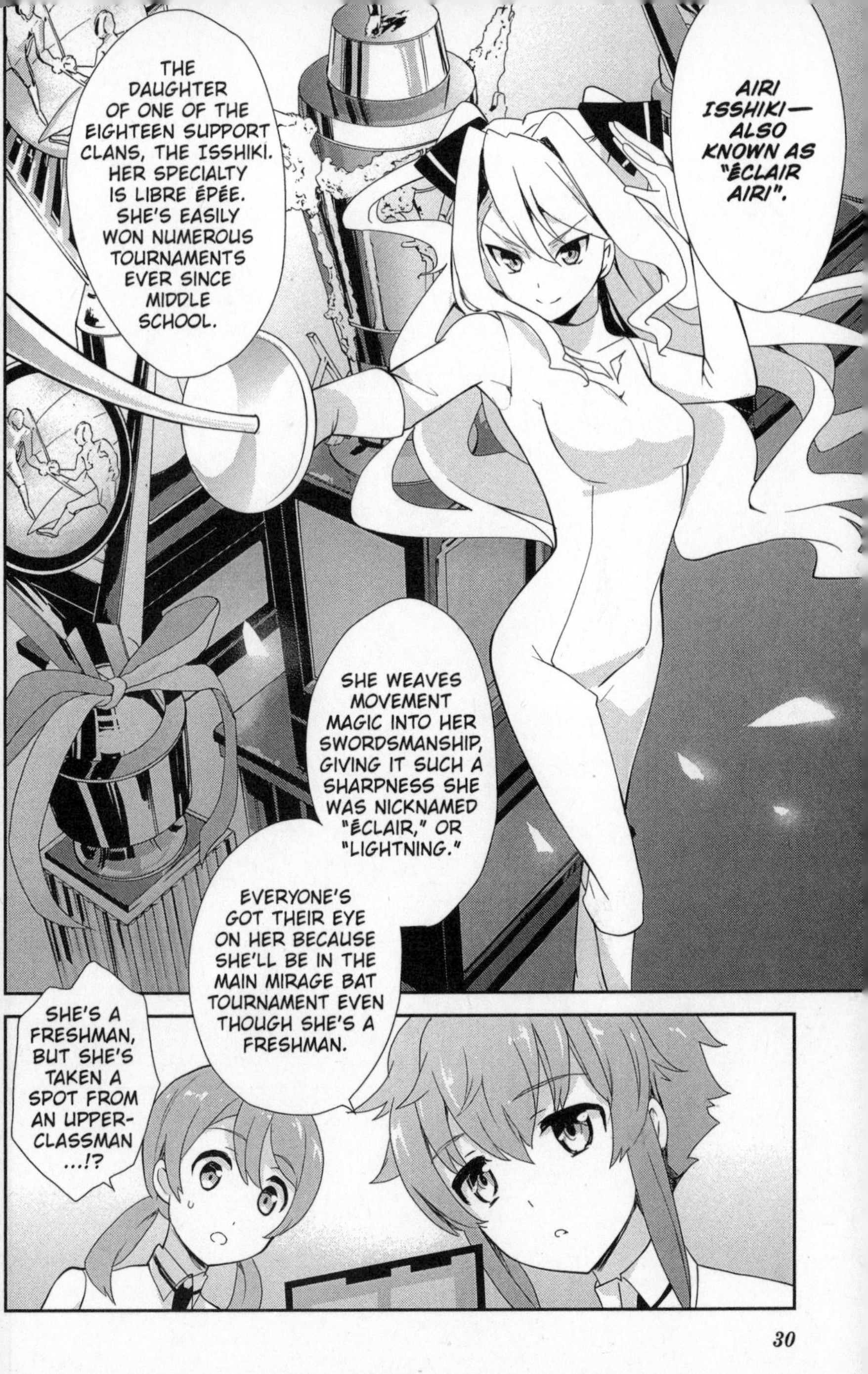
AIRI ISSHIKI—ALSO KNOWN AS "ÉCLAIR AIRI".
THE DAUGHTER OF ONE OF THE EIGHTEEN SUPPORT CLANS, THE ISSHIKI. HER SPECIALTY IS LIBRE ÉPÉE. SHE'S EASILY WON NUMEROUS TOURNAMENTS EVER SINCE MIDDLE SCHOOL.
SHE WEAVES MOVEMENT MAGIC INTO HER SWORDSMANSHIP, GIVING IT SUCH A SHARPNESS SHE WAS NICKNAMED "ÉCLAIR," OR "LIGHTNING."
EVERYONE'S GOT THEIR EYE ON HER BECAUSE SHE'LL BE IN THE MAIN MIRAGE BAT TOURNAMENT EVEN THOUGH SHE'S A FRESHMAN.
SHE'S A FRESHMAN, BUT SHE'S TAKEN A SPOT FROM AN UPPER-CLASSMAN ...!?

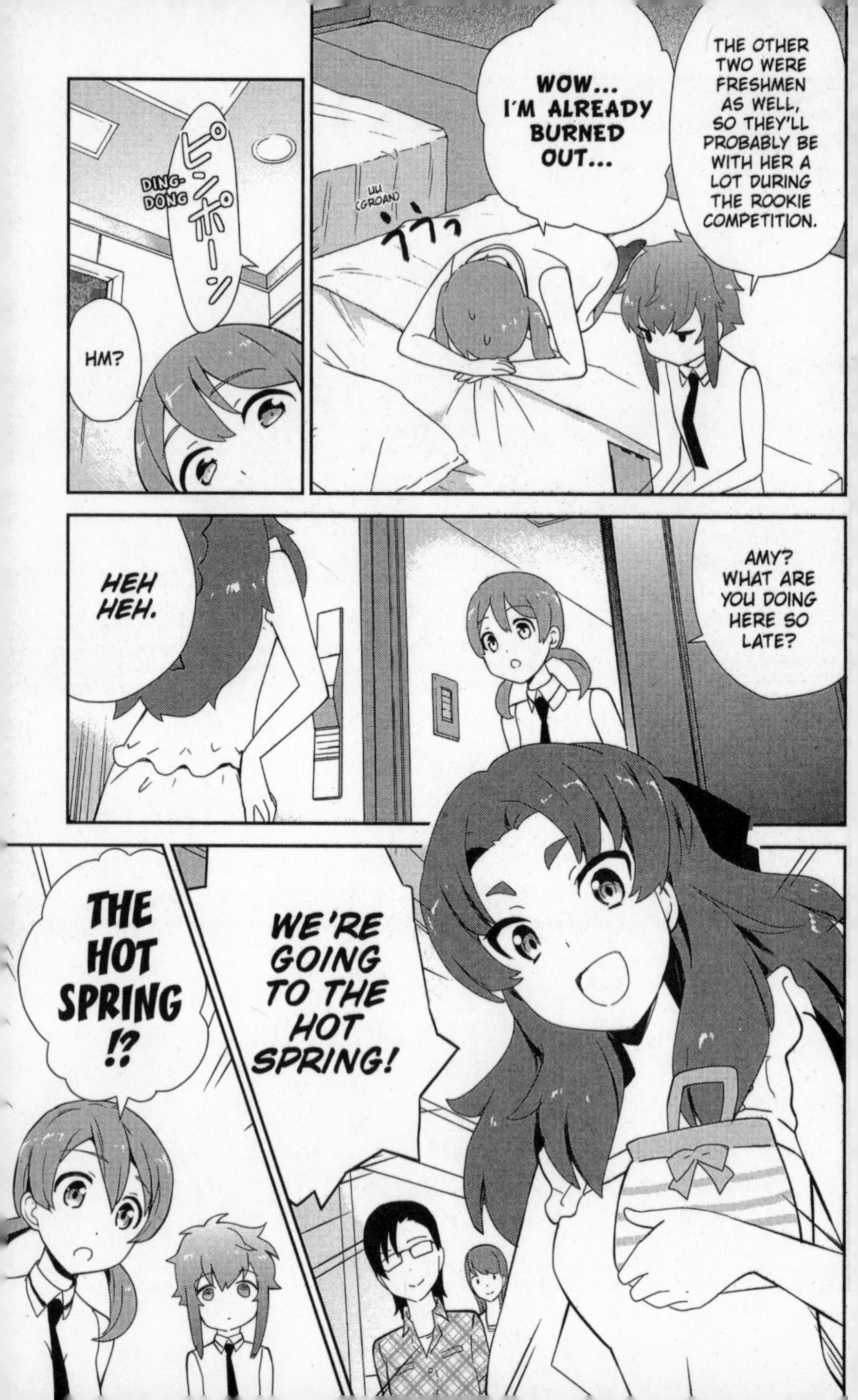
THE OTHER TWO WERE FRESHMEN AS WELL, SO THEY'LL PROBABLY BE WITH HER A LOT DURING THE ROOKIE COMPETITION.
WOW... I'M ALREADY BURNED OUT...
UU (GROAN)
ピンポーン
DING-DONG
HM?
AMY? WHAT ARE YOU DOING HERE SO LATE?
HEH HEH.
WE'RE GOING TO THE HOT SPRING!
THE HOT SPRING!?

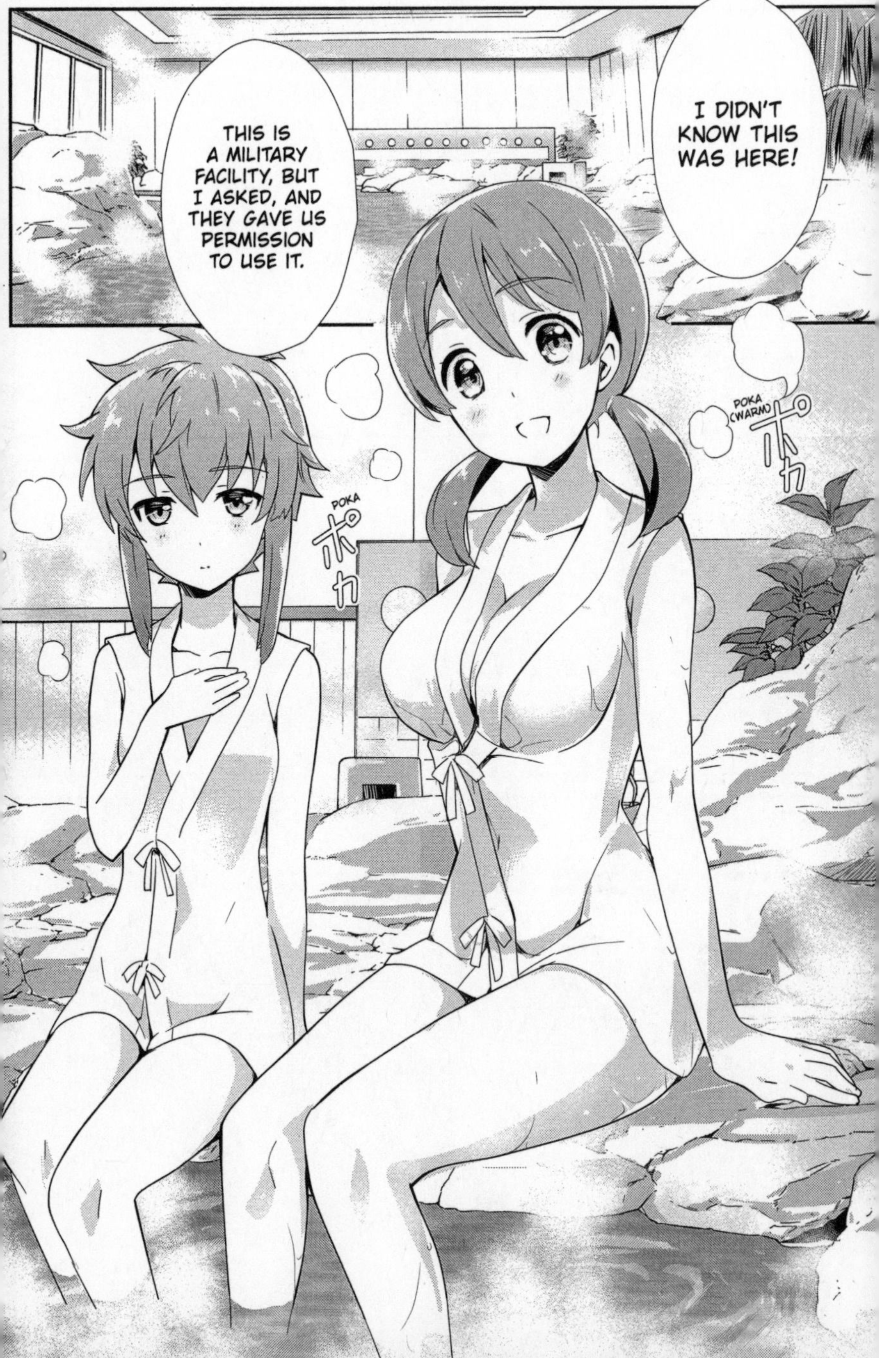
I DIDN'T KNOW THIS WAS HERE!
THIS IS A MILITARY FACILITY, BUT I ASKED, AND THEY GAVE US PERMISSION TO USE IT.
POKA (WARM)
ポカ
POKA
ポカ

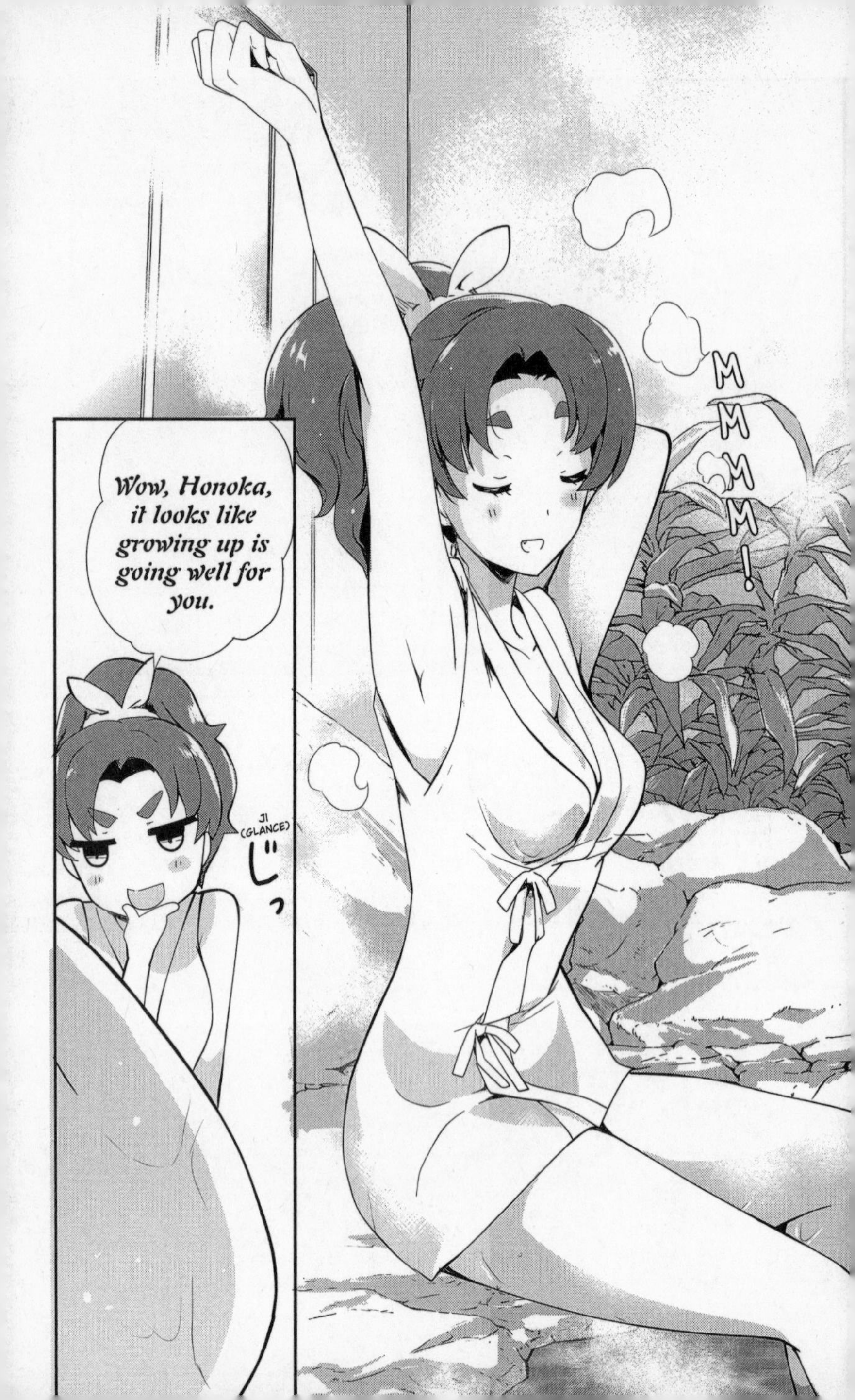
MMMM!
Wow, Honoka, it looks like growing up is going well for you.
JI (GLANCE)
じっ

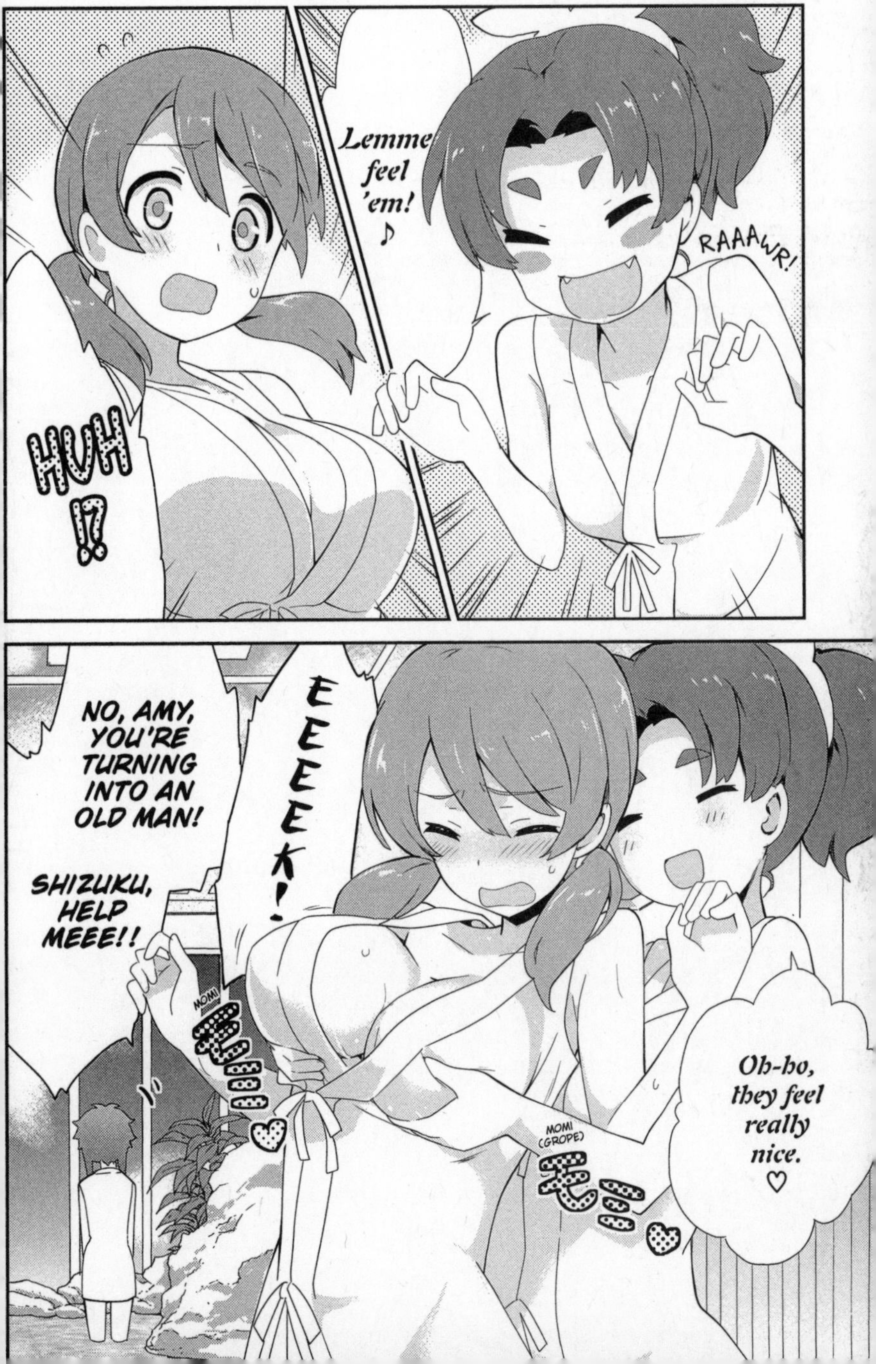

Lemme feel 'em! ♪
RAAAWR!
HUH !?
Oh-ho, they feel really nice. ♡
MOMI (GROPE)
EEEEEK!
MOMI
NO, AMY, YOU'RE TURNING INTO AN OLD MAN!
SHIZUKU, HELP MEEE!!

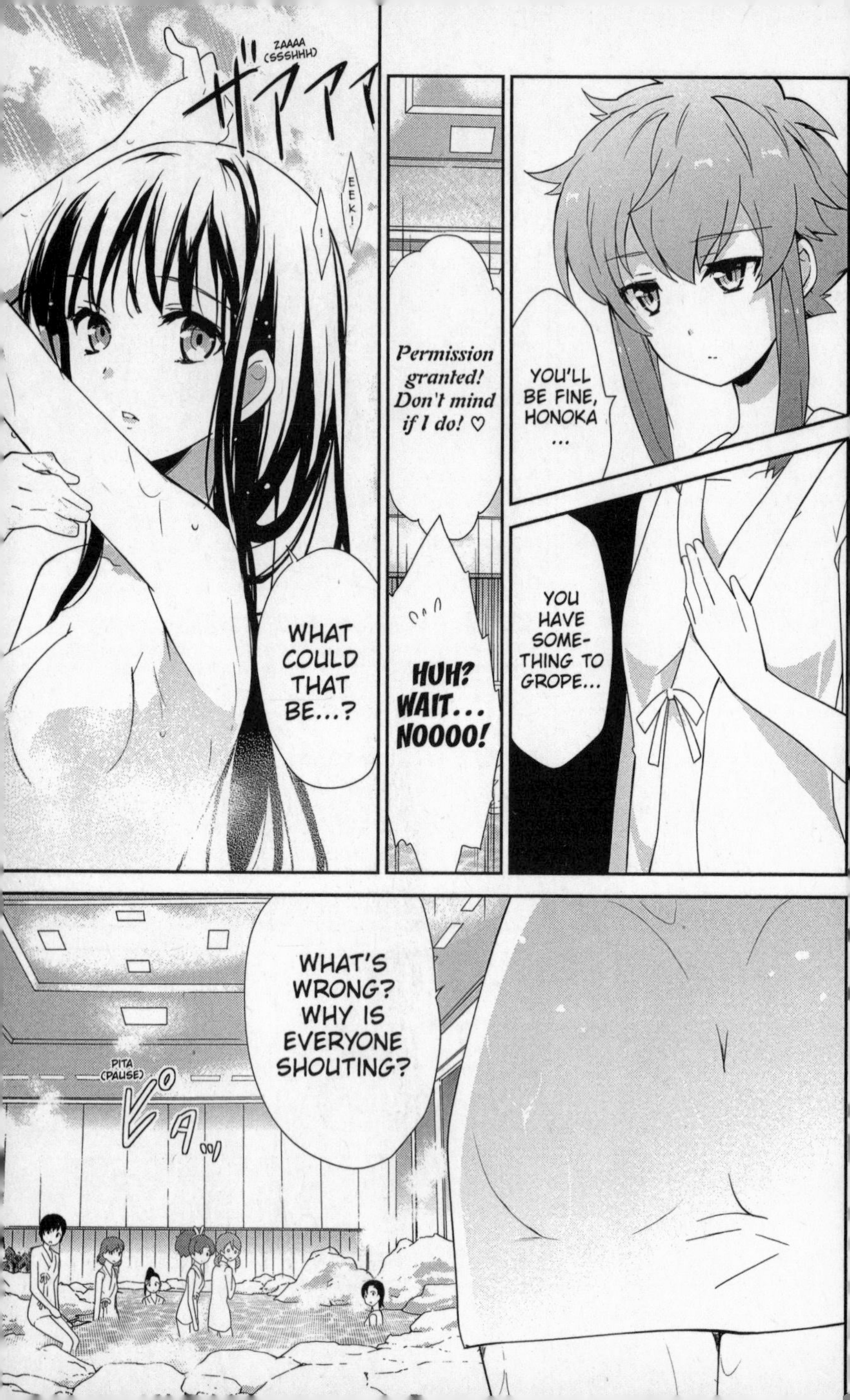
YOU'LL BE FINE, HONOKA ...
YOU HAVE SOME-THING TO GROPE...
Permission granted! Don't mind if I do! ♡
HUH? WAIT... NOOOO!
ZAAAA (SSSHHH)
EEK!
!
WHAT COULD THAT BE...?
WHAT'S WRONG? WHY IS EVERYONE SHOUTING?
PITA (PAUSE)

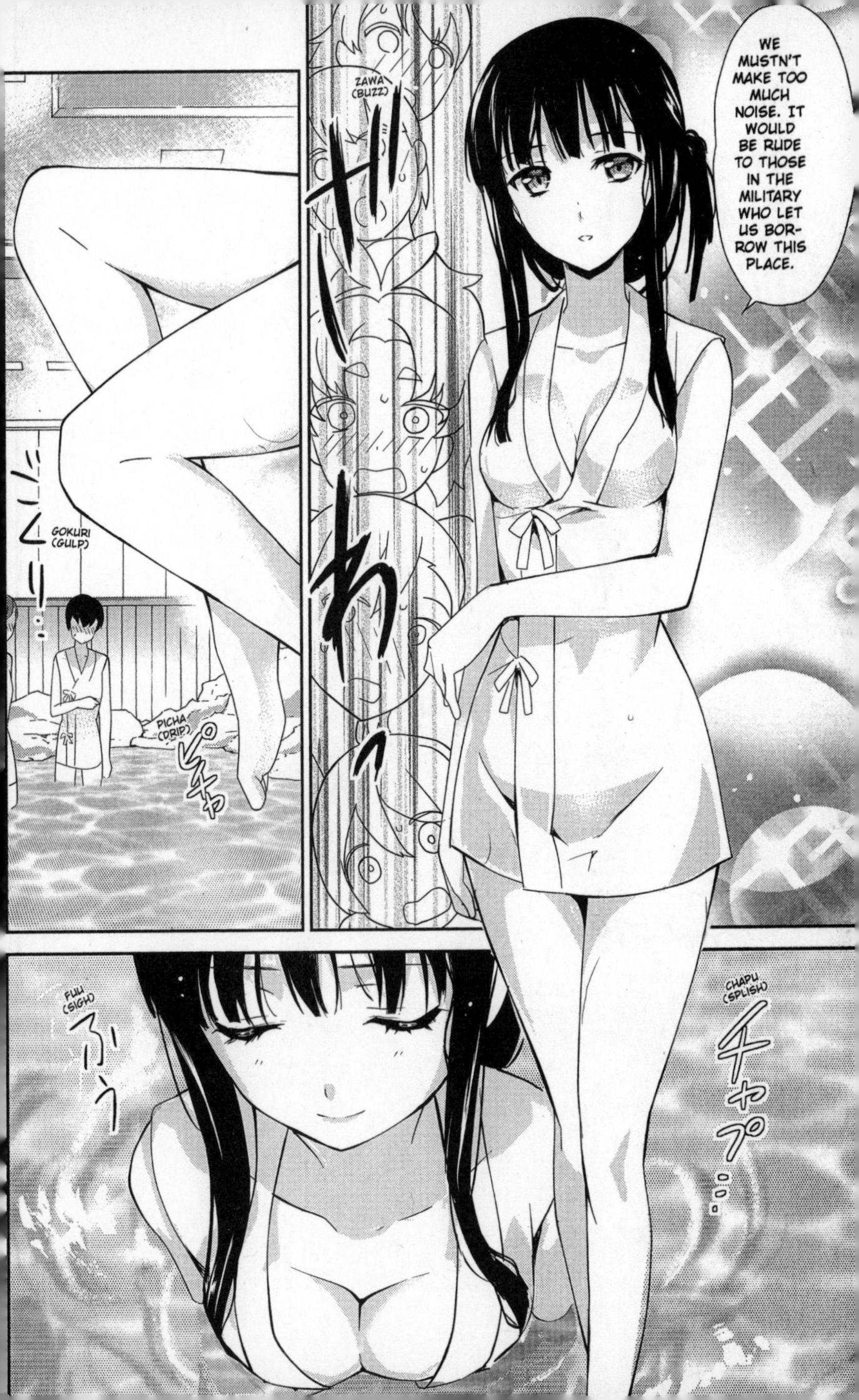
WE MUSTN'T MAKE TOO MUCH NOISE. IT WOULD BE RUDE TO THOSE IN THE MILITARY WHO LET US BOR-ROW THIS PLACE.
ZAWA (BUZZ)
GOKURI (GULP)
PICHA (DRIP)
CHAPU (SPLISH)
FUU (SIGH)

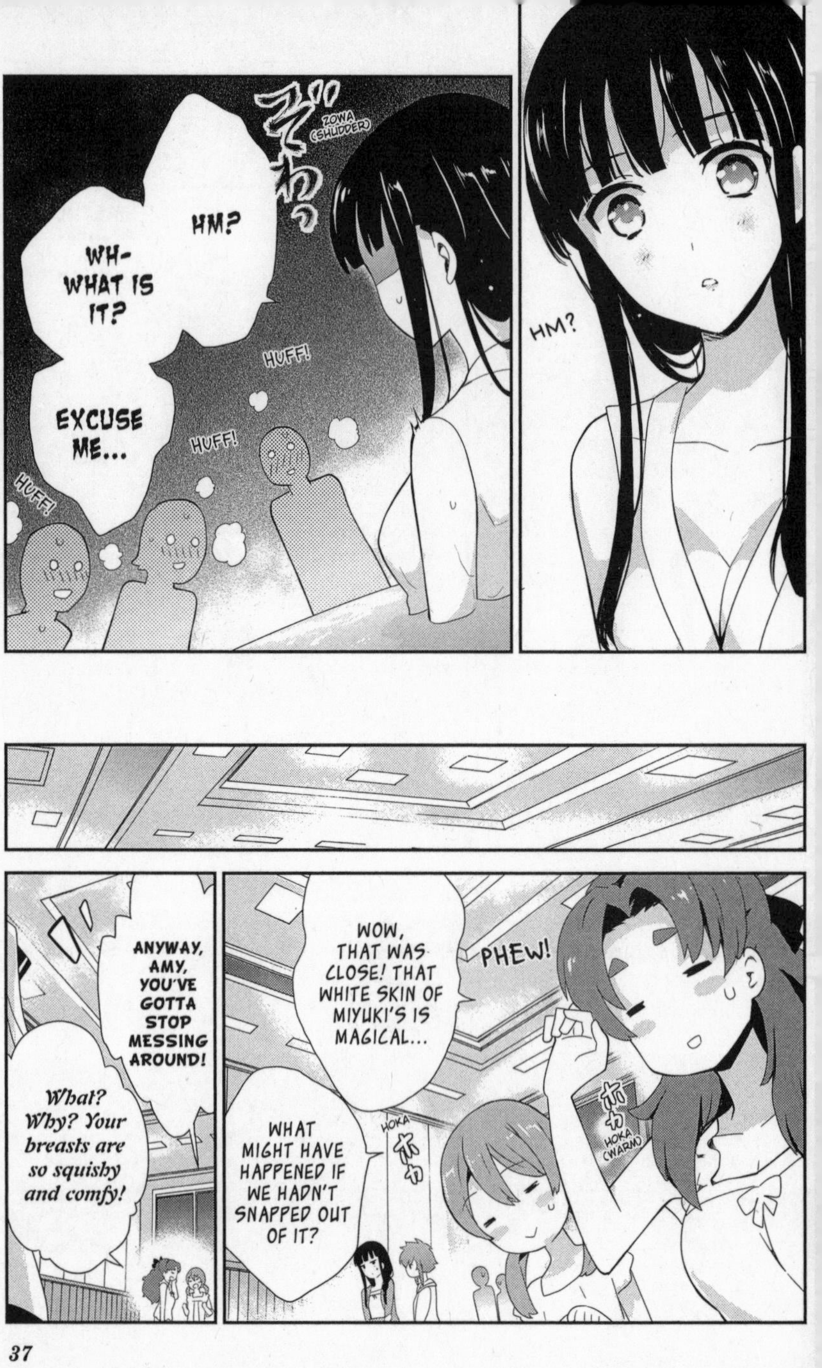
HM?
ZOWA (SHUDDER)
HM?
WH- WHAT IS IT?
HUFF!
EXCUSE ME...
HUFF!
HUFF!
PHEW!
WOW, THAT WAS CLOSE! THAT WHITE SKIN OF MIYUKI'S IS MAGICAL...
HOKA (WARM)
HOKA
WHAT MIGHT HAVE HAPPENED IF WE HADN'T SNAPPED OUT OF IT?
ANYWAY, AMY, YOU'VE GOTTA STOP MESSING AROUND!
What? Why? Your breasts are so squishy and comfy!

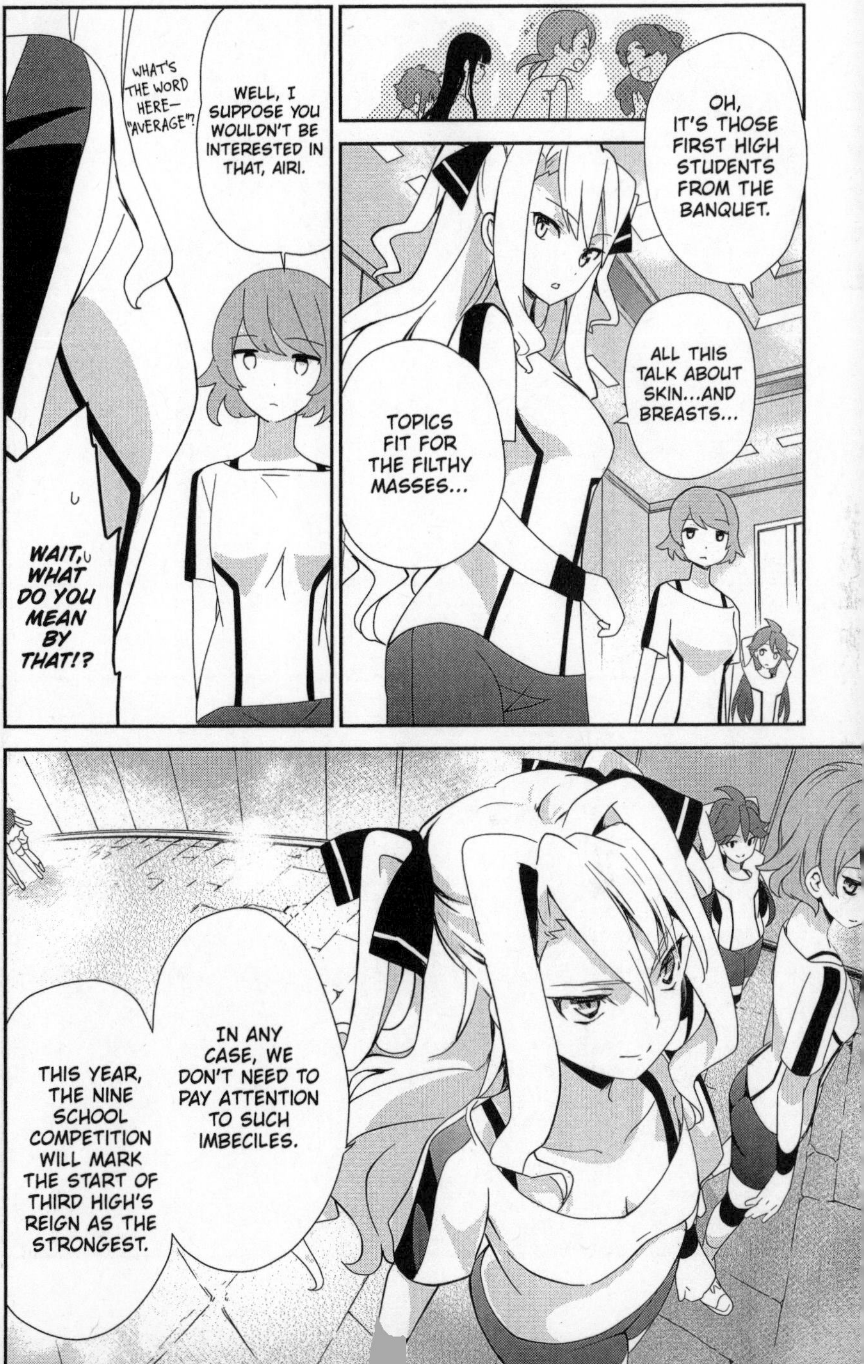
OH, IT'S THOSE FIRST HIGH STUDENTS FROM THE BANQUET.
ALL THIS TALK ABOUT SKIN...AND BREASTS...
TOPICS FIT FOR THE FILTHY MASSES...
WELL, I SUPPOSE YOU WOULDN'T BE INTERESTED IN THAT, AIRI.
WHAT'S THE WORD HERE—"AVERAGE"?
WAIT, WHAT DO YOU MEAN BY THAT!?
IN ANY CASE, WE DON'T NEED TO PAY ATTENTION TO SUCH IMBECILES.
THIS YEAR, THE NINE SCHOOL COMPETITION WILL MARK THE START OF THIRD HIGH'S REIGN AS THE STRONGEST.

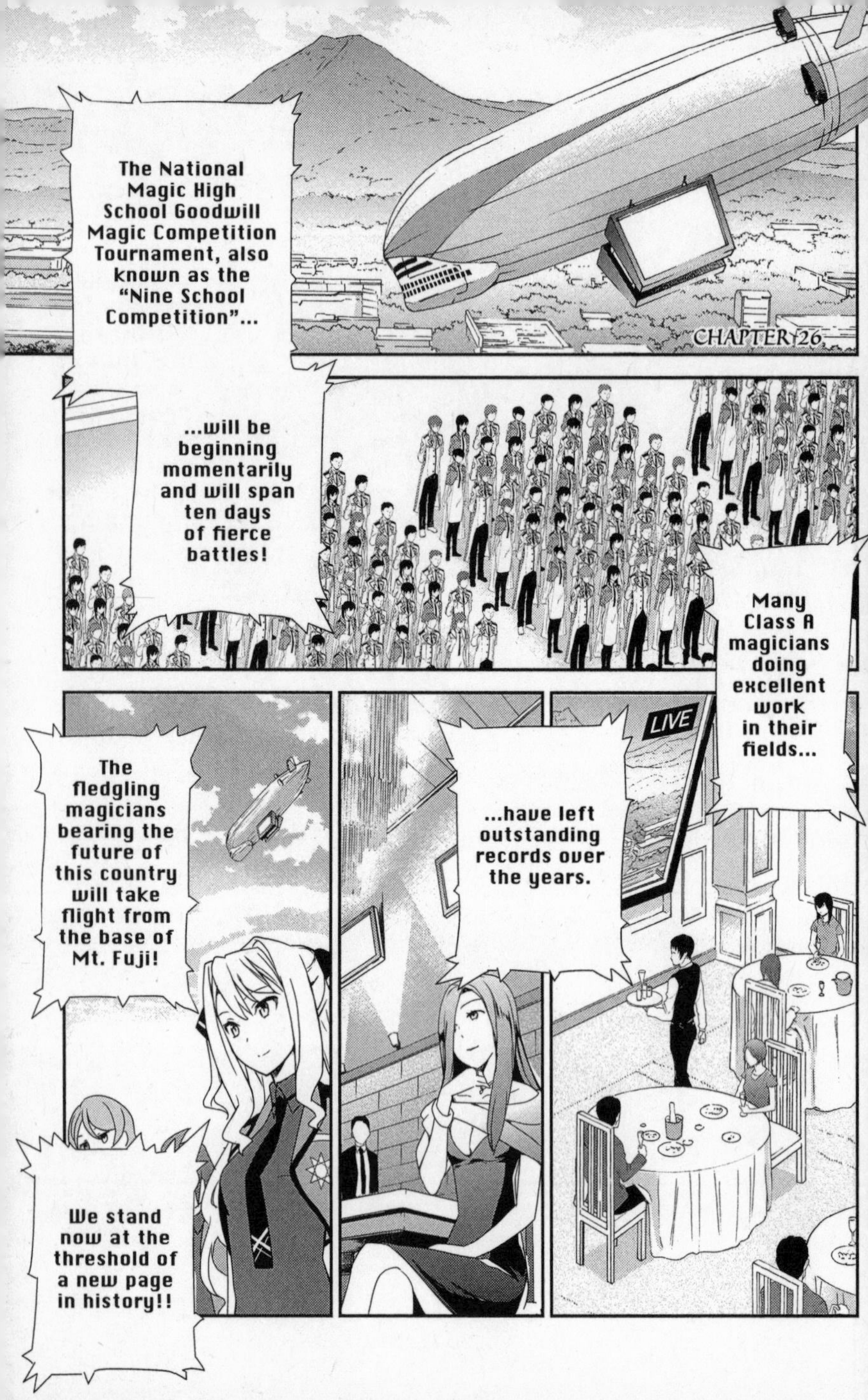
The National Magic High School Goodwill Magic Competition Tournament, also known as the "Nine School Competition"...
CHAPTER 26
...will be beginning momentarily and will span ten days of fierce battles!
Many Class A magicians doing excellent work in their fields...
LIVE
...have left outstanding records over the years.
The fledgling magicians bearing the future of this country will take flight from the base of Mt. Fuji!
We stand now at the threshold of a new page in history!!

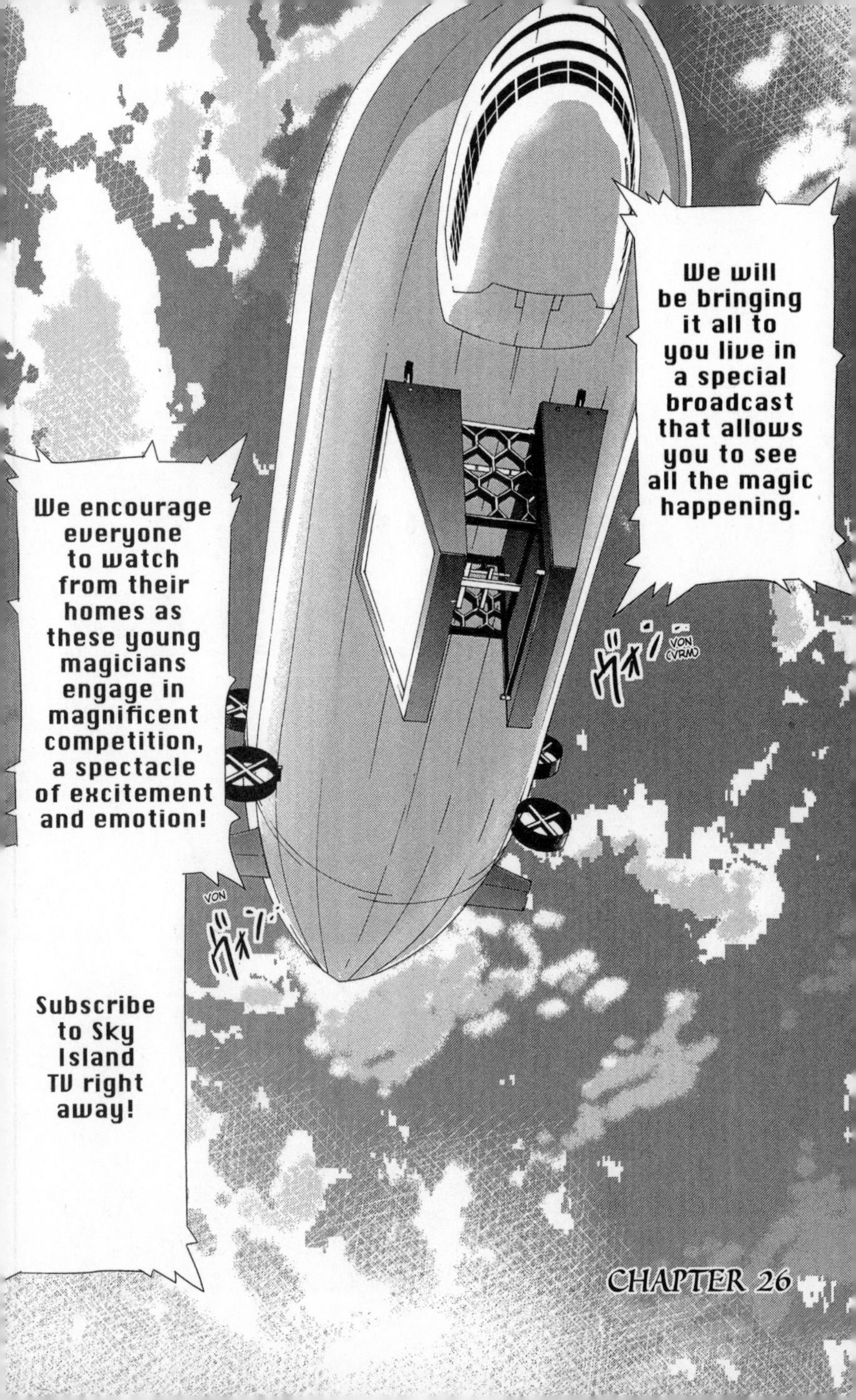
We will be bringing it all to you live in a special broadcast that allows you to see all the magic happening.
VON (VRM)
We encourage everyone to watch from their homes as these young magicians engage in magnificent competition, a spectacle of excitement and emotion!
VON
Subscribe to Sky Island TV right away!

# CHAPTER 26

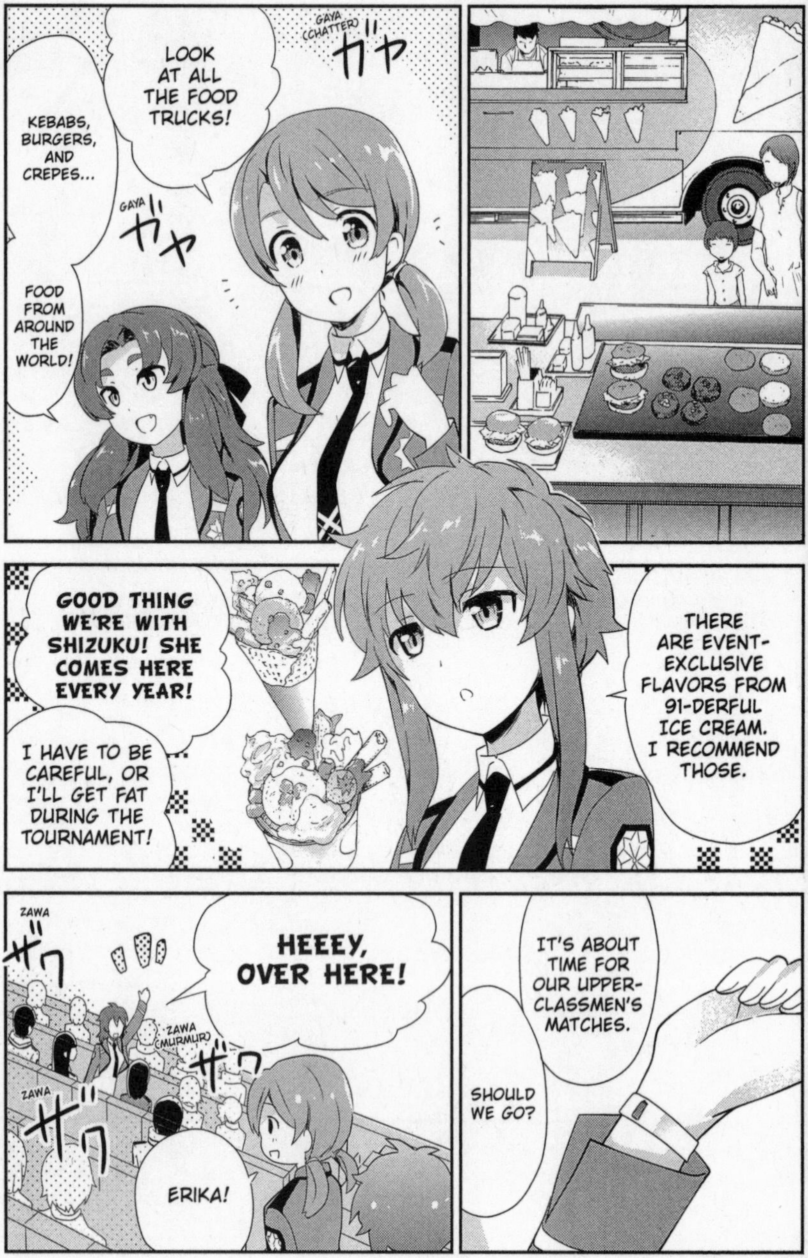
GAYA (CHATTER) ガヤ
LOOK AT ALL THE FOOD TRUCKS!
KEBABS, BURGERS, AND CREPES...
GAYA ガヤ
FOOD FROM AROUND THE WORLD!
THERE ARE EVENT-EXCLUSIVE FLAVORS FROM 91-DERFUL ICE CREAM. I RECOMMEND THOSE.
GOOD THING WE'RE WITH SHIZUKU! SHE COMES HERE EVERY YEAR!
I HAVE TO BE CAREFUL, OR I'LL GET FAT DURING THE TOURNAMENT!
IT'S ABOUT TIME FOR OUR UPPER-CLASSMEN'S MATCHES.
SHOULD WE GO?
HEEEY, OVER HERE!
ZAWA ザワ
ZAWA (MURMUR) ザワ
ZAWA ザワ
ERIKA!

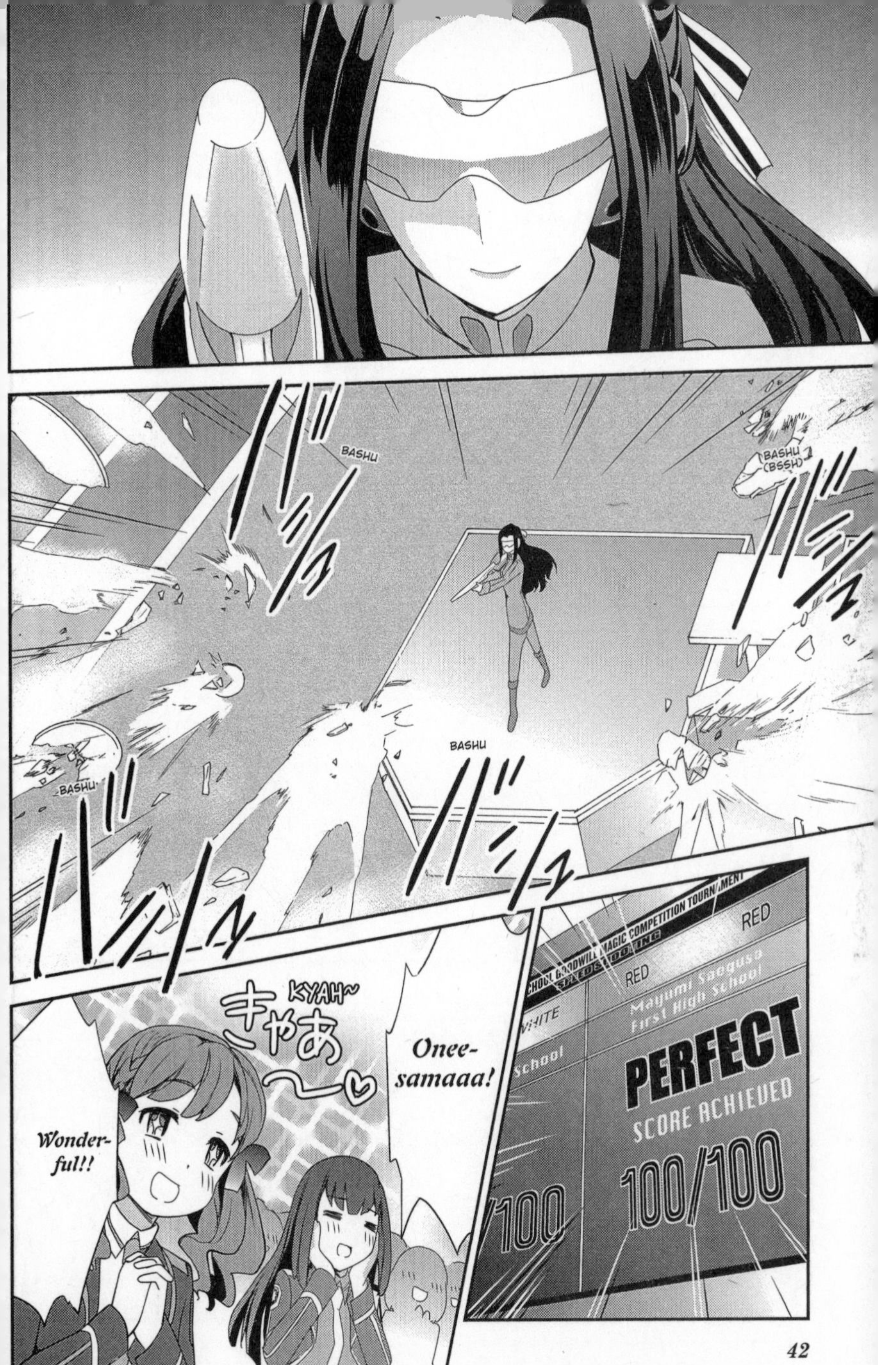
BASHU (BSSH)
BASHU
BASHU
BASHU
MAGIC COMPETITION TOURN
RED
RED
Mayumi Saegusa
First High School
WHITE
School
PERFECT
SCORE ACHIEVED
100/100
/100
Onee-samaaa!
きゃあ〜♡
KYAH~
Wonder-ful!!

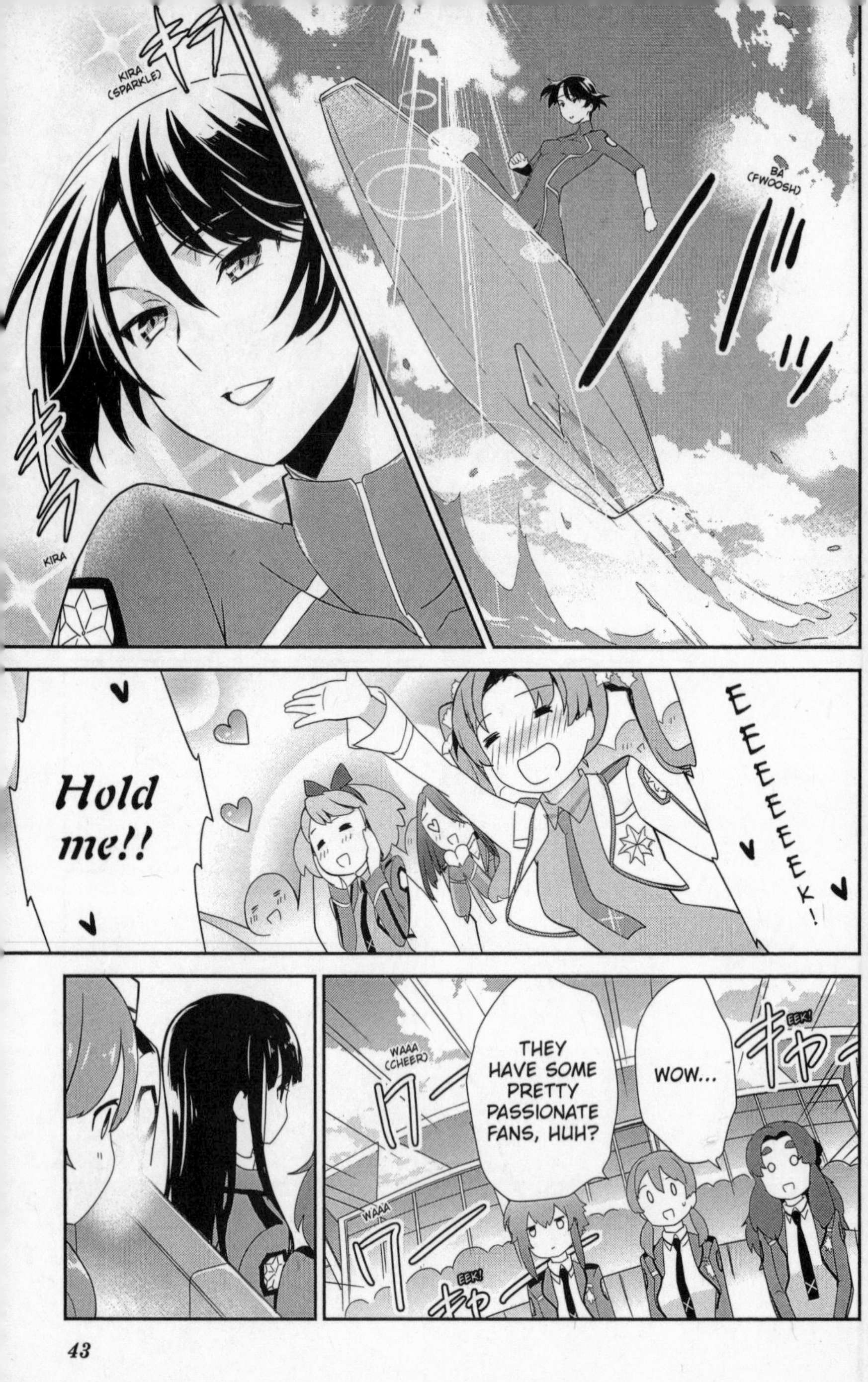
BA (FWOOSH)
KIRA (SPARKLE)
KIRA
EEEEEEEEK!
Hold me!!
EEK!
WOW...
THEY HAVE SOME PRETTY PASSIONATE FANS, HUH?
WAAA (CHEER)
WAAA
EEK!

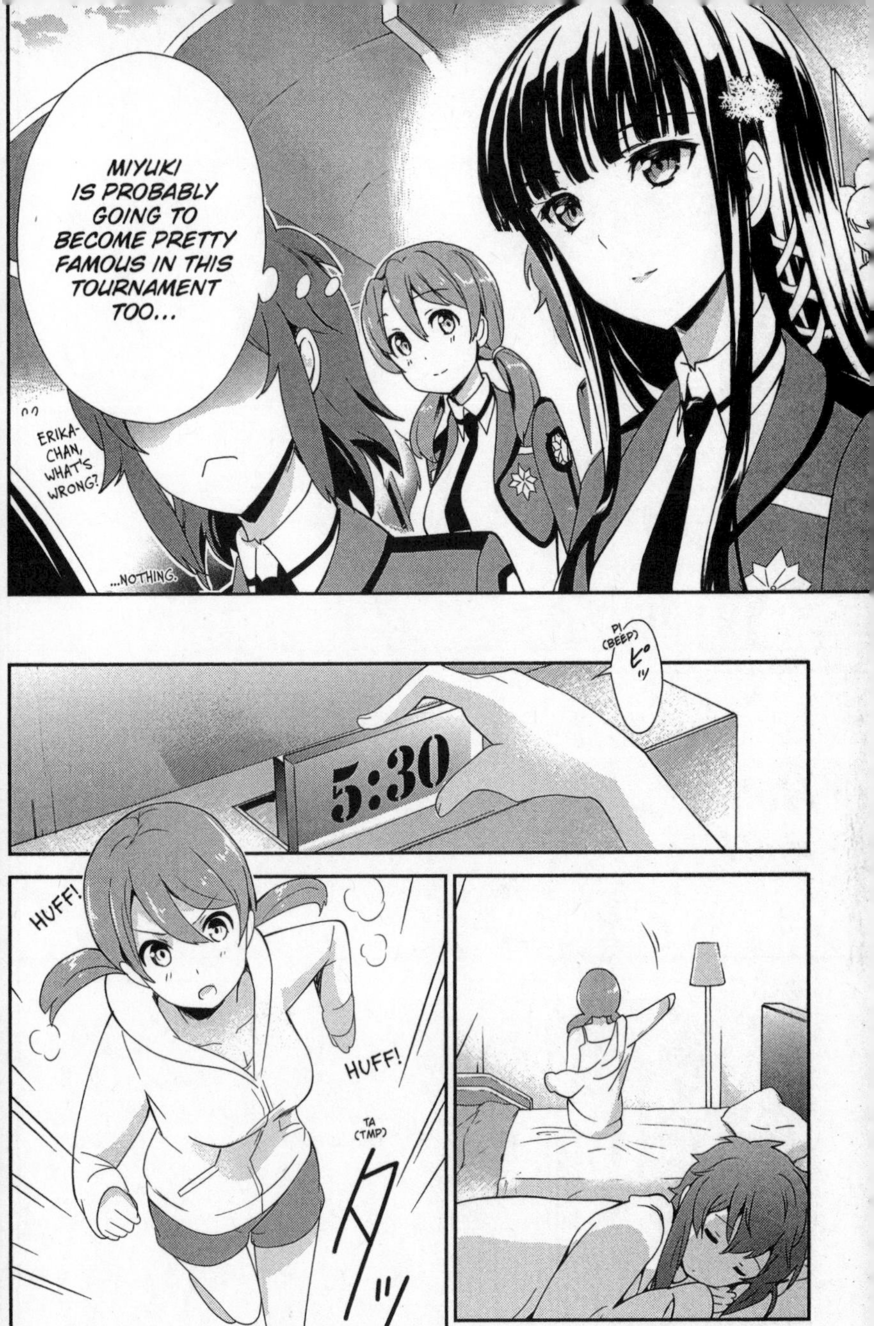
MIYUKI IS PROBABLY GOING TO BECOME PRETTY FAMOUS IN THIS TOURNAMENT TOO...
ERIKA-CHAN, WHAT'S WRONG?
...NOTHING.
PI (BEEP)
ピッ
5:30
HUFF!
HUFF!
TA (TMP)
タッ

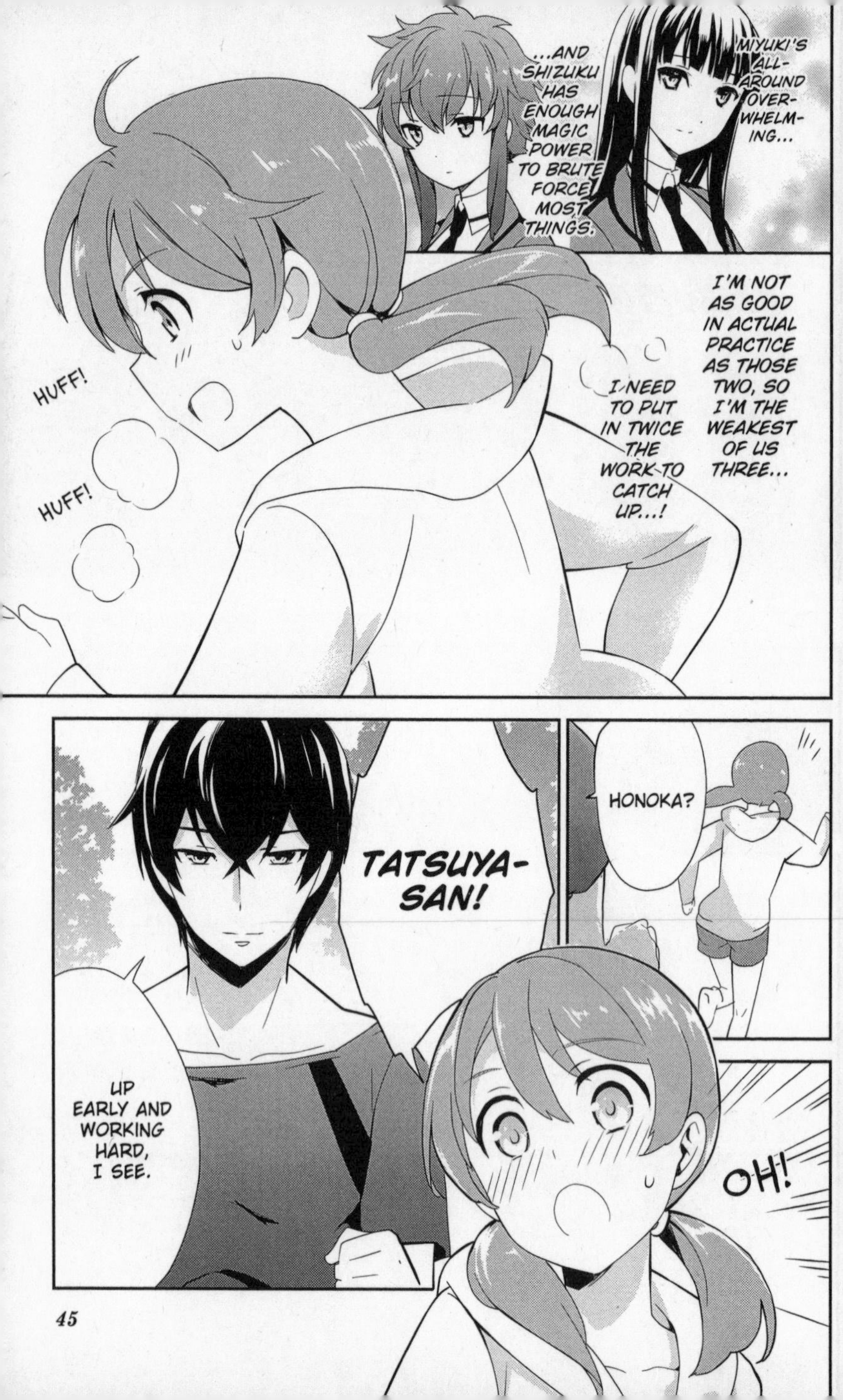
MIYUKI'S ALL-AROUND OVER-WHELMING...
...AND SHIZUKU HAS ENOUGH MAGIC POWER TO BRUTE FORCE MOST THINGS.
I'M NOT AS GOOD IN ACTUAL PRACTICE AS THOSE TWO, SO I'M THE WEAKEST OF US THREE...
I NEED TO PUT IN TWICE THE WORK TO CATCH UP...!
HUFF!
HUFF!
HONOKA?
TATSUYA-SAN!
OH!
UP EARLY AND WORKING HARD, I SEE.

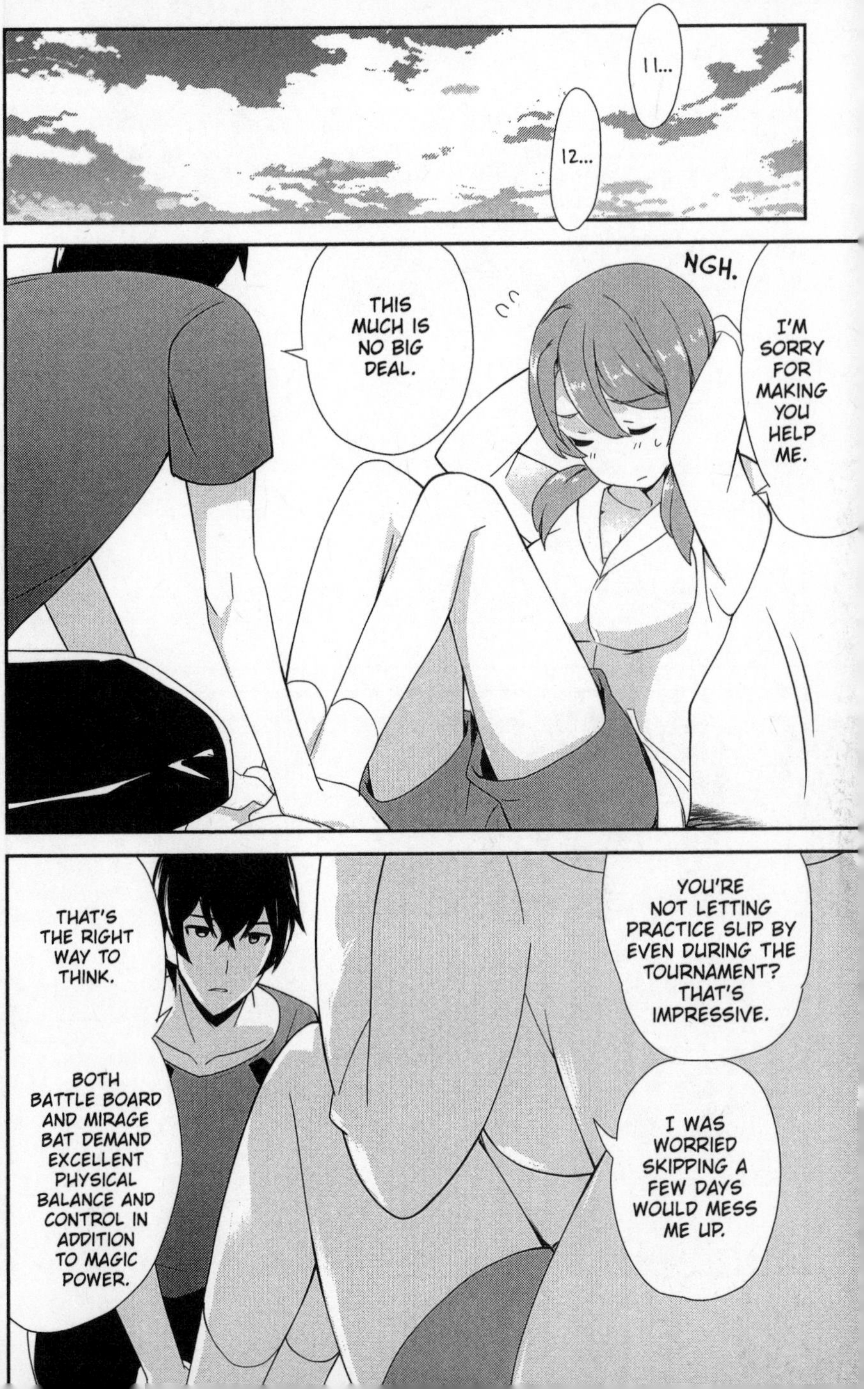
11...
12...
NGH.
I'M SORRY FOR MAKING YOU HELP ME.
THIS MUCH IS NO BIG DEAL.
YOU'RE NOT LETTING PRACTICE SLIP BY EVEN DURING THE TOURNAMENT? THAT'S IMPRESSIVE.
I WAS WORRIED SKIPPING A FEW DAYS WOULD MESS ME UP.
THAT'S THE RIGHT WAY TO THINK.
BOTH BATTLE BOARD AND MIRAGE BAT DEMAND EXCELLENT PHYSICAL BALANCE AND CONTROL IN ADDITION TO MAGIC POWER.

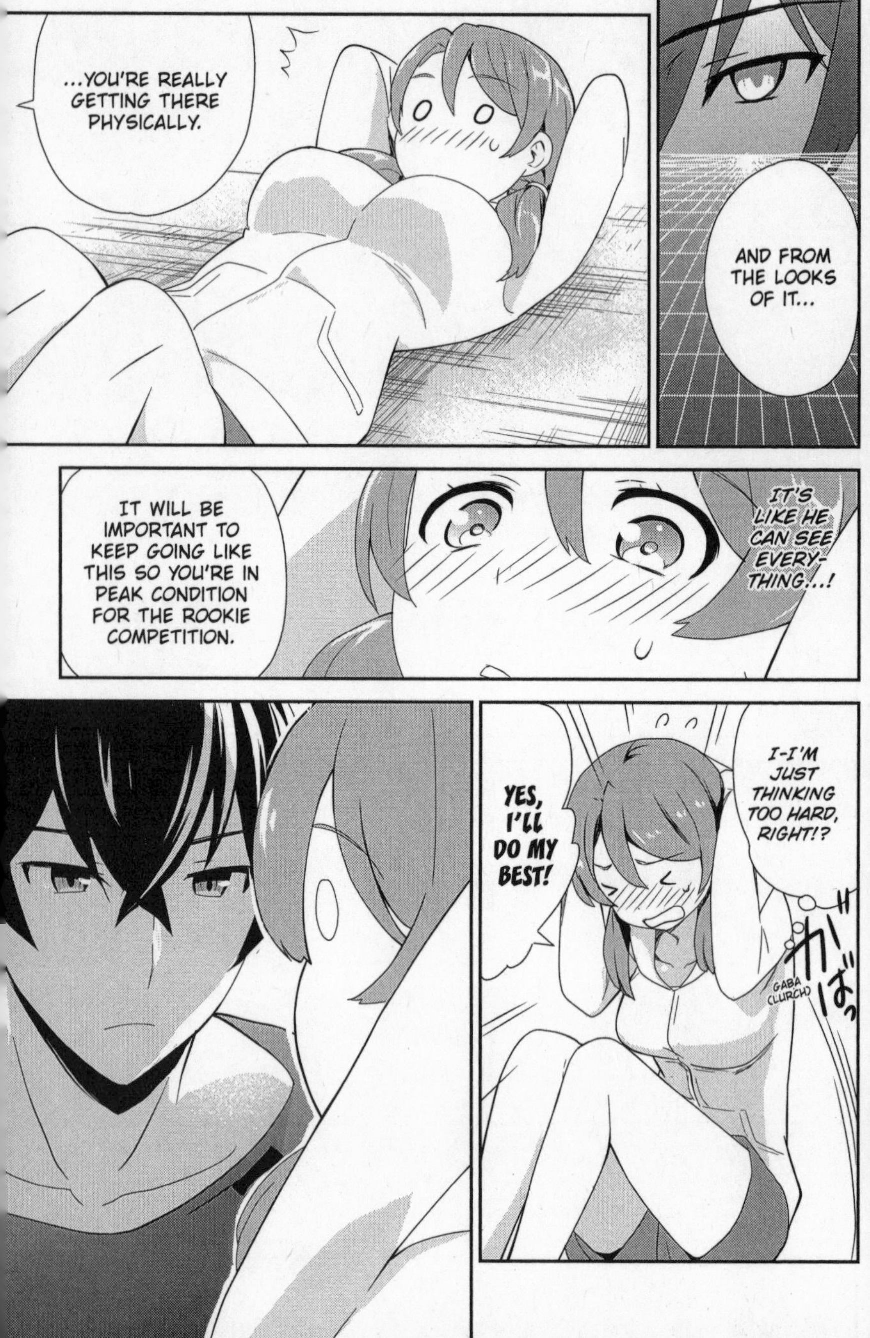
AND FROM THE LOOKS OF IT...
...YOU'RE REALLY GETTING THERE PHYSICALLY.
IT'S LIKE HE CAN SEE EVERY-THING...!
IT WILL BE IMPORTANT TO KEEP GOING LIKE THIS SO YOU'RE IN PEAK CONDITION FOR THE ROOKIE COMPETITION.
I-I'M JUST THINKING TOO HARD, RIGHT!?
がばっ
GABA (LURCH)
YES, I'LL DO MY BEST!

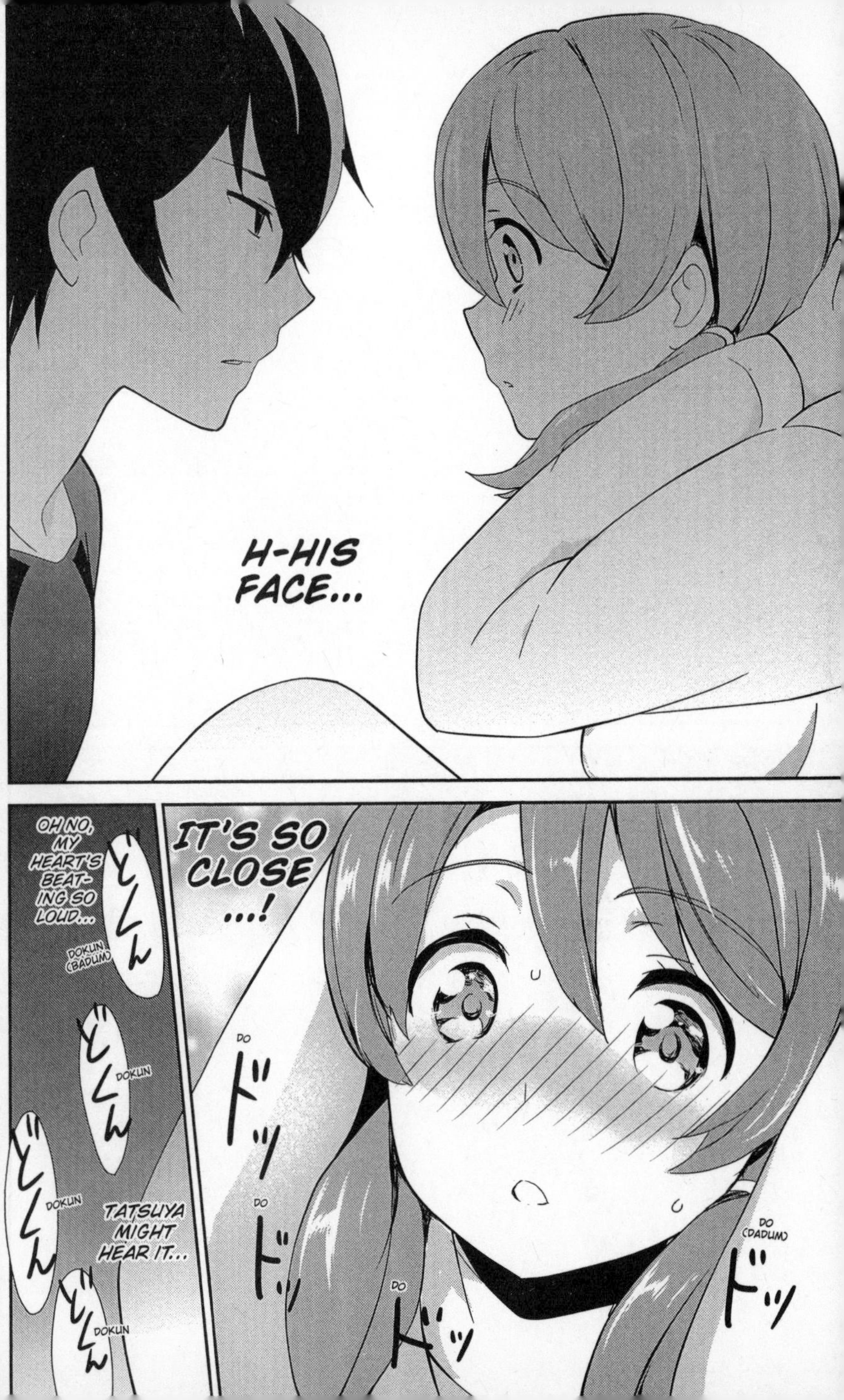
H-HIS FACE...
IT'S SO CLOSE ...!
ドッ DO
ドッ DO
ドッ DO
ドッ DO (DADUM)
OH NO, MY HEART'S BEAT-ING SO LOUD...
どくん DOKUN (BADUM)
どくん DOKUN
どくん DOKUN
TATSUYA MIGHT HEAR IT...
どくん DOKUN

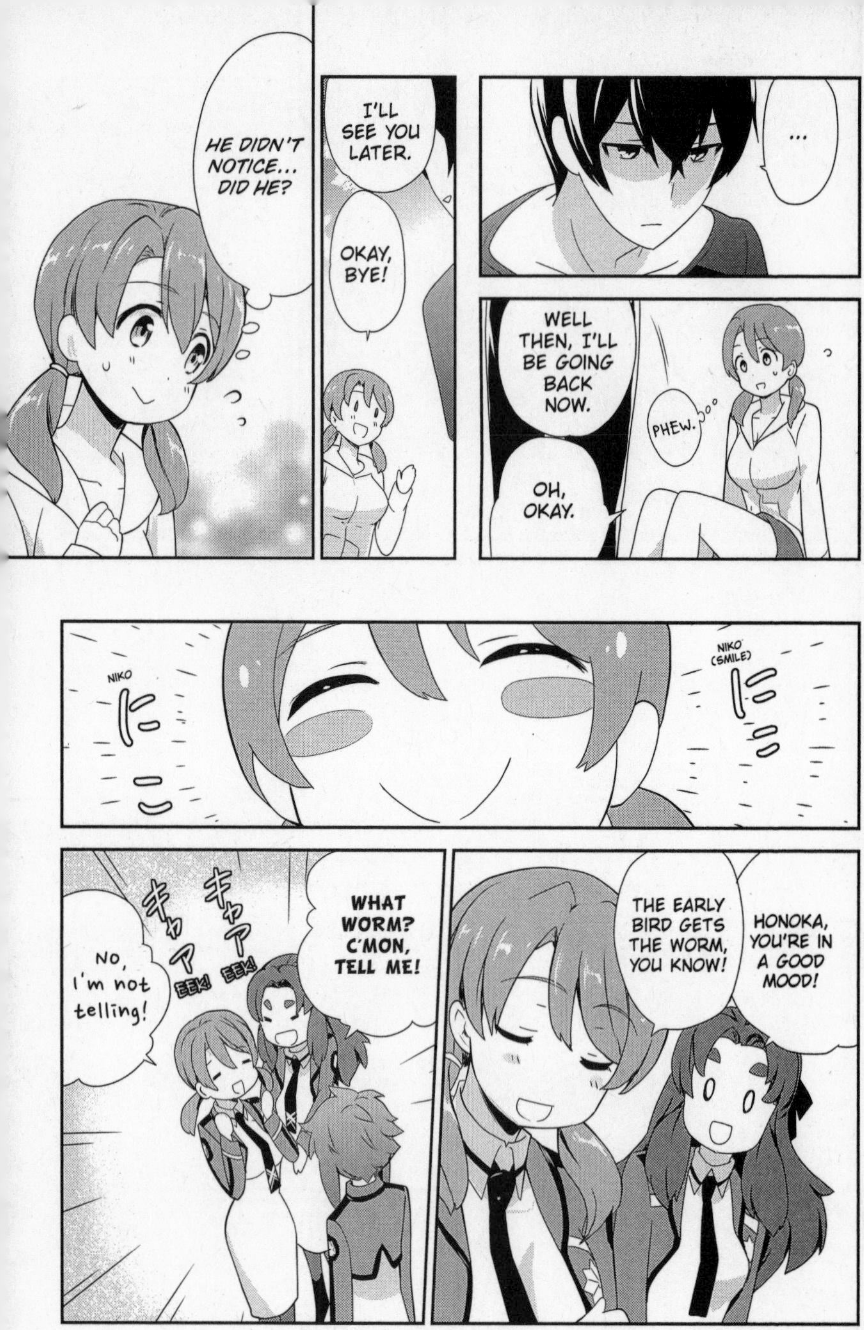
...
WELL THEN, I'LL BE GOING BACK NOW.
OH, OKAY.
PHEW.
I'LL SEE YOU LATER.
OKAY, BYE!
HE DIDN'T NOTICE... DID HE?
NIKO (SMILE)
NIKO
HONOKA, YOU'RE IN A GOOD MOOD!
THE EARLY BIRD GETS THE WORM, YOU KNOW!
WHAT WORM? C'MON, TELL ME!
EEK!
EEK!
No, I'm not telling!

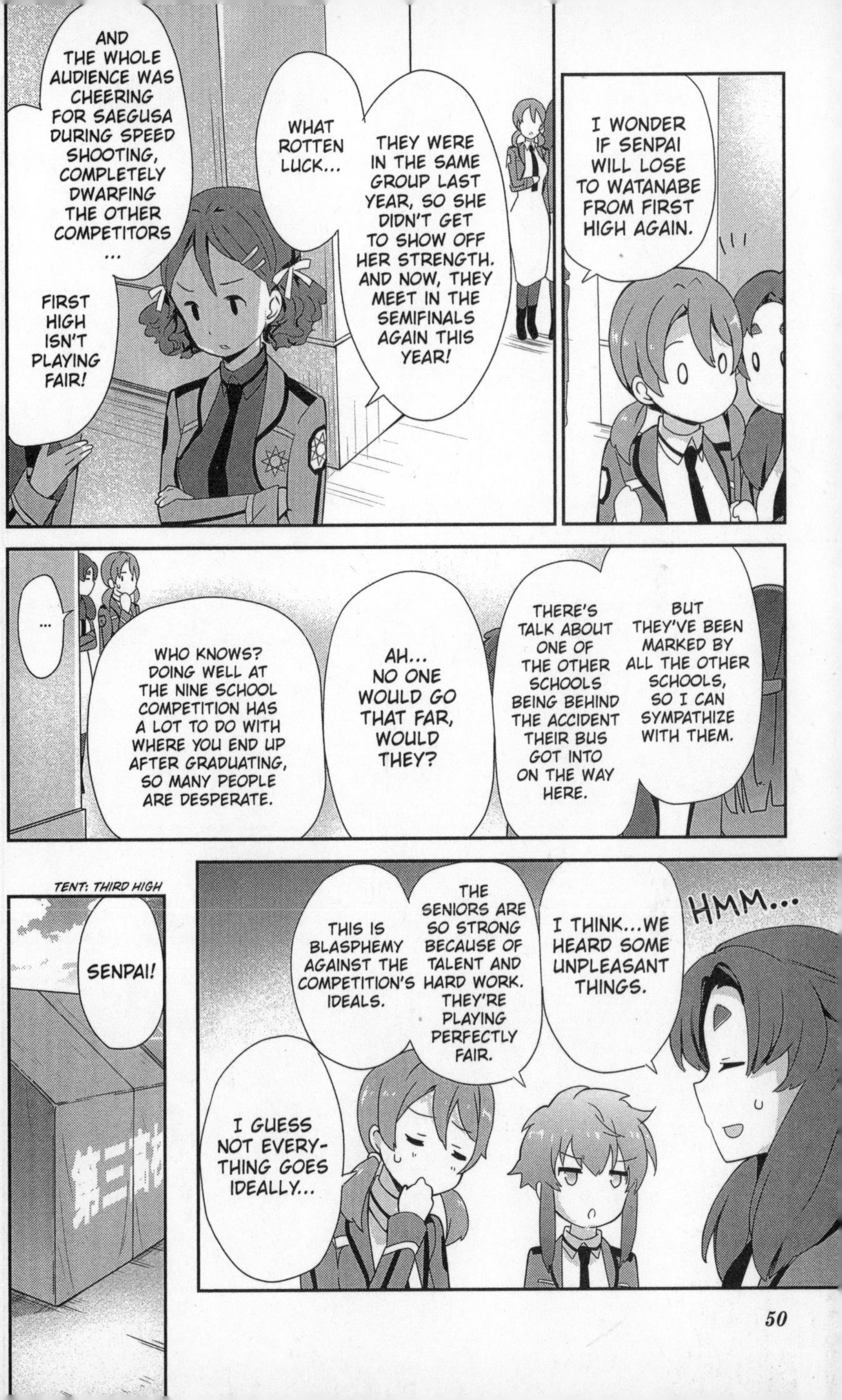
I WONDER IF SENPAI WILL LOSE TO WATANABE FROM FIRST HIGH AGAIN.
THEY WERE IN THE SAME GROUP LAST YEAR, SO SHE DIDN'T GET TO SHOW OFF HER STRENGTH. AND NOW, THEY MEET IN THE SEMIFINALS AGAIN THIS YEAR!
WHAT ROTTEN LUCK...
AND THE WHOLE AUDIENCE WAS CHEERING FOR SAEGUSA DURING SPEED SHOOTING, COMPLETELY DWARFING THE OTHER COMPETITORS...
FIRST HIGH ISN'T PLAYING FAIR!
BUT THEY'VE BEEN MARKED BY ALL THE OTHER SCHOOLS, SO I CAN SYMPATHIZE WITH THEM.
THERE'S TALK ABOUT ONE OF THE OTHER SCHOOLS BEING BEHIND THE ACCIDENT THEIR BUS GOT INTO ON THE WAY HERE.
AH... NO ONE WOULD GO THAT FAR, WOULD THEY?
WHO KNOWS? DOING WELL AT THE NINE SCHOOL COMPETITION HAS A LOT TO DO WITH WHERE YOU END UP AFTER GRADUATING, SO MANY PEOPLE ARE DESPERATE.
...
HMM...
I THINK...WE HEARD SOME UNPLEASANT THINGS.
THE SENIORS ARE SO STRONG BECAUSE OF TALENT AND HARD WORK. THEY'RE PLAYING PERFECTLY FAIR.
THIS IS BLASPHEMY AGAINST THE COMPETITION'S IDEALS.
I GUESS NOT EVERYTHING GOES IDEALLY...
TENT: THIRD HIGH
SENPAI!

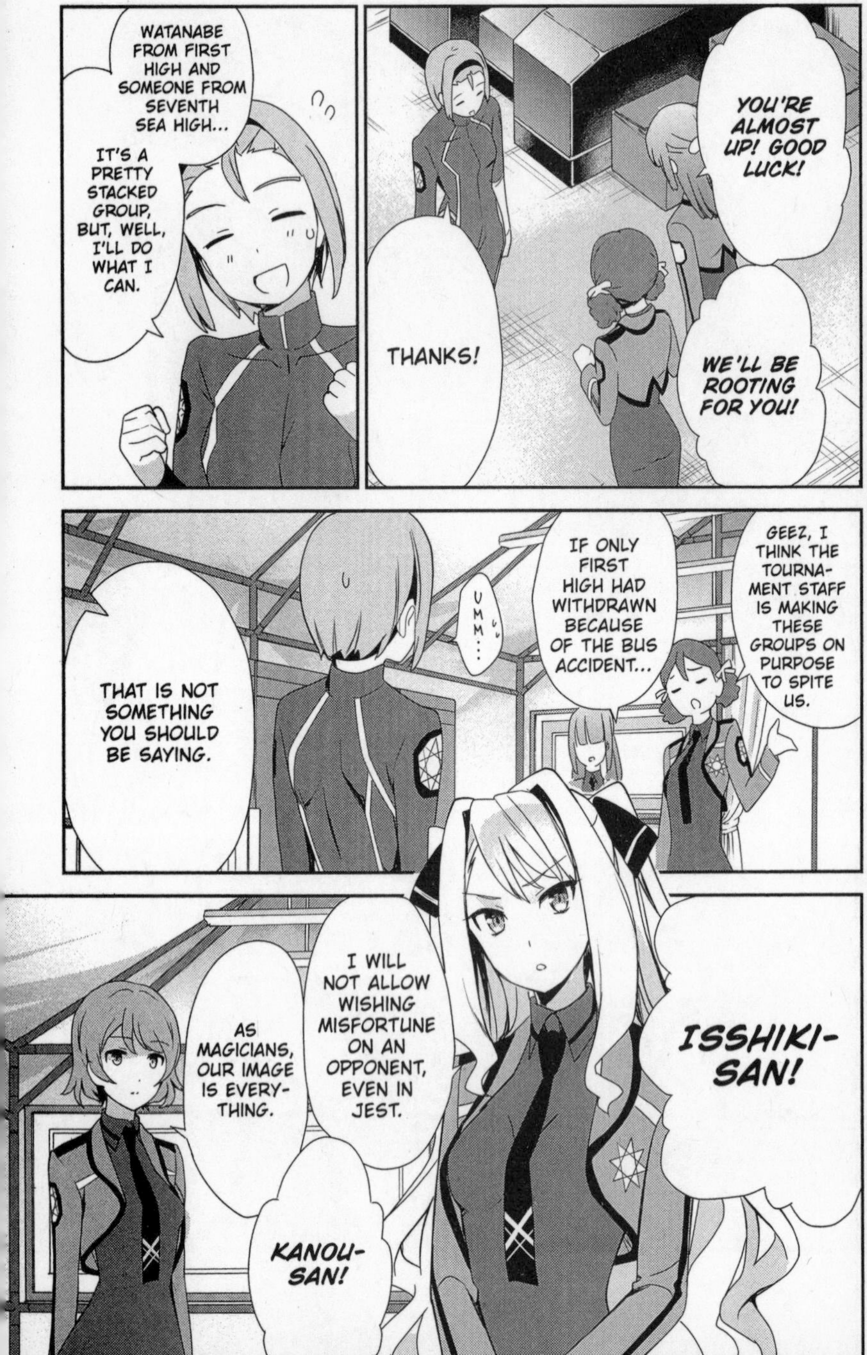
YOU'RE ALMOST UP! GOOD LUCK!
WE'LL BE ROOTING FOR YOU!
THANKS!
WATANABE FROM FIRST HIGH AND SOMEONE FROM SEVENTH SEA HIGH...
IT'S A PRETTY STACKED GROUP, BUT, WELL, I'LL DO WHAT I CAN.
GEEZ, I THINK THE TOURNAMENT STAFF IS MAKING THESE GROUPS ON PURPOSE TO SPITE US.
IF ONLY FIRST HIGH HAD WITHDRAWN BECAUSE OF THE BUS ACCIDENT...
UMM...
THAT IS NOT SOMETHING YOU SHOULD BE SAYING.
ISSHIKI-SAN!
I WILL NOT ALLOW WISHING MISFORTUNE ON AN OPPONENT, EVEN IN JEST.
AS MAGICIANS, OUR IMAGE IS EVERYTHING.
KANOU-SAN!

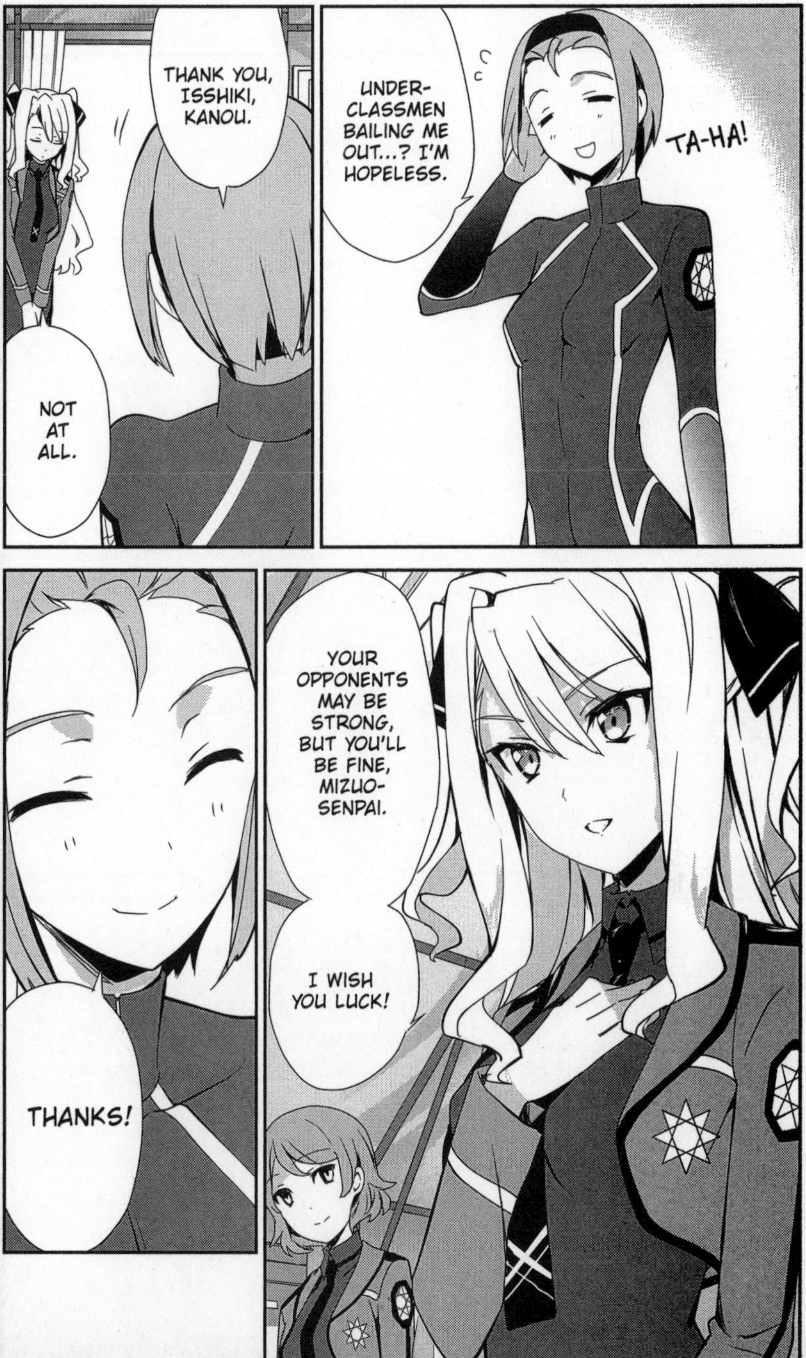
UNDER-CLASSMEN BAILING ME OUT...? I'M HOPELESS.
TA-HA!
THANK YOU, ISSHIKI, KANOU.
NOT AT ALL.
YOUR OPPONENTS MAY BE STRONG, BUT YOU'LL BE FINE, MIZUO-SENPAI.
I WISH YOU LUCK!
THANKS!

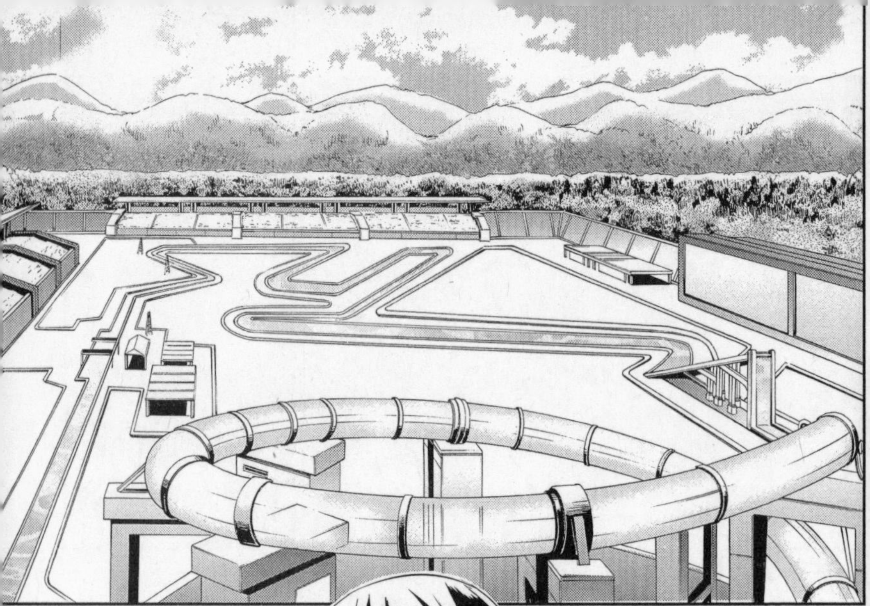

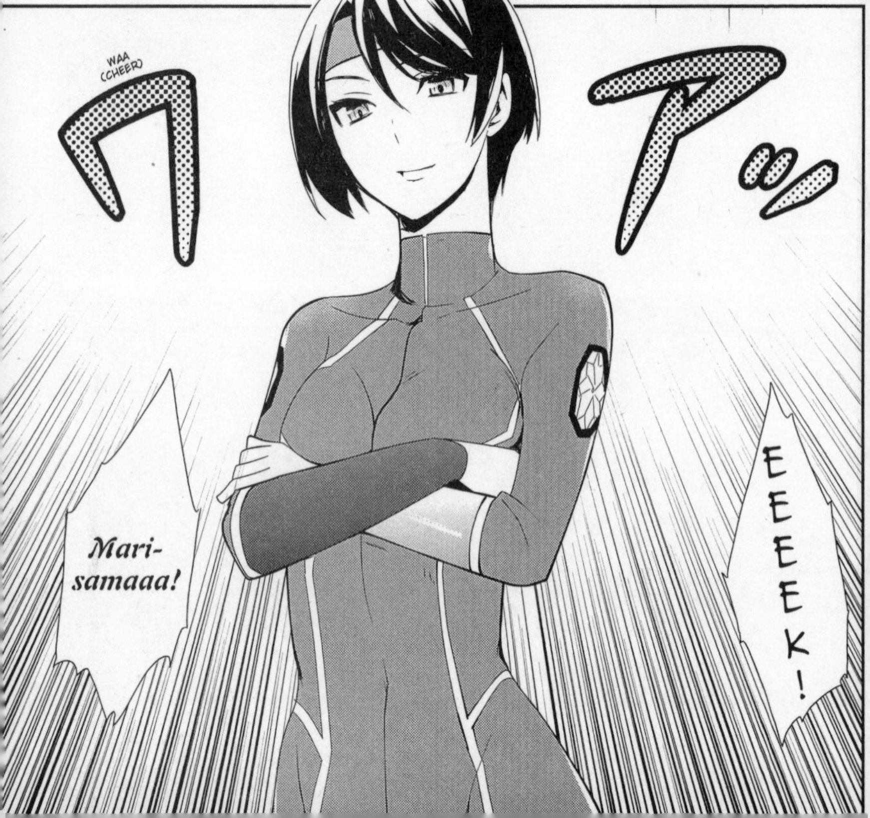
ワァッ
WAA (CHEER)
EEEEK!
Mari-samaaa!

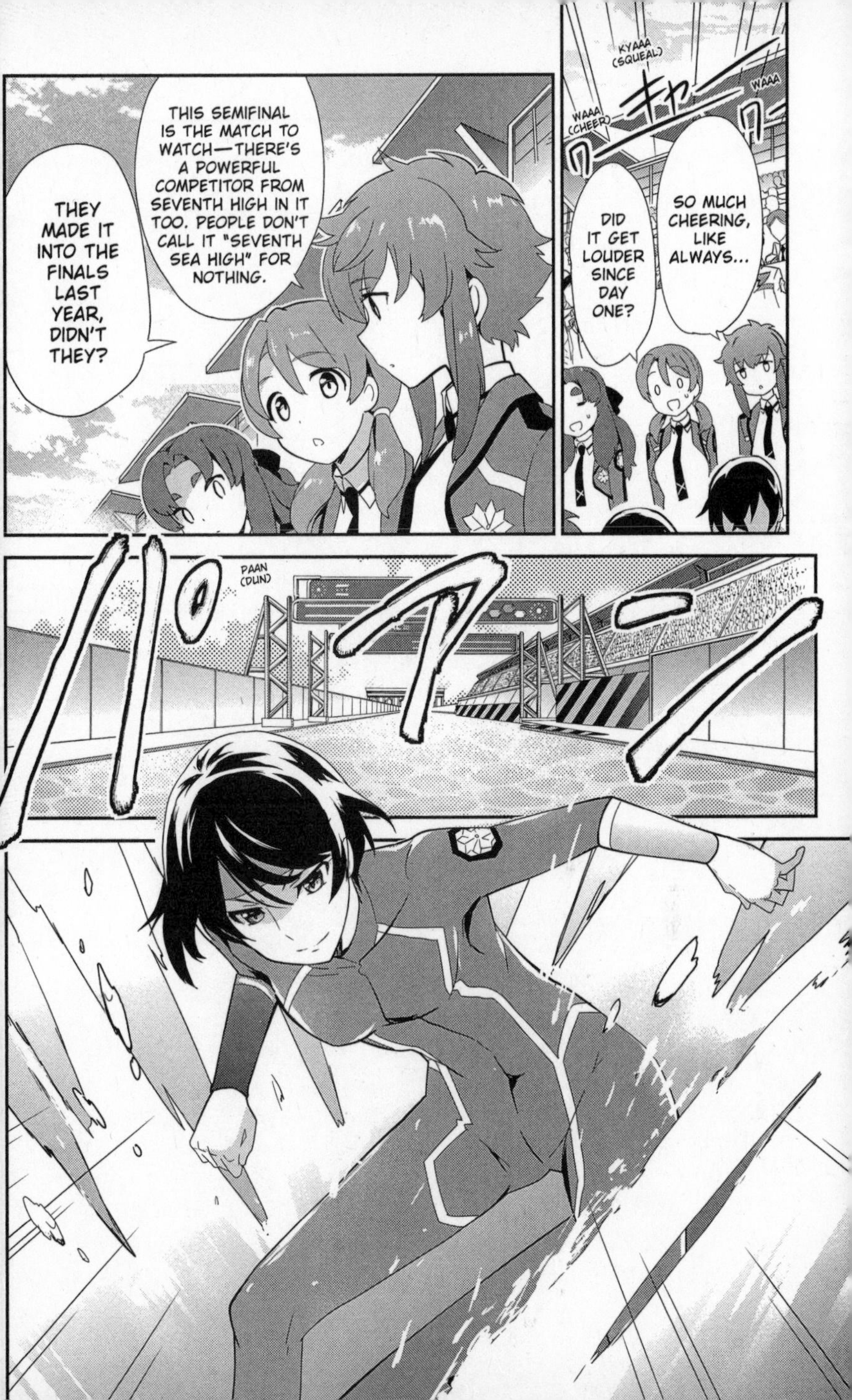
KYAAA (SQUEAL)
WAAA
WAAA (CHEER)
SO MUCH CHEERING, LIKE ALWAYS...
DID IT GET LOUDER SINCE DAY ONE?
THIS SEMIFINAL IS THE MATCH TO WATCH—THERE'S A POWERFUL COMPETITOR FROM SEVENTH HIGH IN IT TOO. PEOPLE DON'T CALL IT "SEVENTH SEA HIGH" FOR NOTHING.
THEY MADE IT INTO THE FINALS LAST YEAR, DIDN'T THEY?
PAAN (DUN)

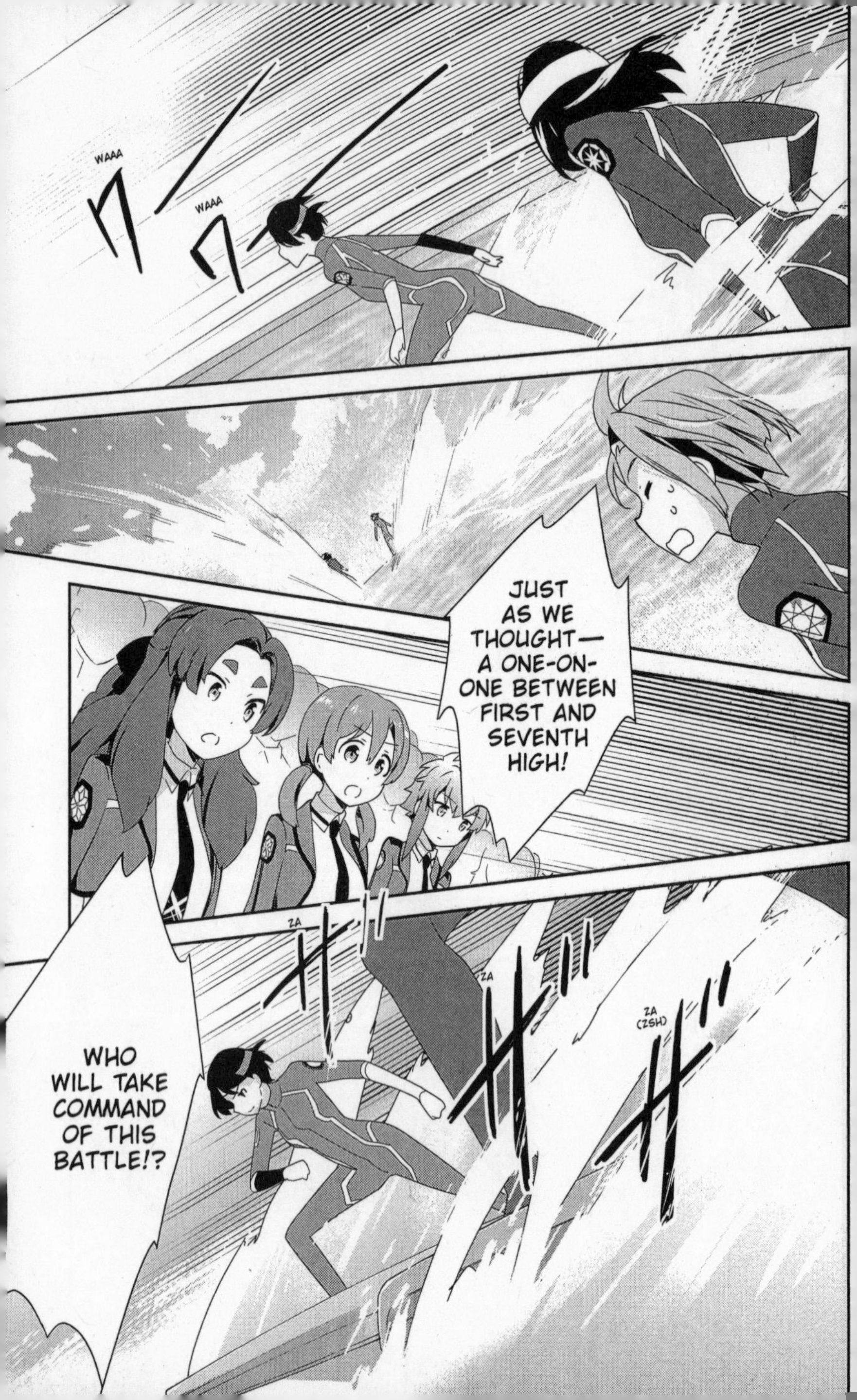
WAAA
WAAA
JUST AS WE THOUGHT—A ONE-ON-ONE BETWEEN FIRST AND SEVENTH HIGH!
ZA (ZSH)
ZA
ZA
WHO WILL TAKE COMMAND OF THIS BATTLE!?

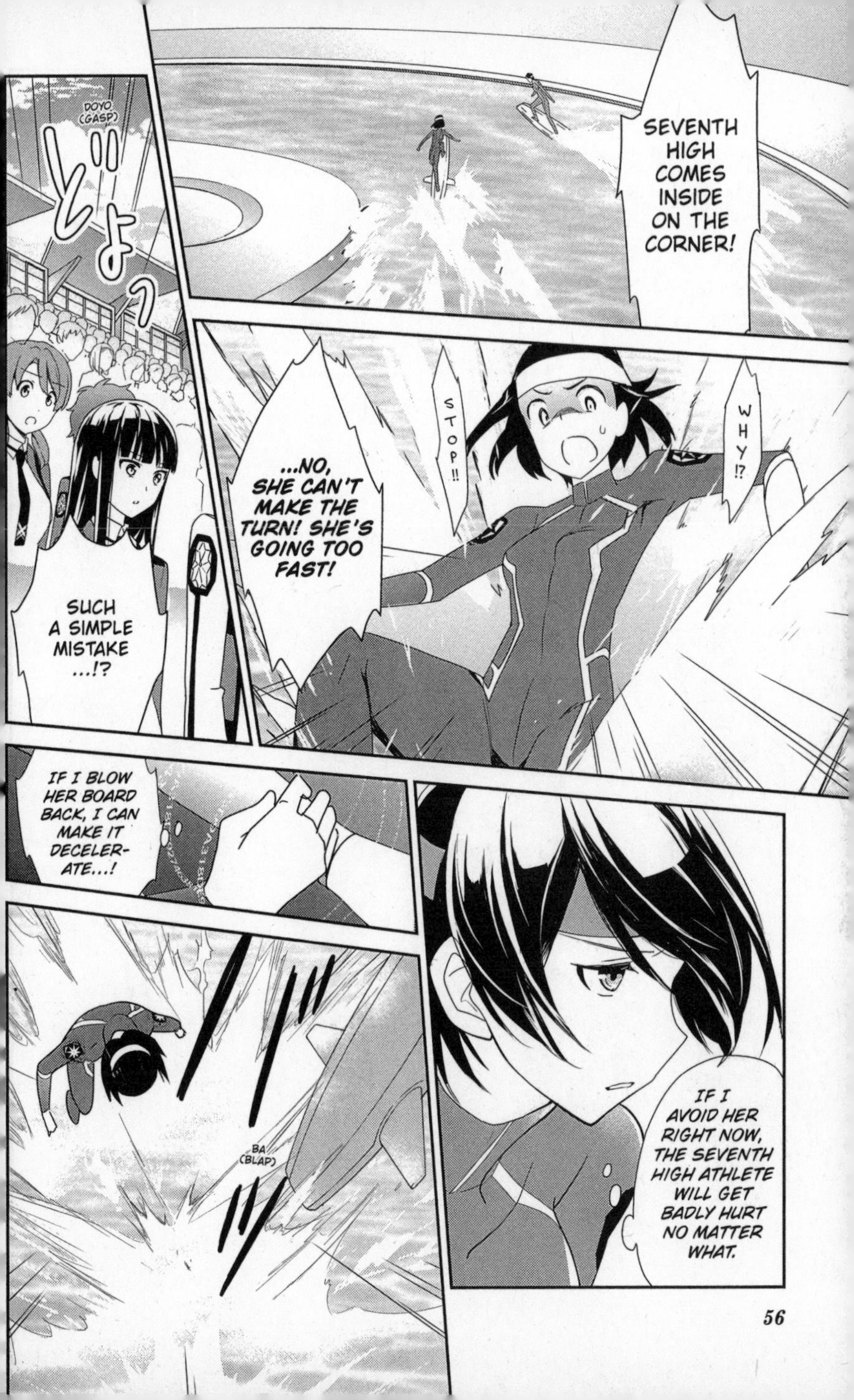

SEVENTH HIGH COMES INSIDE ON THE CORNER!
WHY!?
STOP!!
...NO, SHE CAN'T MAKE THE TURN! SHE'S GOING TOO FAST!
DOYO (GASP)
SUCH A SIMPLE MISTAKE ...!?
IF I AVOID HER RIGHT NOW, THE SEVENTH HIGH ATHLETE WILL GET BADLY HURT NO MATTER WHAT.
IF I BLOW HER BOARD BACK, I CAN MAKE IT DECELER-ATE...!
BA (BLAP)

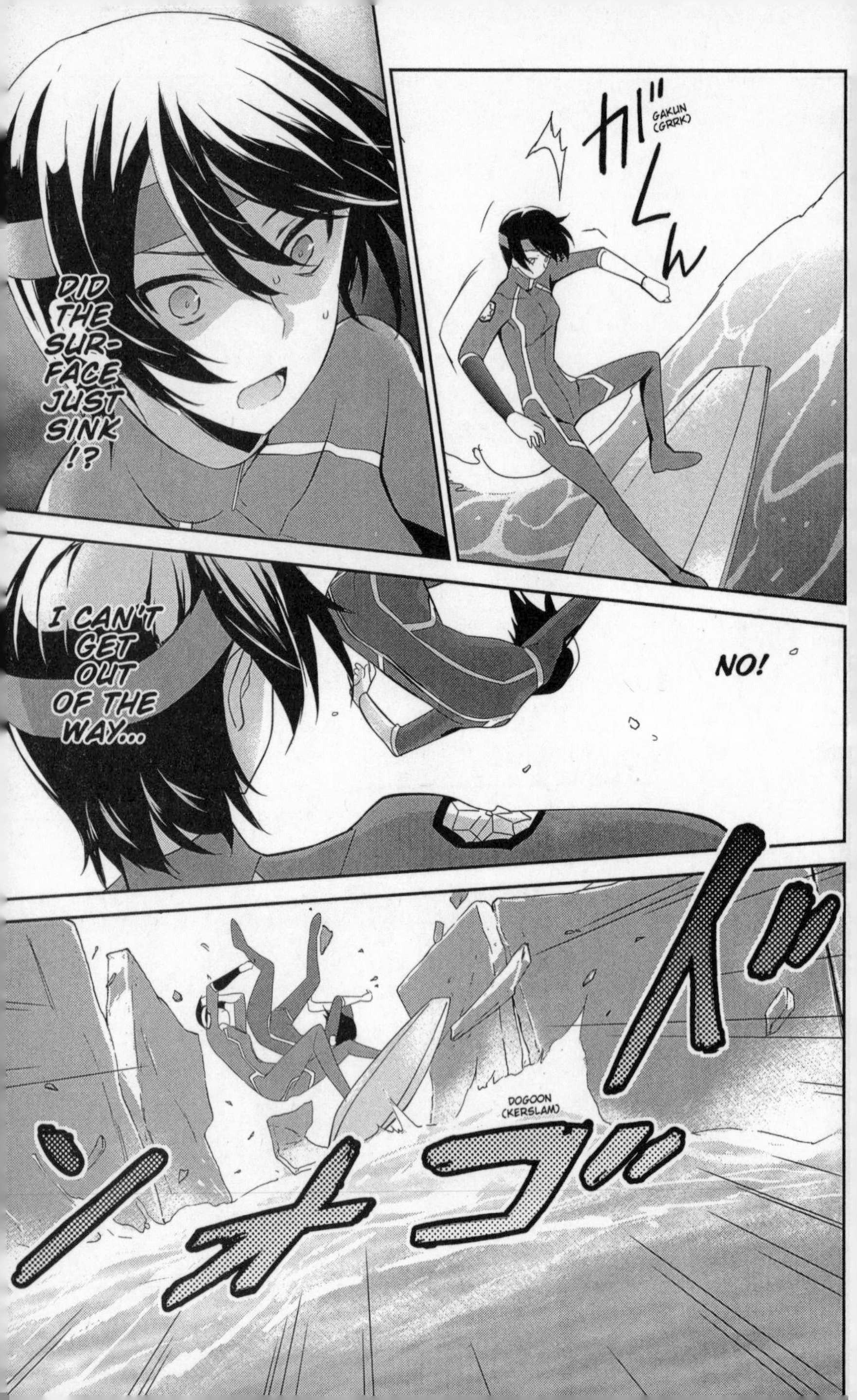
ガくん
GAKUN (GRRK)
DID THE SUR-FACE JUST SINK!?
NO!
I CAN'T GET OUT OF THE WAY...
DOGOON (KERSLAM)

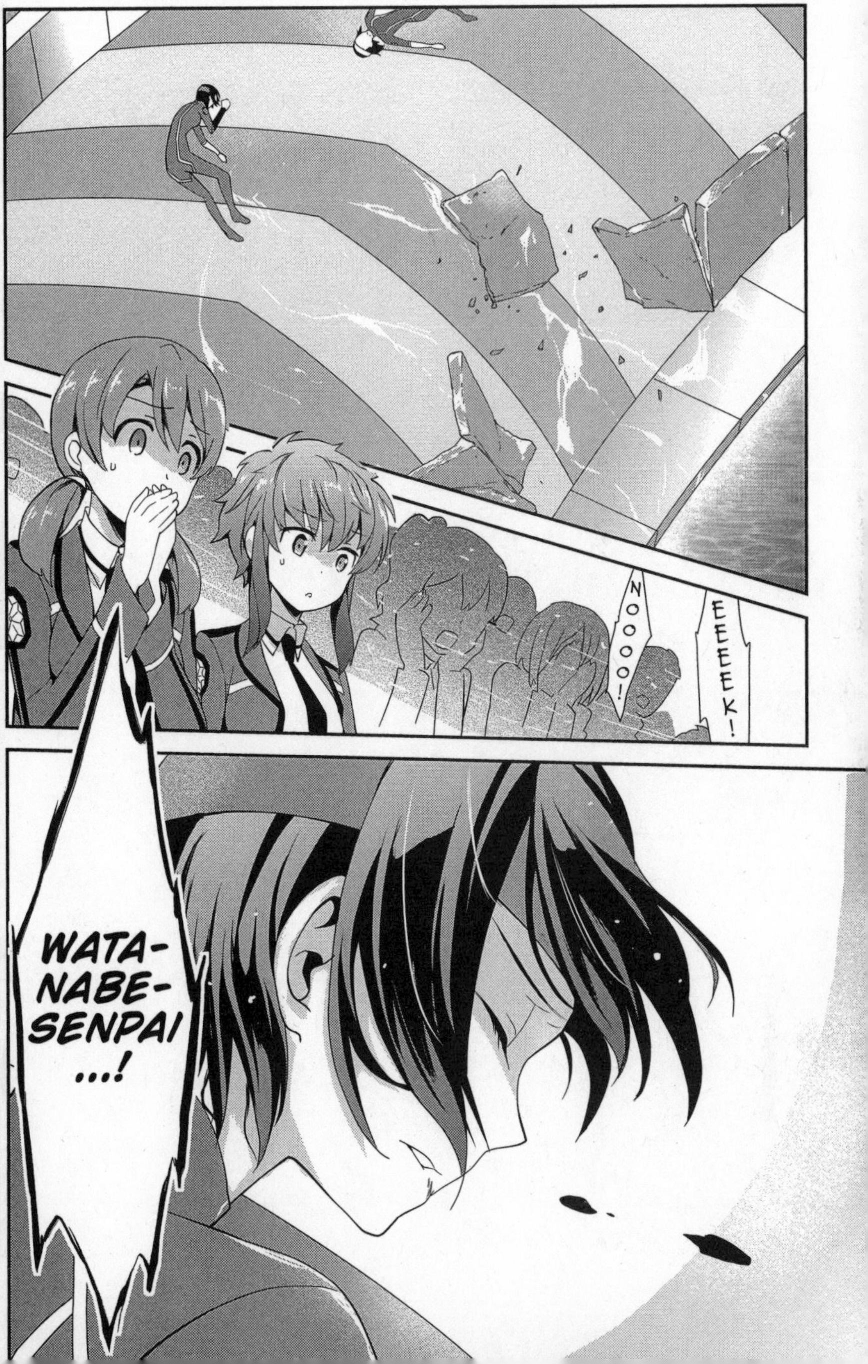
EEEEK!
NOOOO!
WATA-NABE-SENPAI ...!

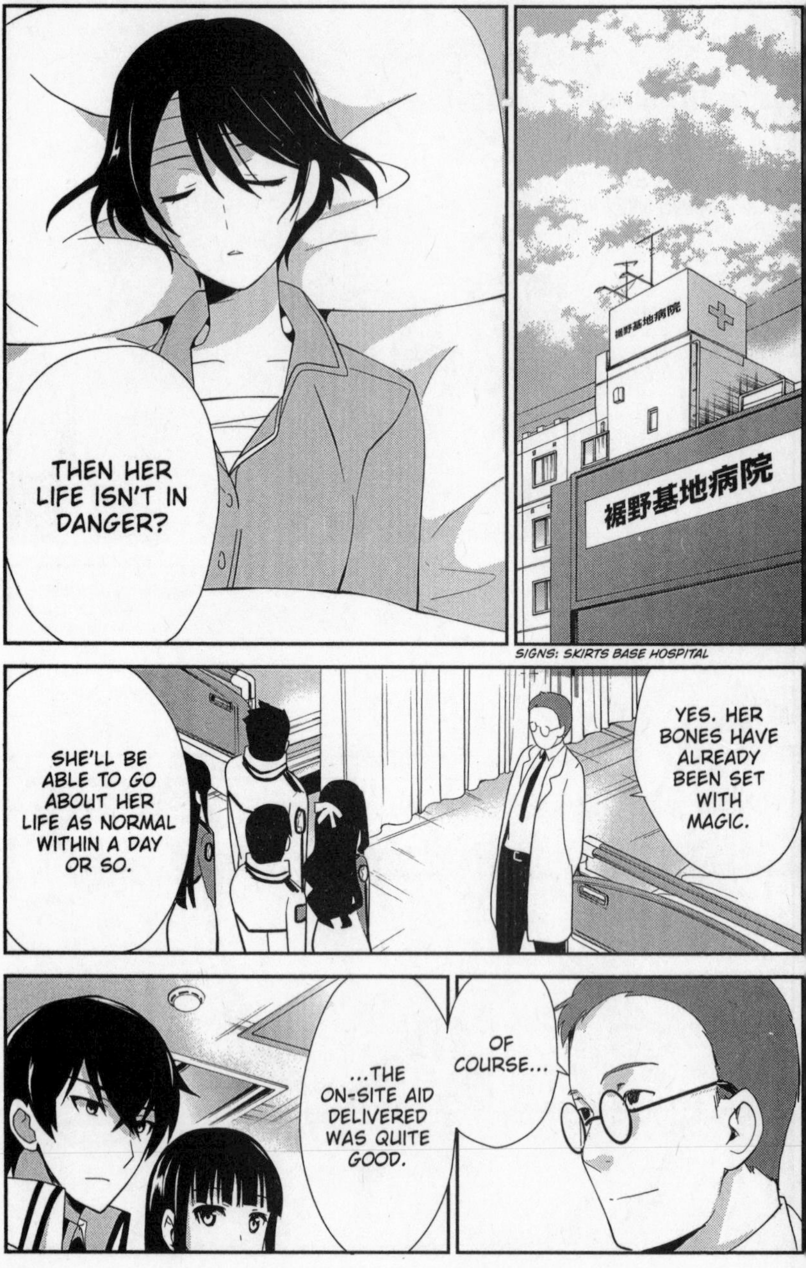
裾野基地病院
裾野基地病院
THEN HER LIFE ISN'T IN DANGER?
YES. HER BONES HAVE ALREADY BEEN SET WITH MAGIC.
SHE'LL BE ABLE TO GO ABOUT HER LIFE AS NORMAL WITHIN A DAY OR SO.
OF COURSE...
...THE ON-SITE AID DELIVERED WAS QUITE GOOD.

SIGNS: SKIRTS BASE HOSPITAL

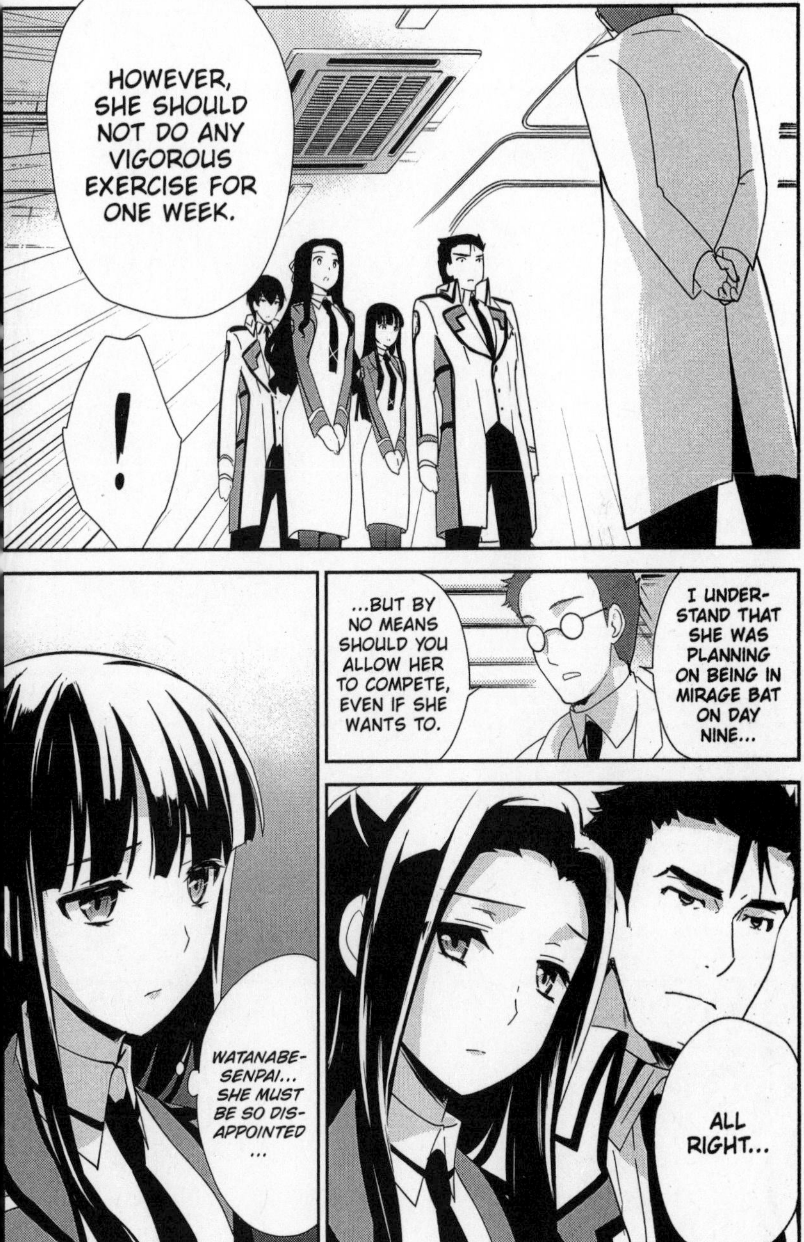
HOWEVER, SHE SHOULD NOT DO ANY VIGOROUS EXERCISE FOR ONE WEEK.
!
I UNDER-STAND THAT SHE WAS PLANNING ON BEING IN MIRAGE BAT ON DAY NINE...
...BUT BY NO MEANS SHOULD YOU ALLOW HER TO COMPETE, EVEN IF SHE WANTS TO.
ALL RIGHT...
WATANABE-SENPAI... SHE MUST BE SO DIS-APPOINTED ...

# CHAPTER 27

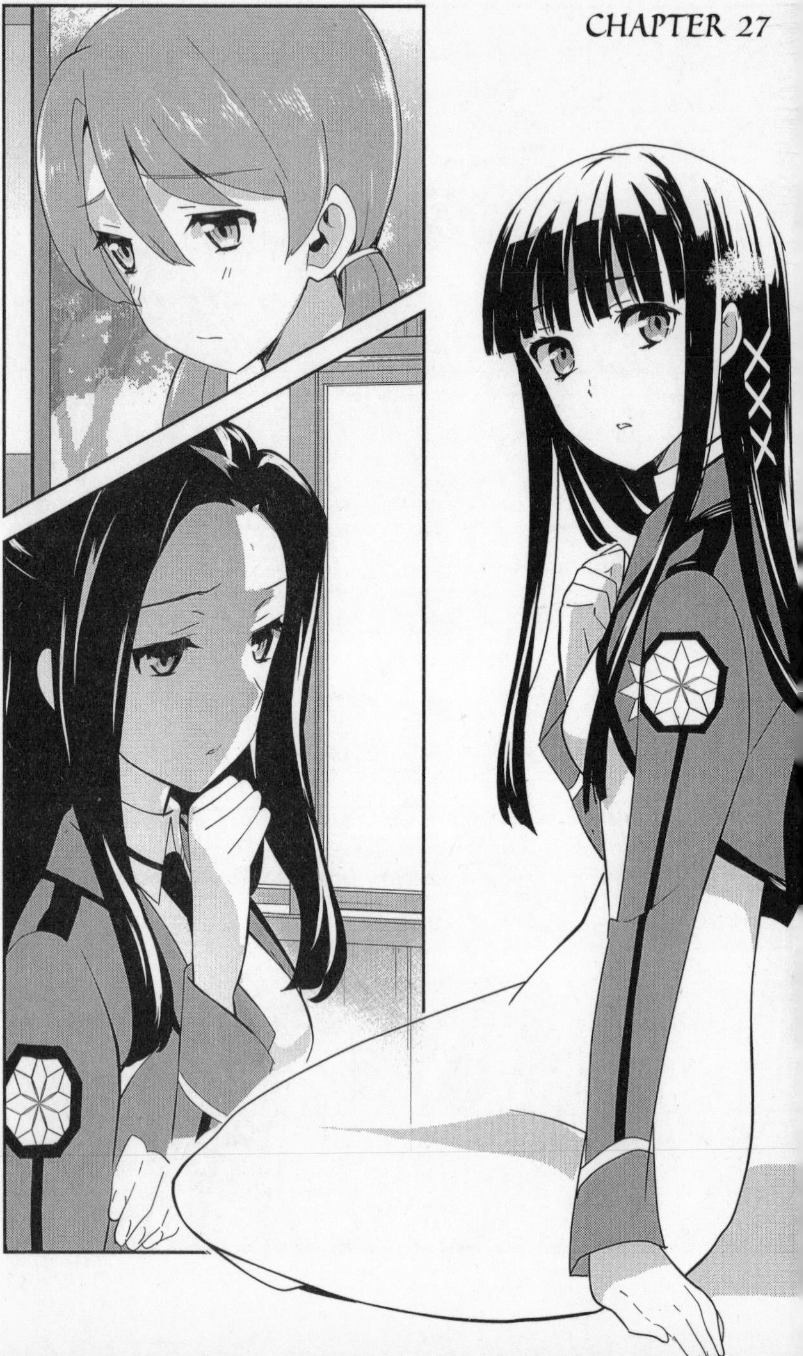

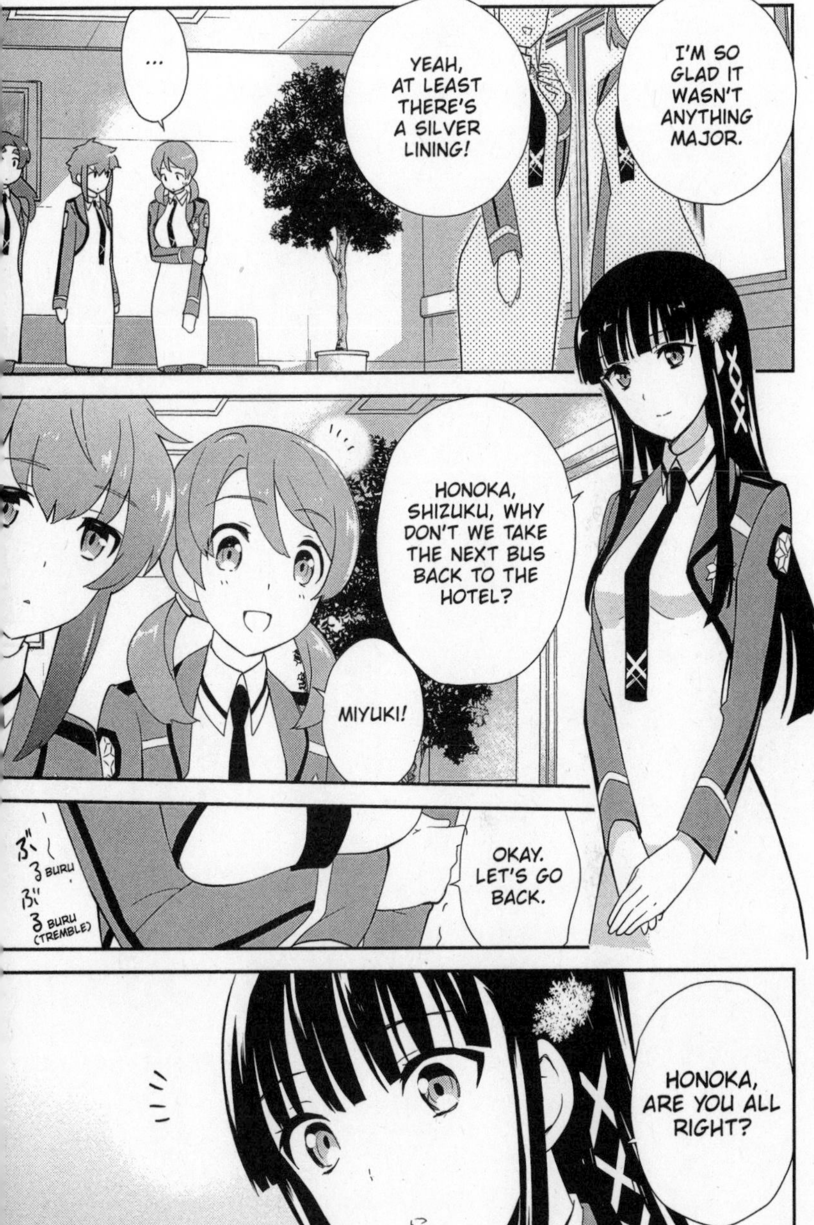
I'M SO GLAD IT WASN'T ANYTHING MAJOR.
YEAH, AT LEAST THERE'S A SILVER LINING!
...
HONOKA, SHIZUKU, WHY DON'T WE TAKE THE NEXT BUS BACK TO THE HOTEL?
MIYUKI!
OKAY. LET'S GO BACK.
ぶる BURU
ぶる BURU (TREMBLE)
HONOKA, ARE YOU ALL RIGHT?

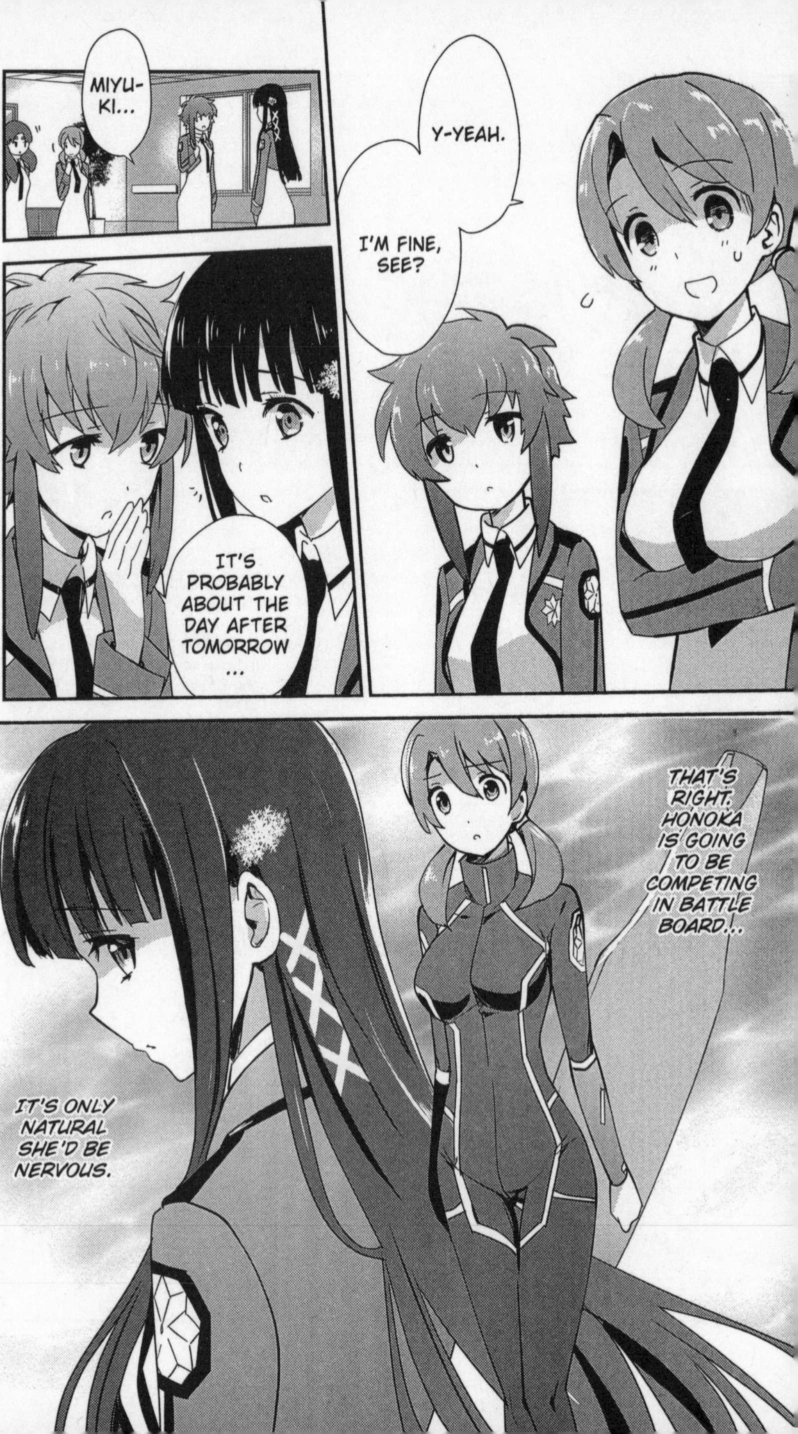
Y-YEAH.
I'M FINE, SEE?
MIYU-KI...
IT'S PROBABLY ABOUT THE DAY AFTER TOMORROW...
THAT'S RIGHT. HONOKA IS GOING TO BE COMPETING IN BATTLE BOARD...
IT'S ONLY NATURAL SHE'D BE NERVOUS.

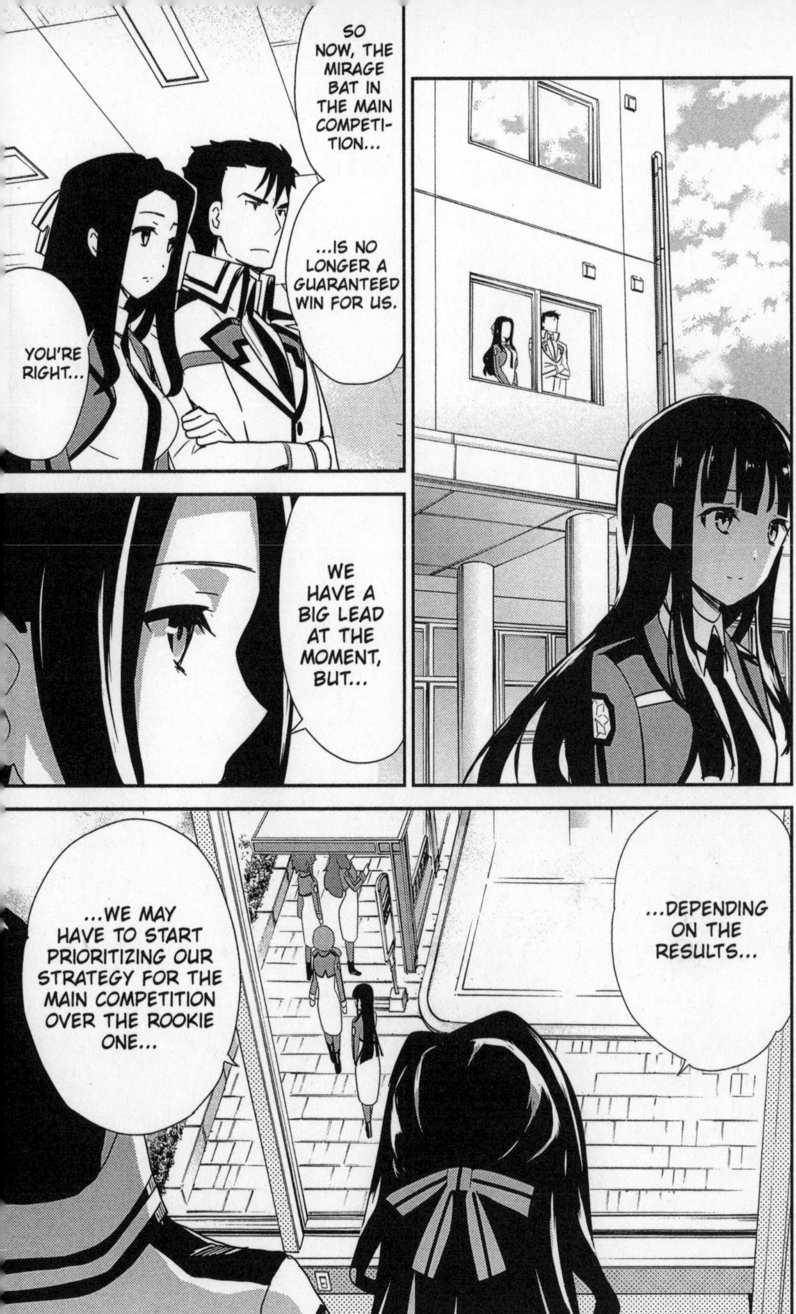
SO NOW, THE MIRAGE BAT IN THE MAIN COMPETITION...
...IS NO LONGER A GUARANTEED WIN FOR US.
YOU'RE RIGHT...
WE HAVE A BIG LEAD AT THE MOMENT, BUT...
...DEPENDING ON THE RESULTS...
...WE MAY HAVE TO START PRIORITIZING OUR STRATEGY FOR THE MAIN COMPETITION OVER THE ROOKIE ONE...

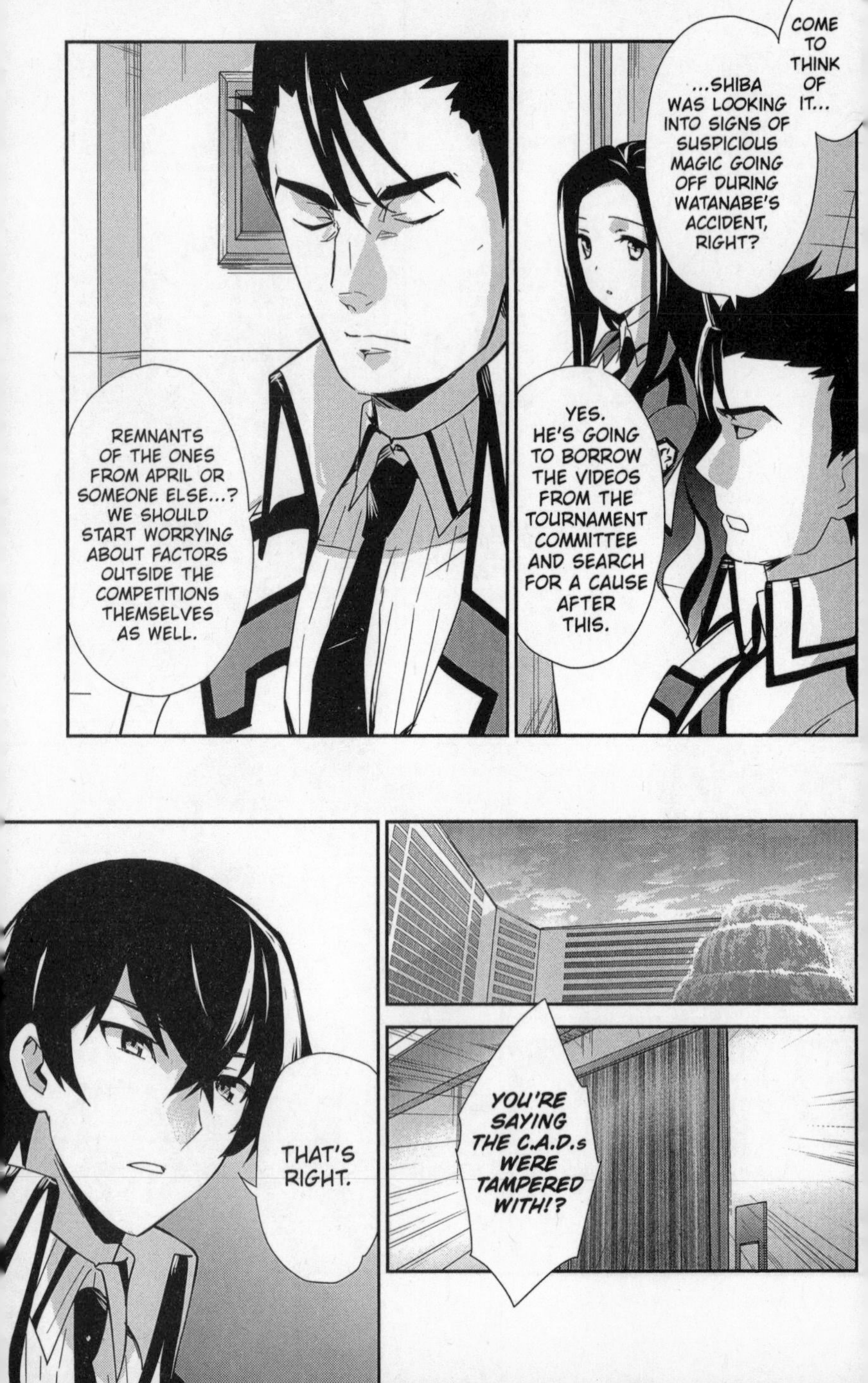
COME TO THINK OF IT...
...SHIBA WAS LOOKING INTO SIGNS OF SUSPICIOUS MAGIC GOING OFF DURING WATANABE'S ACCIDENT, RIGHT?
YES. HE'S GOING TO BORROW THE VIDEOS FROM THE TOURNAMENT COMMITTEE AND SEARCH FOR A CAUSE AFTER THIS.
REMNANTS OF THE ONES FROM APRIL OR SOMEONE ELSE...? WE SHOULD START WORRYING ABOUT FACTORS OUTSIDE THE COMPETITIONS THEMSELVES AS WELL.
YOU'RE SAYING THE C.A.D.s WERE TAMPERED WITH!?
THAT'S RIGHT.

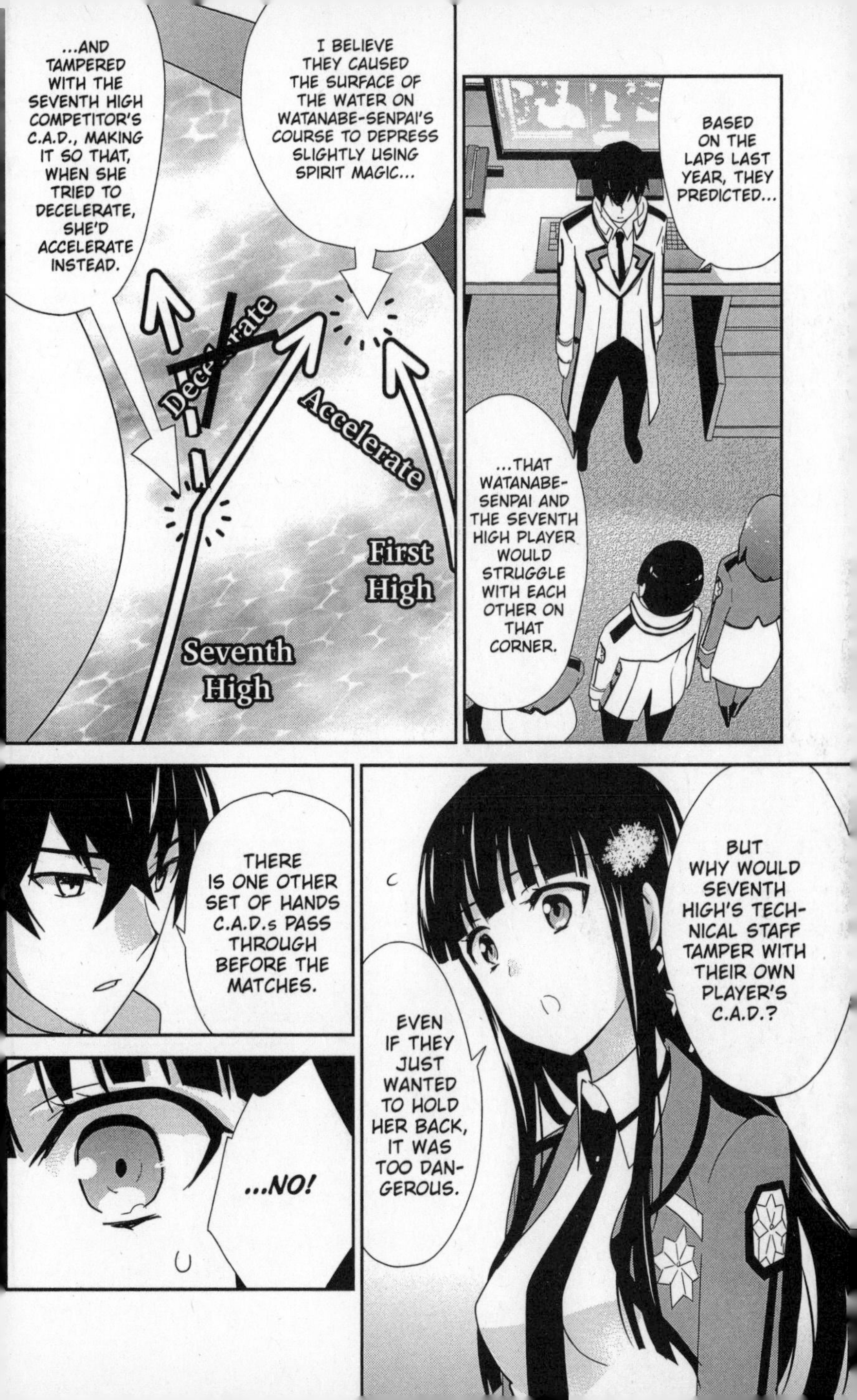
BASED ON THE LAPS LAST YEAR, THEY PREDICTED...
...THAT WATANABE-SENPAI AND THE SEVENTH HIGH PLAYER WOULD STRUGGLE WITH EACH OTHER ON THAT CORNER.
I BELIEVE THEY CAUSED THE SURFACE OF THE WATER ON WATANABE-SENPAI'S COURSE TO DEPRESS SLIGHTLY USING SPIRIT MAGIC...
...AND TAMPERED WITH THE SEVENTH HIGH COMPETITOR'S C.A.D., MAKING IT SO THAT, WHEN SHE TRIED TO DECELERATE, SHE'D ACCELERATE INSTEAD.
Decelerate
Accelerate
First High
Seventh High
BUT WHY WOULD SEVENTH HIGH'S TECH-NICAL STAFF TAMPER WITH THEIR OWN PLAYER'S C.A.D.?
EVEN IF THEY JUST WANTED TO HOLD HER BACK, IT WAS TOO DAN-GEROUS.
THERE IS ONE OTHER SET OF HANDS C.A.D.s PASS THROUGH BEFORE THE MATCHES.
...NO!

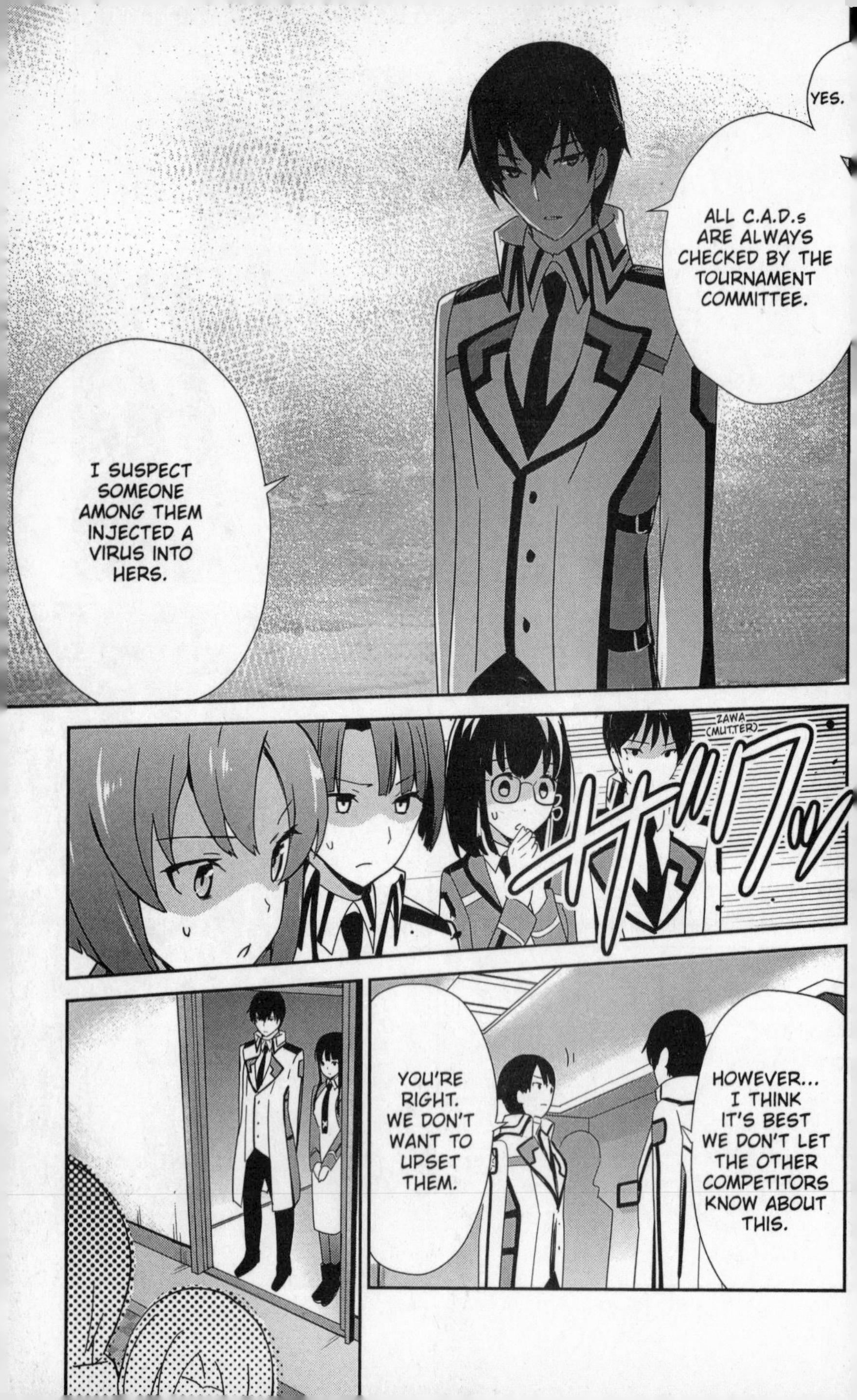
YES.
ALL C.A.D.s ARE ALWAYS CHECKED BY THE TOURNAMENT COMMITTEE.
I SUSPECT SOMEONE AMONG THEM INJECTED A VIRUS INTO HERS.
ZAWA (MUTTER)
HOWEVER... I THINK IT'S BEST WE DON'T LET THE OTHER COMPETITORS KNOW ABOUT THIS.
YOU'RE RIGHT. WE DON'T WANT TO UPSET THEM.

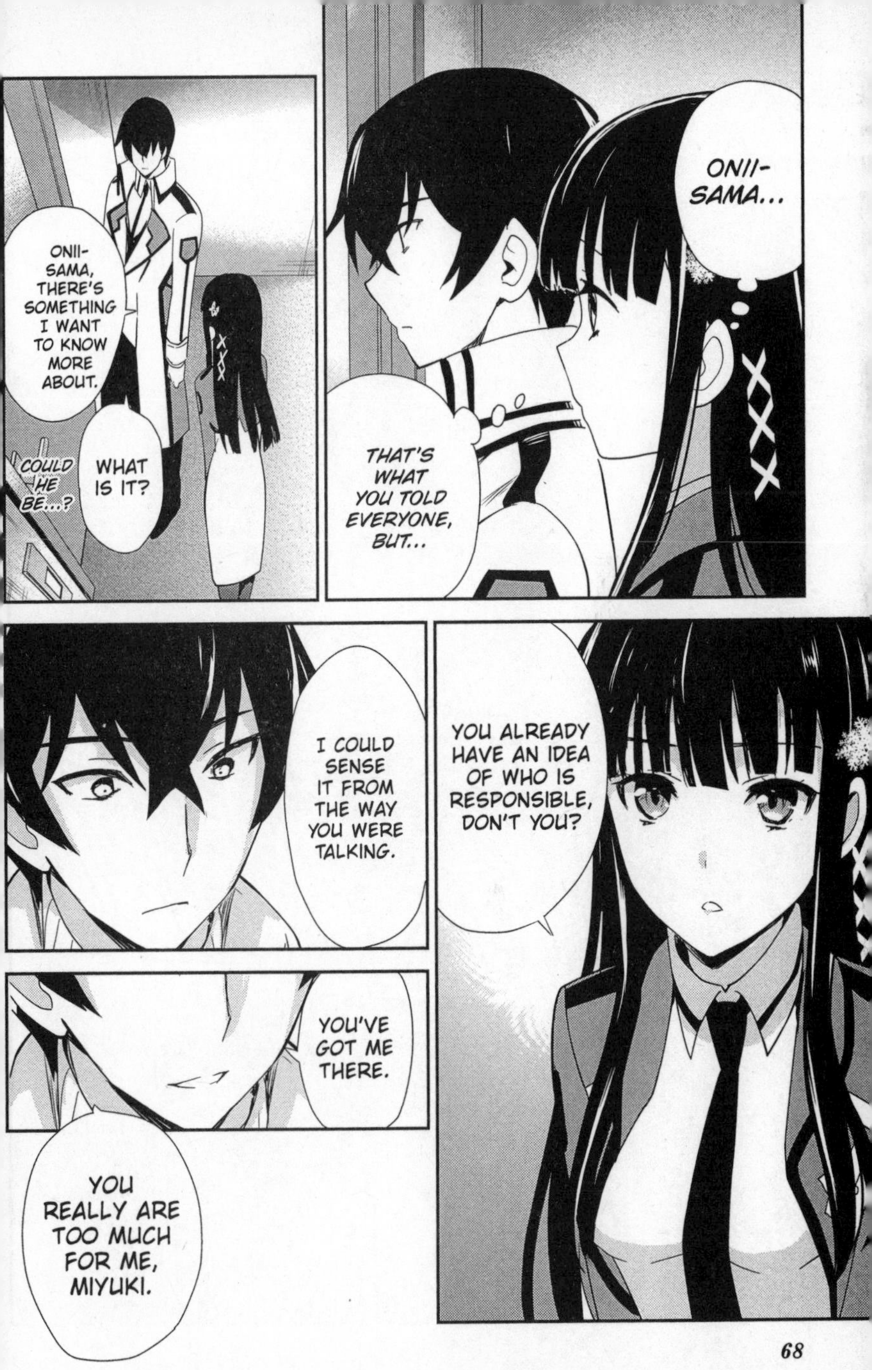
ONII-SAMA...
THAT'S WHAT YOU TOLD EVERYONE, BUT...
ONII-SAMA, THERE'S SOMETHING I WANT TO KNOW MORE ABOUT.
WHAT IS IT?
COULD HE BE...?
YOU ALREADY HAVE AN IDEA OF WHO IS RESPONSIBLE, DON'T YOU?
I COULD SENSE IT FROM THE WAY YOU WERE TALKING.
YOU'VE GOT ME THERE.
YOU REALLY ARE TOO MUCH FOR ME, MIYUKI.

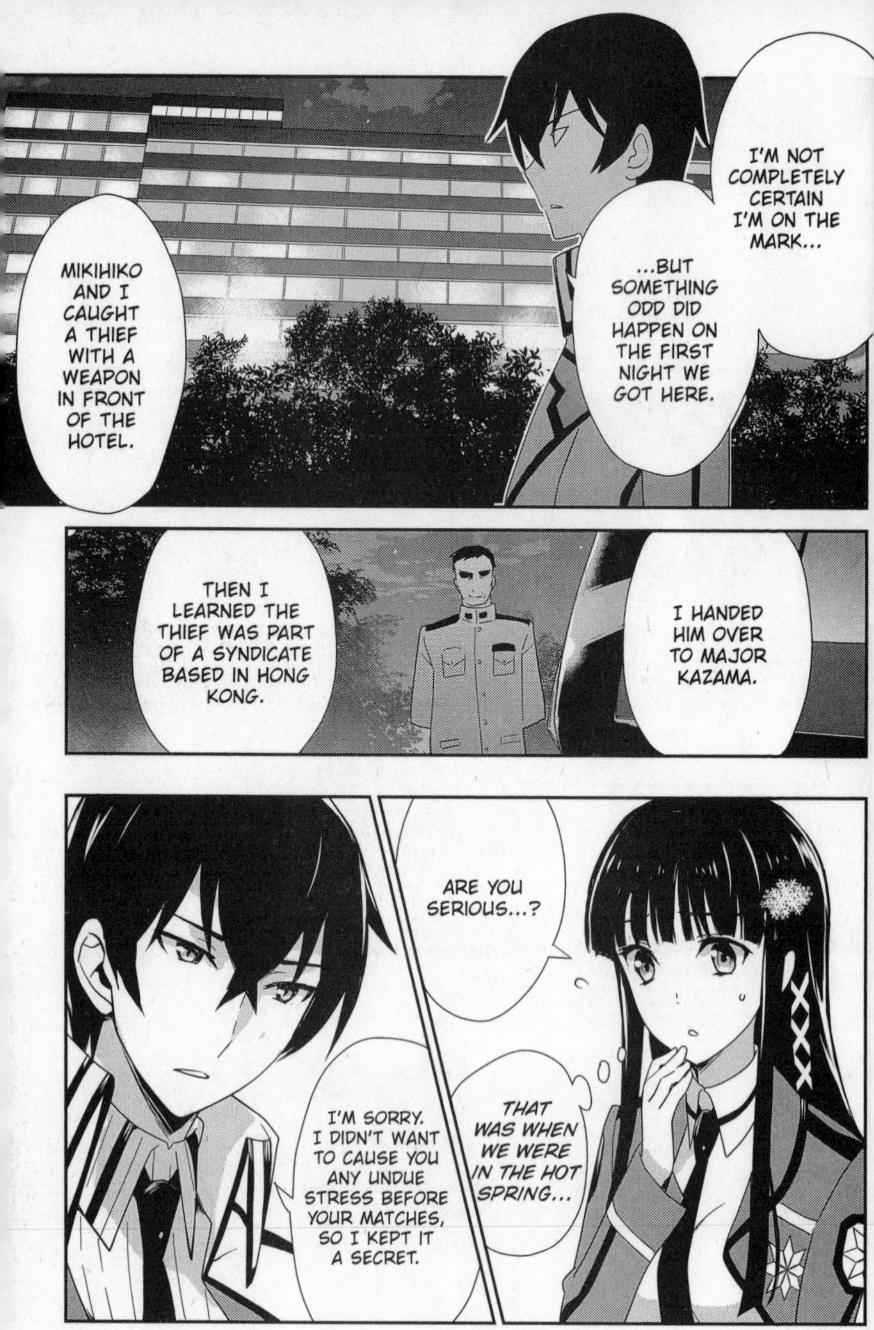
I'M NOT COMPLETELY CERTAIN I'M ON THE MARK...
...BUT SOMETHING ODD DID HAPPEN ON THE FIRST NIGHT WE GOT HERE.
MIKIHIKO AND I CAUGHT A THIEF WITH A WEAPON IN FRONT OF THE HOTEL.
I HANDED HIM OVER TO MAJOR KAZAMA.
THEN I LEARNED THE THIEF WAS PART OF A SYNDICATE BASED IN HONG KONG.
ARE YOU SERIOUS...?
THAT WAS WHEN WE WERE IN THE HOT SPRING...
I'M SORRY. I DIDN'T WANT TO CAUSE YOU ANY UNDUE STRESS BEFORE YOUR MATCHES, SO I KEPT IT A SECRET.

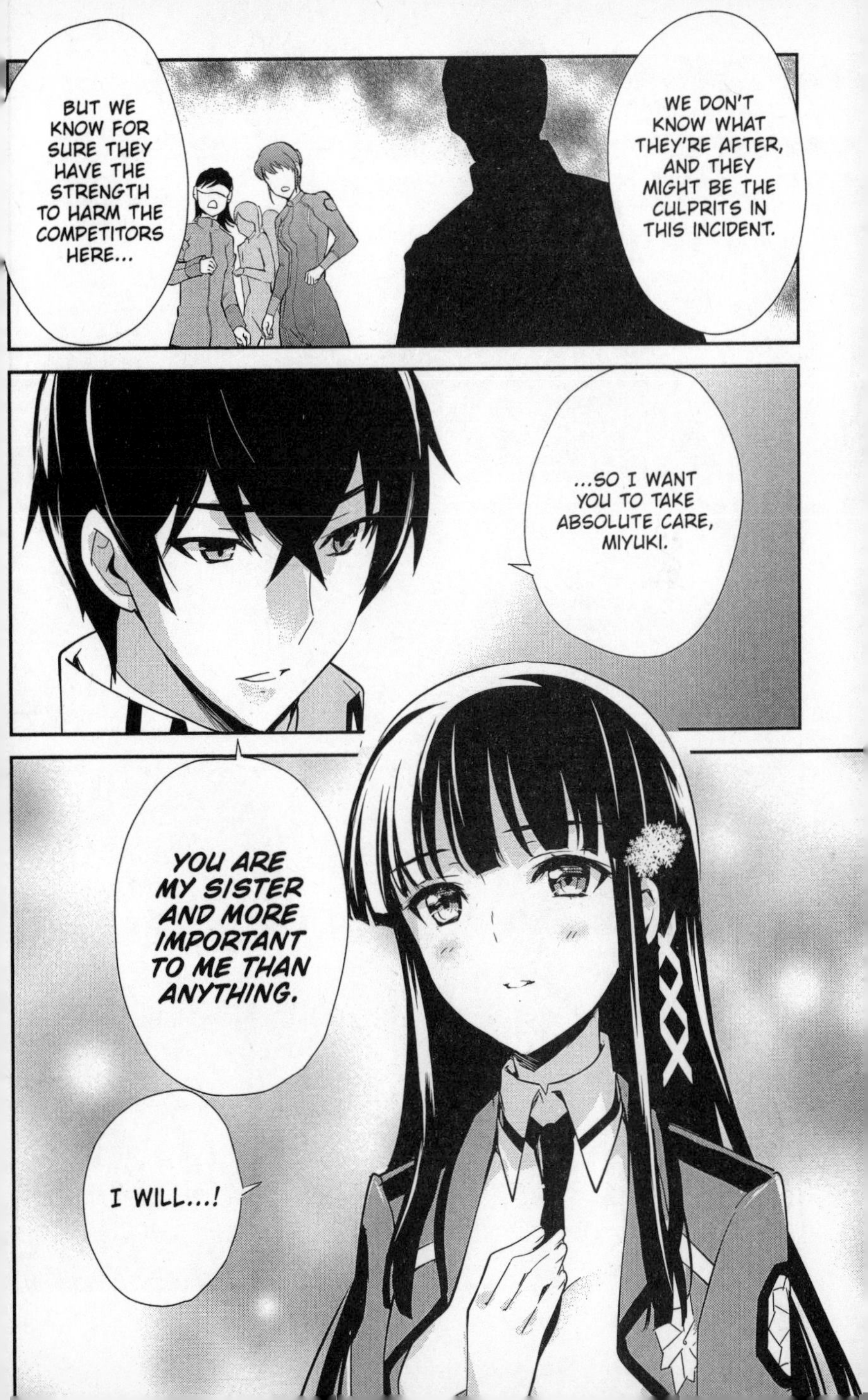
WE DON'T KNOW WHAT THEY'RE AFTER, AND THEY MIGHT BE THE CULPRITS IN THIS INCIDENT.
BUT WE KNOW FOR SURE THEY HAVE THE STRENGTH TO HARM THE COMPETITORS HERE...
...SO I WANT YOU TO TAKE ABSOLUTE CARE, MIYUKI.
YOU ARE MY SISTER AND MORE IMPORTANT TO ME THAN ANYTHING.
I WILL...!

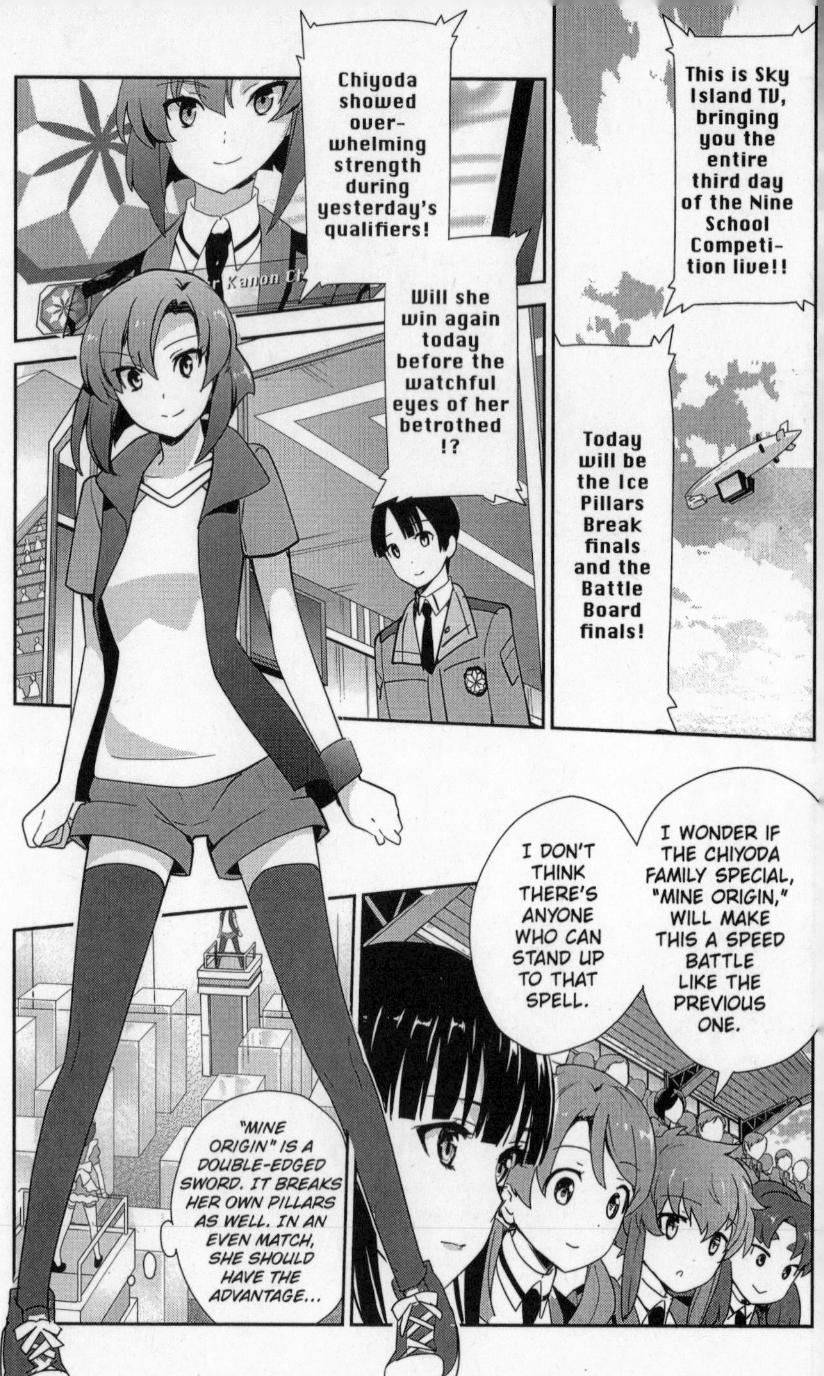
This is Sky Island TV, bringing you the entire third day of the Nine School Competition live!!
Today will be the Ice Pillars Break finals and the Battle Board finals!
Chiyoda showed overwhelming strength during yesterday's qualifiers!
Will she win again today before the watchful eyes of her betrothed!?
I WONDER IF THE CHIYODA FAMILY SPECIAL, "MINE ORIGIN," WILL MAKE THIS A SPEED BATTLE LIKE THE PREVIOUS ONE.
I DON'T THINK THERE'S ANYONE WHO CAN STAND UP TO THAT SPELL.
"MINE ORIGIN" IS A DOUBLE-EDGED SWORD. IT BREAKS HER OWN PILLARS AS WELL. IN AN EVEN MATCH, SHE SHOULD HAVE THE ADVANTAGE...

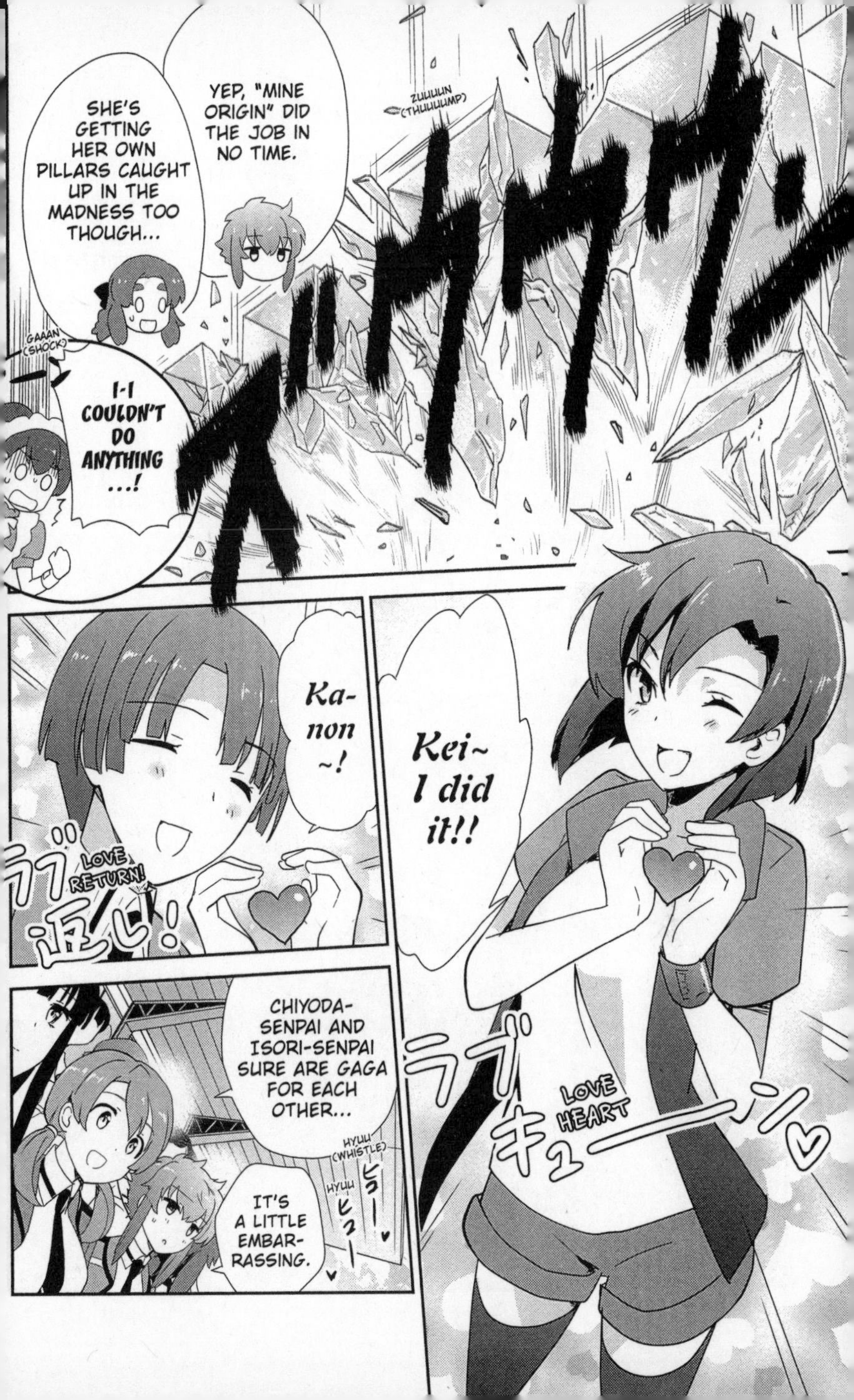
ZUUUUUN (THUUUUMP)
YEP, "MINE ORIGIN" DID THE JOB IN NO TIME.
SHE'S GETTING HER OWN PILLARS CAUGHT UP IN THE MADNESS TOO THOUGH...
GAAAN (SHOCK)
I-I COULDN'T DO ANYTHING ...!
Kei~ I did it!!
ラブキュ―――ン♡
LOVE HEART
Ka-non ~!
ラブ返し!
LOVE RETURN!
CHIYODA-SENPAI AND ISORI-SENPAI SURE ARE GAGA FOR EACH OTHER...
HYUU (WHISTLE)
ヒュー
HYUU
ヒュー
IT'S A LITTLE EMBARRASSING.

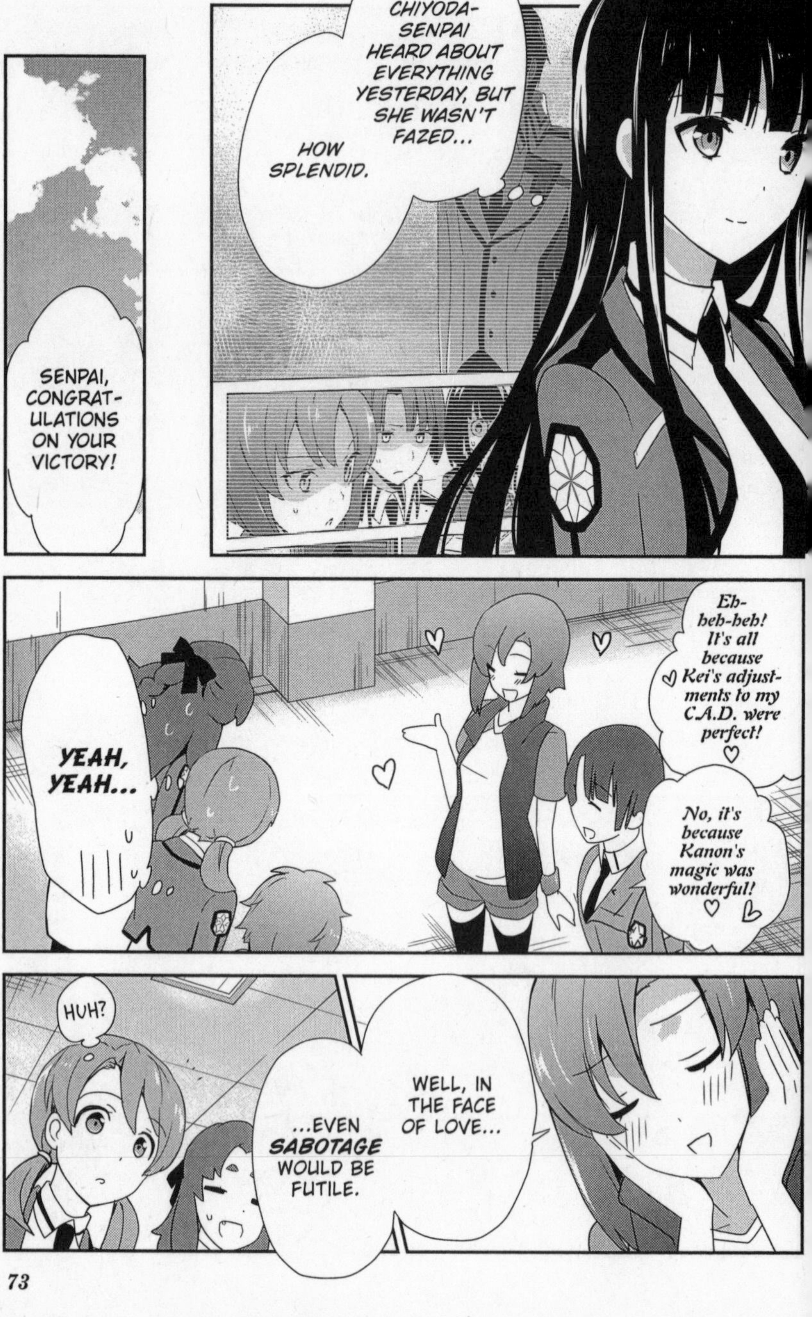
CHIYODA-SENPAI HEARD ABOUT EVERYTHING YESTERDAY, BUT SHE WASN'T FAZED...
HOW SPLENDID.
SENPAI, CONGRAT-ULATIONS ON YOUR VICTORY!
Eh-heh-heh! It's all because Kei's adjust-ments to my C.A.D. were perfect!
No, it's because Kanon's magic was wonderful!
YEAH, YEAH...
WELL, IN THE FACE OF LOVE...
...EVEN SABOTAGE WOULD BE FUTILE.
HUH?

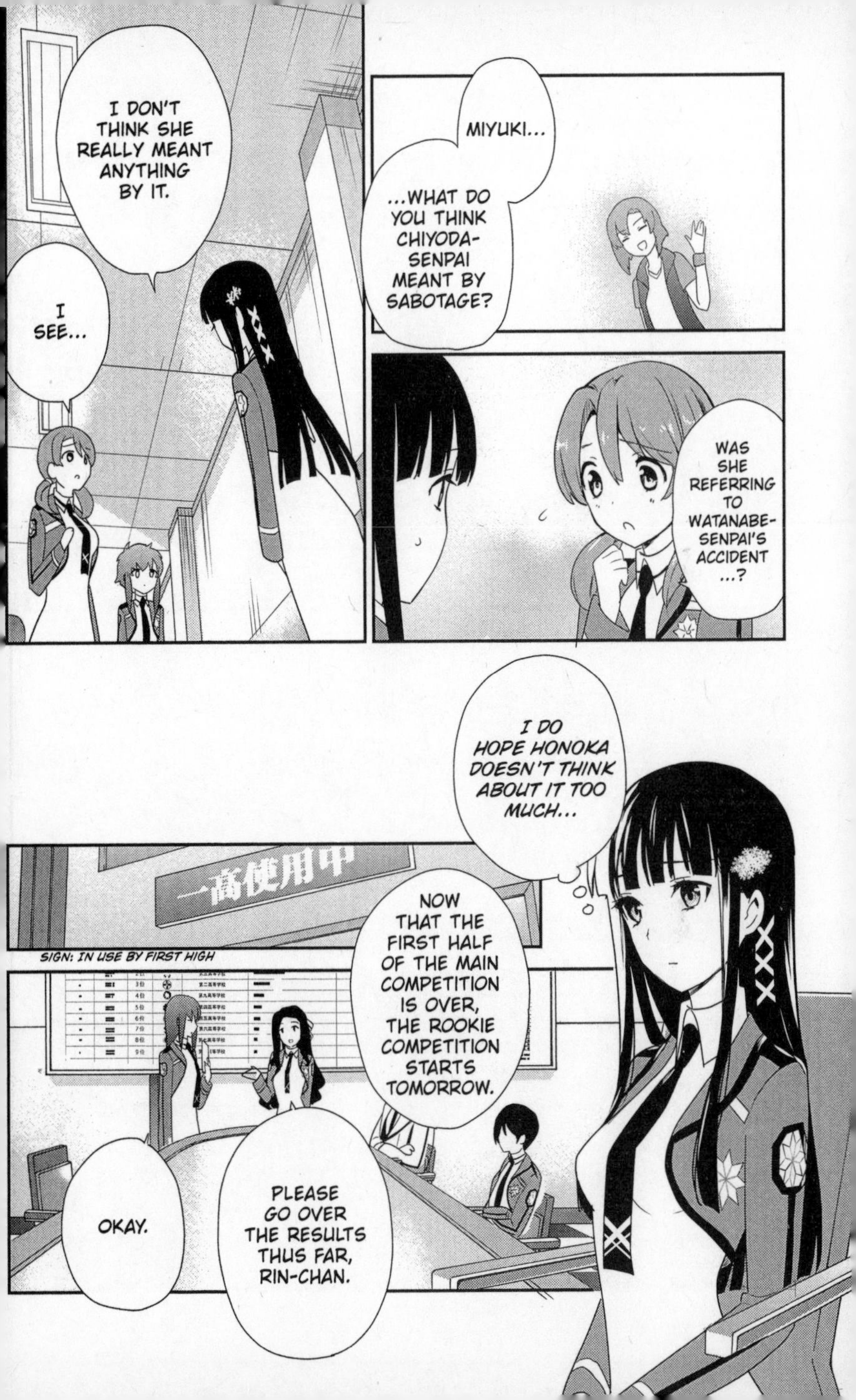
MIYUKI...
...WHAT DO YOU THINK CHIYODA-SENPAI MEANT BY SABOTAGE?
WAS SHE REFERRING TO WATANABE-SENPAI'S ACCIDENT ...?
I DON'T THINK SHE REALLY MEANT ANYTHING BY IT.
I SEE...
I DO HOPE HONOKA DOESN'T THINK ABOUT IT TOO MUCH...
一高使用中
SIGN: IN USE BY FIRST HIGH
NOW THAT THE FIRST HALF OF THE MAIN COMPETITION IS OVER, THE ROOKIE COMPETITION STARTS TOMORROW.
PLEASE GO OVER THE RESULTS THUS FAR, RIN-CHAN.
OKAY.

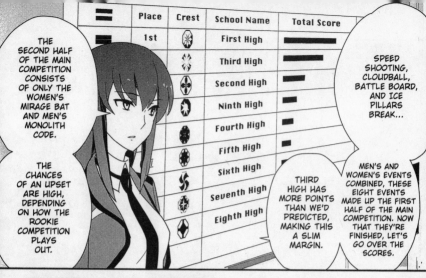

| | Place | Crest | School Name | Total Score |
|---|---|---|---|---|
| | 1st | | First High | |
| | | | Third High | |
| | | | Second High | |
| | | | Ninth High | |
| | | | Fourth High | |
| | | | Fifth High | |
| | | | Sixth High | |
| | | | Seventh High | |
| | | | Eighth High | |

THE SECOND HALF OF THE MAIN COMPETITION CONSISTS OF ONLY THE WOMEN'S MIRAGE BAT AND MEN'S MONOLITH CODE.

THE CHANCES OF AN UPSET ARE HIGH, DEPENDING ON HOW THE ROOKIE COMPETITION PLAYS OUT.

THIRD HIGH HAS MORE POINTS THAN WE'D PREDICTED, MAKING THIS A SLIM MARGIN.

MEN'S AND WOMEN'S EVENTS COMBINED, THESE EIGHT EVENTS MADE UP THE FIRST HALF OF THE MAIN COMPETITION. NOW THAT THEY'RE FINISHED, LET'S GO OVER THE SCORES.

SPEED SHOOTING, CLOUDBALL, BATTLE BOARD, AND ICE PILLARS BREAK...

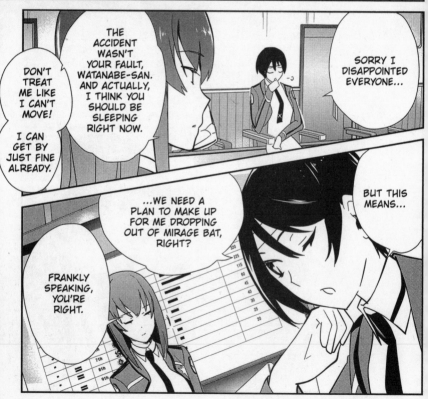

DON'T TREAT ME LIKE I CAN'T MOVE!

I CAN GET BY JUST FINE ALREADY.

THE ACCIDENT WASN'T YOUR FAULT, WATANABE-SAN. AND ACTUALLY, I THINK YOU SHOULD BE SLEEPING RIGHT NOW.

SORRY I DISAPPOINTED EVERYONE...

BUT THIS MEANS...

...WE NEED A PLAN TO MAKE UP FOR ME DROPPING OUT OF MIRAGE BAT, RIGHT?

FRANKLY SPEAKING, YOU'RE RIGHT.

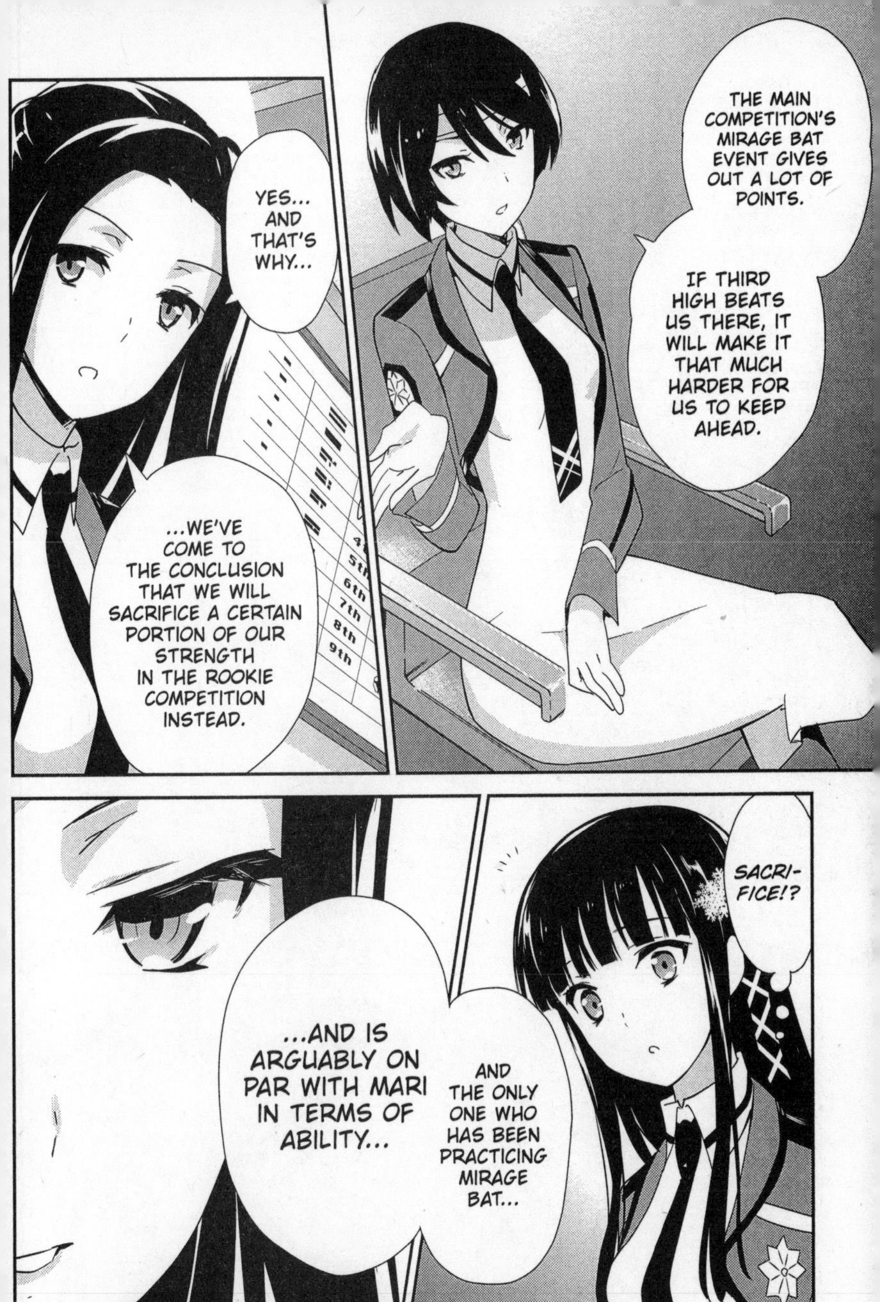
THE MAIN COMPETITION'S MIRAGE BAT EVENT GIVES OUT A LOT OF POINTS.
IF THIRD HIGH BEATS US THERE, IT WILL MAKE IT THAT MUCH HARDER FOR US TO KEEP AHEAD.
YES... AND THAT'S WHY...
...WE'VE COME TO THE CONCLUSION THAT WE WILL SACRIFICE A CERTAIN PORTION OF OUR STRENGTH IN THE ROOKIE COMPETITION INSTEAD.
SACRI-FICE!?
AND THE ONLY ONE WHO HAS BEEN PRACTICING MIRAGE BAT...
...AND IS ARGUABLY ON PAR WITH MARI IN TERMS OF ABILITY...

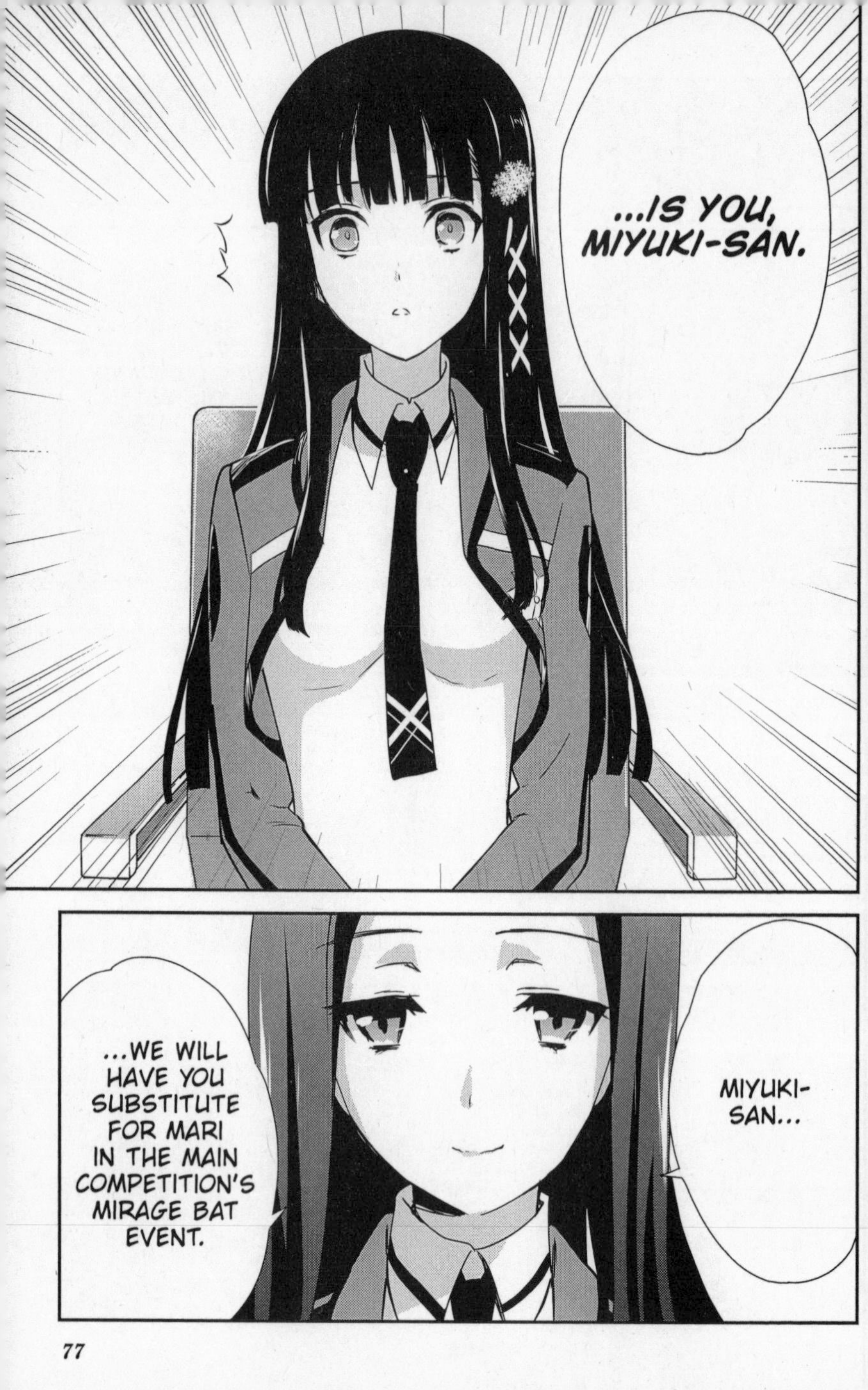
...IS YOU, MIYUKI-SAN.
MIYUKI-SAN...
...WE WILL HAVE YOU SUBSTITUTE FOR MARI IN THE MAIN COMPETITION'S MIRAGE BAT EVENT.

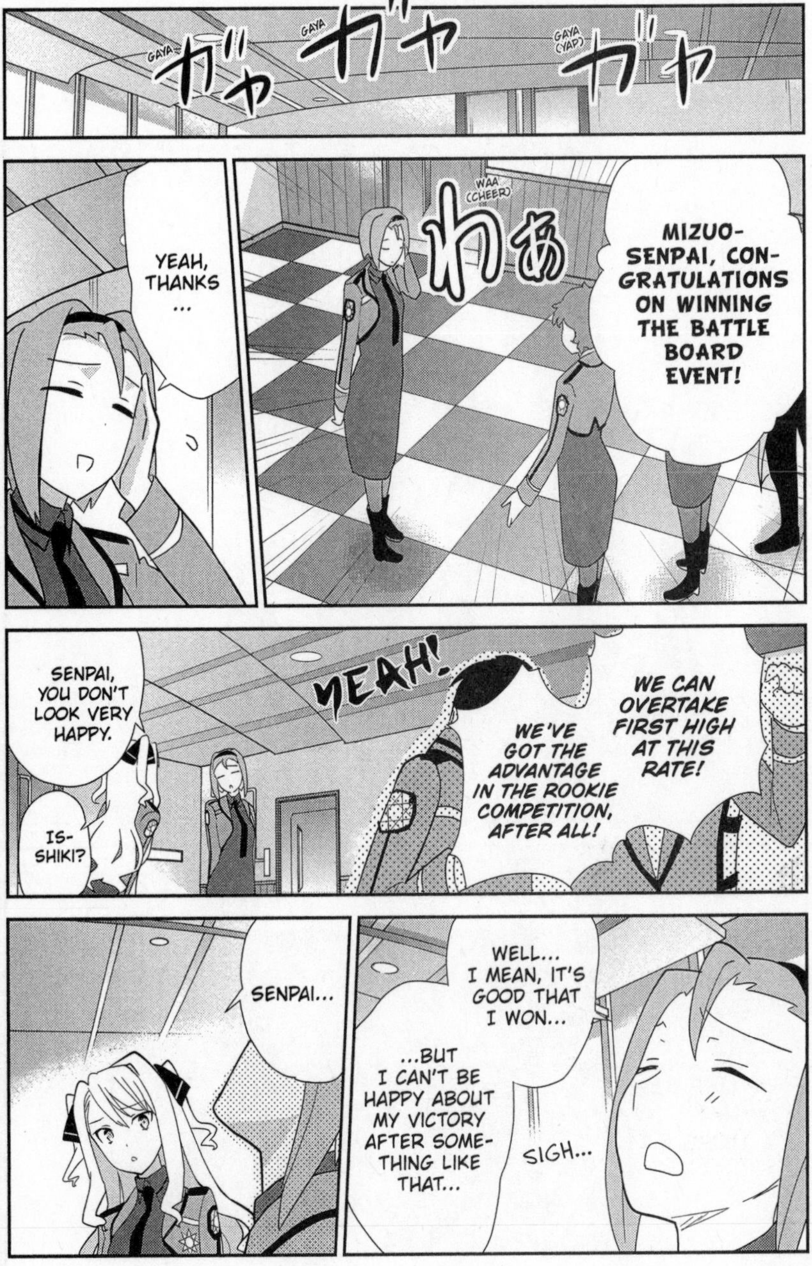
ガヤ
GAYA (YAP)
ガヤ
GAYA
ガヤ
GAYA
MIZUO-SENPAI, CONGRATULATIONS ON WINNING THE BATTLE BOARD EVENT!
わぁ
WAA (CHEER)
YEAH, THANKS ...
WE CAN OVERTAKE FIRST HIGH AT THIS RATE!
WE'VE GOT THE ADVANTAGE IN THE ROOKIE COMPETITION, AFTER ALL!
YEAH!
SENPAI, YOU DON'T LOOK VERY HAPPY.
ISSHIKI?
WELL... I MEAN, IT'S GOOD THAT I WON...
...BUT I CAN'T BE HAPPY ABOUT MY VICTORY AFTER SOMETHING LIKE THAT...
SIGH...
SENPAI...

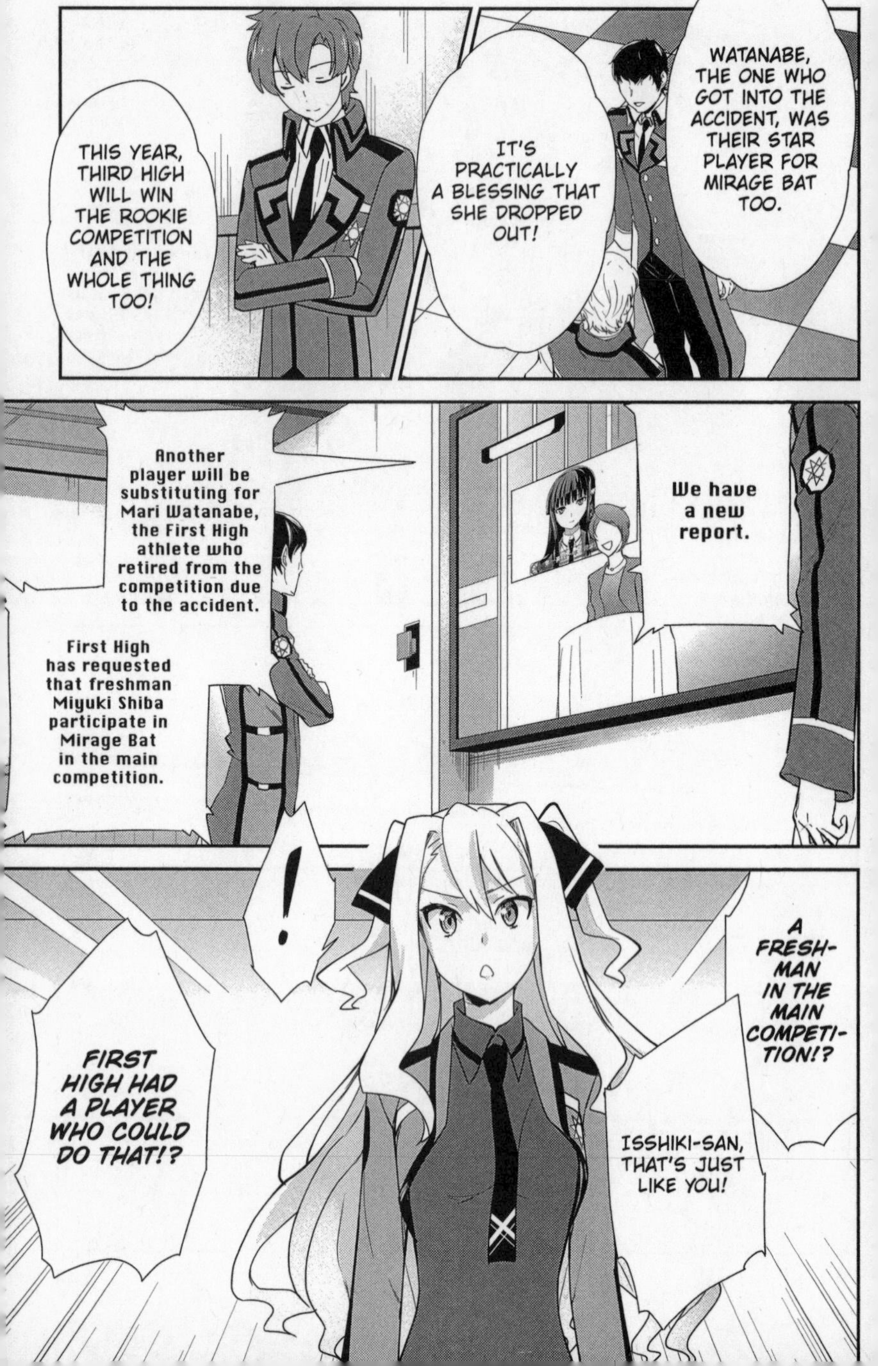
WATANABE, THE ONE WHO GOT INTO THE ACCIDENT, WAS THEIR STAR PLAYER FOR MIRAGE BAT TOO.
IT'S PRACTICALLY A BLESSING THAT SHE DROPPED OUT!
THIS YEAR, THIRD HIGH WILL WIN THE ROOKIE COMPETITION AND THE WHOLE THING TOO!
We have a new report.
Another player will be substituting for Mari Watanabe, the First High athlete who retired from the competition due to the accident.
First High has requested that freshman Miyuki Shiba participate in Mirage Bat in the main competition.
A FRESHMAN IN THE MAIN COMPETITION!?
!
ISSHIKI-SAN, THAT'S JUST LIKE YOU!
FIRST HIGH HAD A PLAYER WHO COULD DO THAT!?

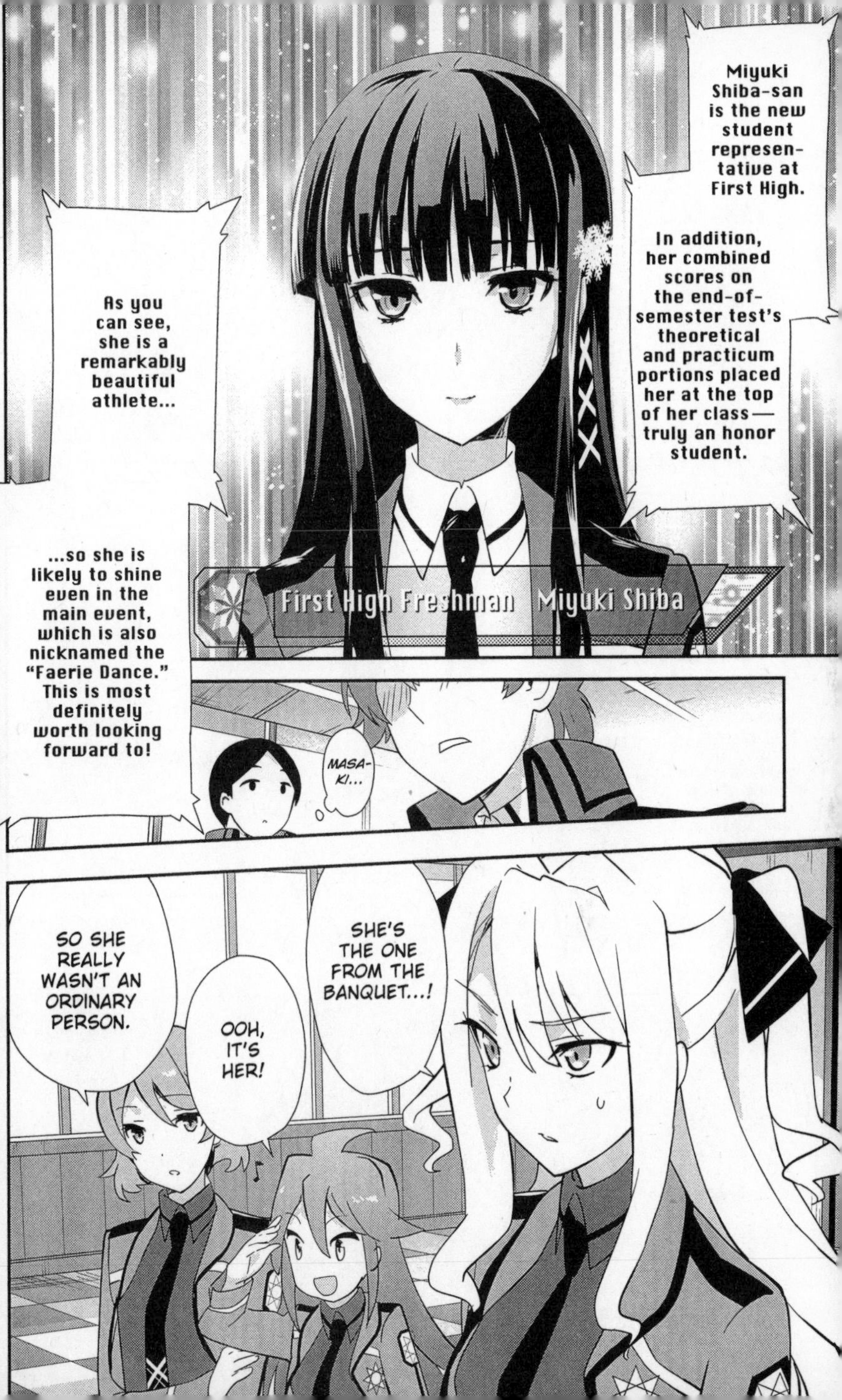
Miyuki Shiba-san is the new student representative at First High.
In addition, her combined scores on the end-of-semester test's theoretical and practicum portions placed her at the top of her class—truly an honor student.
As you can see, she is a remarkably beautiful athlete...
First High Freshman Miyuki Shiba
...so she is likely to shine even in the main event, which is also nicknamed the "Faerie Dance." This is most definitely worth looking forward to!
MASA-KI...
SHE'S THE ONE FROM THE BANQUET...!
OOH, IT'S HER!
SO SHE REALLY WASN'T AN ORDINARY PERSON.

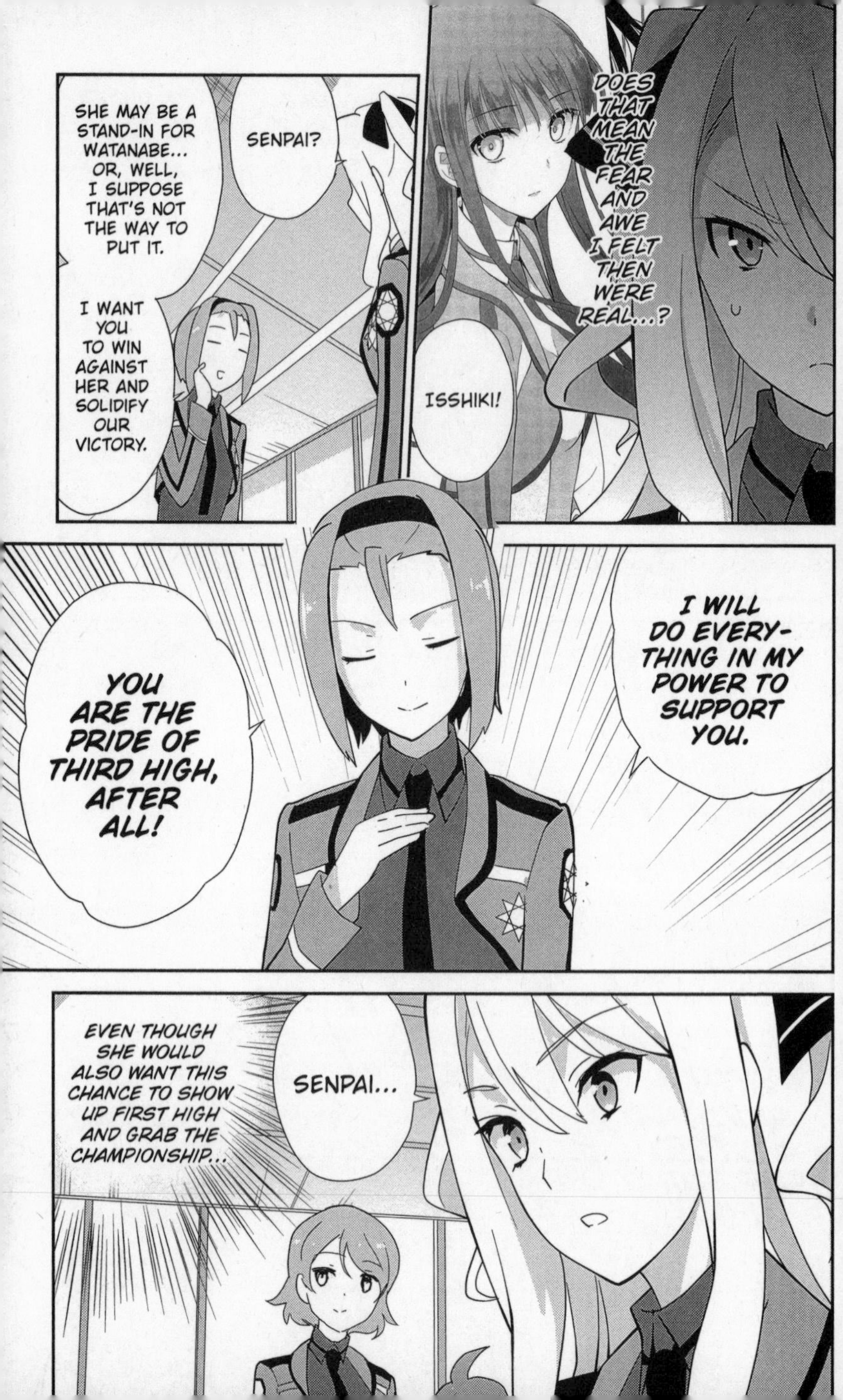
DOES THAT MEAN THE FEAR AND AWE I FELT THEN WERE REAL...?
ISSHIKI!
SENPAI?
SHE MAY BE A STAND-IN FOR WATANABE... OR, WELL, I SUPPOSE THAT'S NOT THE WAY TO PUT IT.
I WANT YOU TO WIN AGAINST HER AND SOLIDIFY OUR VICTORY.
I WILL DO EVERY-THING IN MY POWER TO SUPPORT YOU.
YOU ARE THE PRIDE OF THIRD HIGH, AFTER ALL!
SENPAI...
EVEN THOUGH SHE WOULD ALSO WANT THIS CHANCE TO SHOW UP FIRST HIGH AND GRAB THE CHAMPIONSHIP...

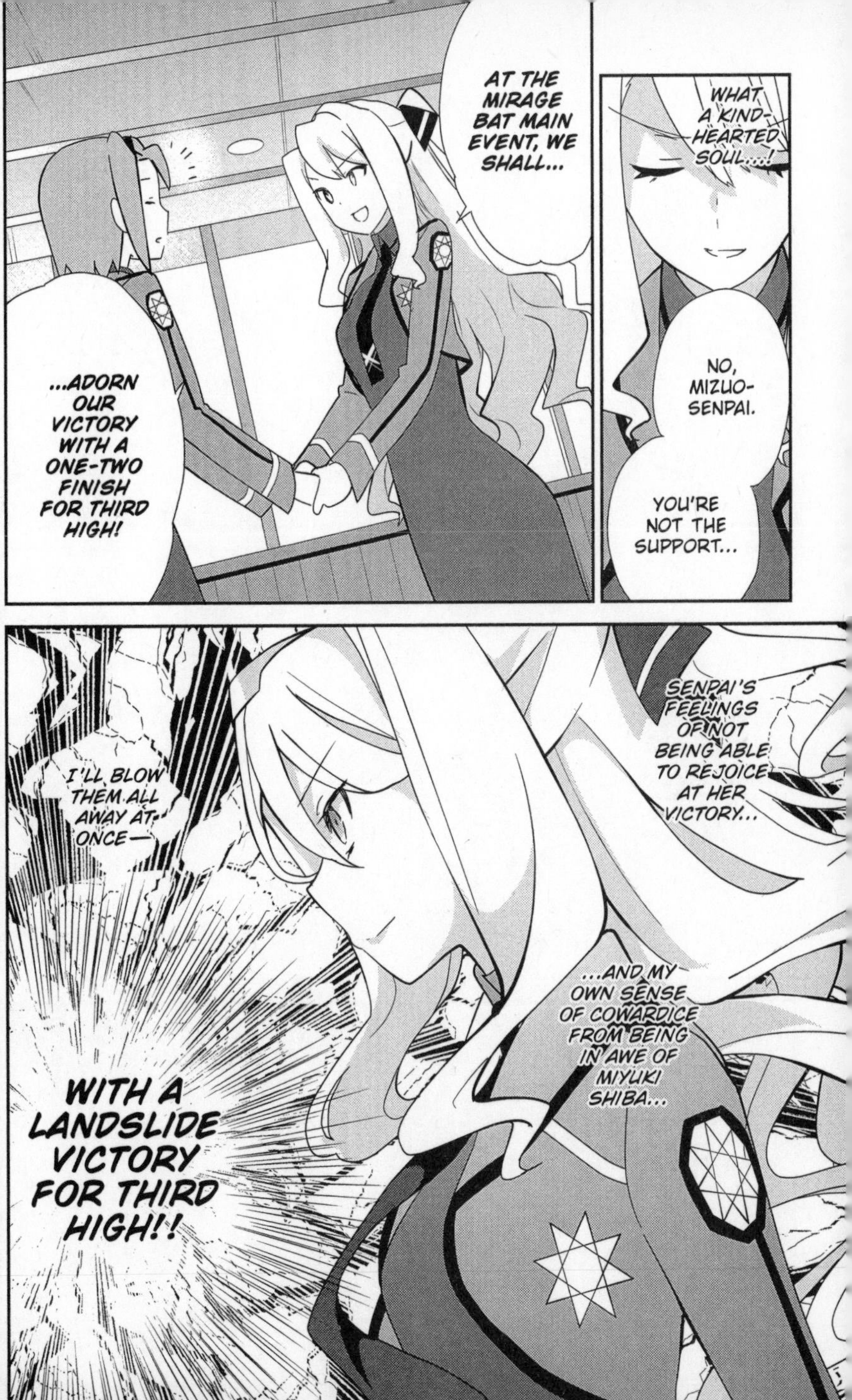
WHAT A KIND-HEARTED SOUL...!
NO, MIZUO-SENPAI.
YOU'RE NOT THE SUPPORT...
AT THE MIRAGE BAT MAIN EVENT, WE SHALL...
...ADORN OUR VICTORY WITH A ONE-TWO FINISH FOR THIRD HIGH!
SENPAI'S FEELINGS OF NOT BEING ABLE TO REJOICE AT HER VICTORY...
...AND MY OWN SENSE OF COWARDICE FROM BEING IN AWE OF MIYUKI SHIBA...
I'LL BLOW THEM ALL AWAY AT ONCE—
WITH A LANDSLIDE VICTORY FOR THIRD HIGH!!

The Honor Student at Magic High School

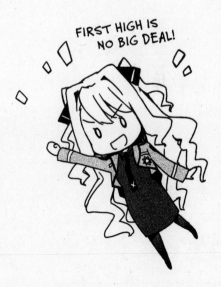

FIRST HIGH IS
NO BIG DEAL!

# CHAPTER 28

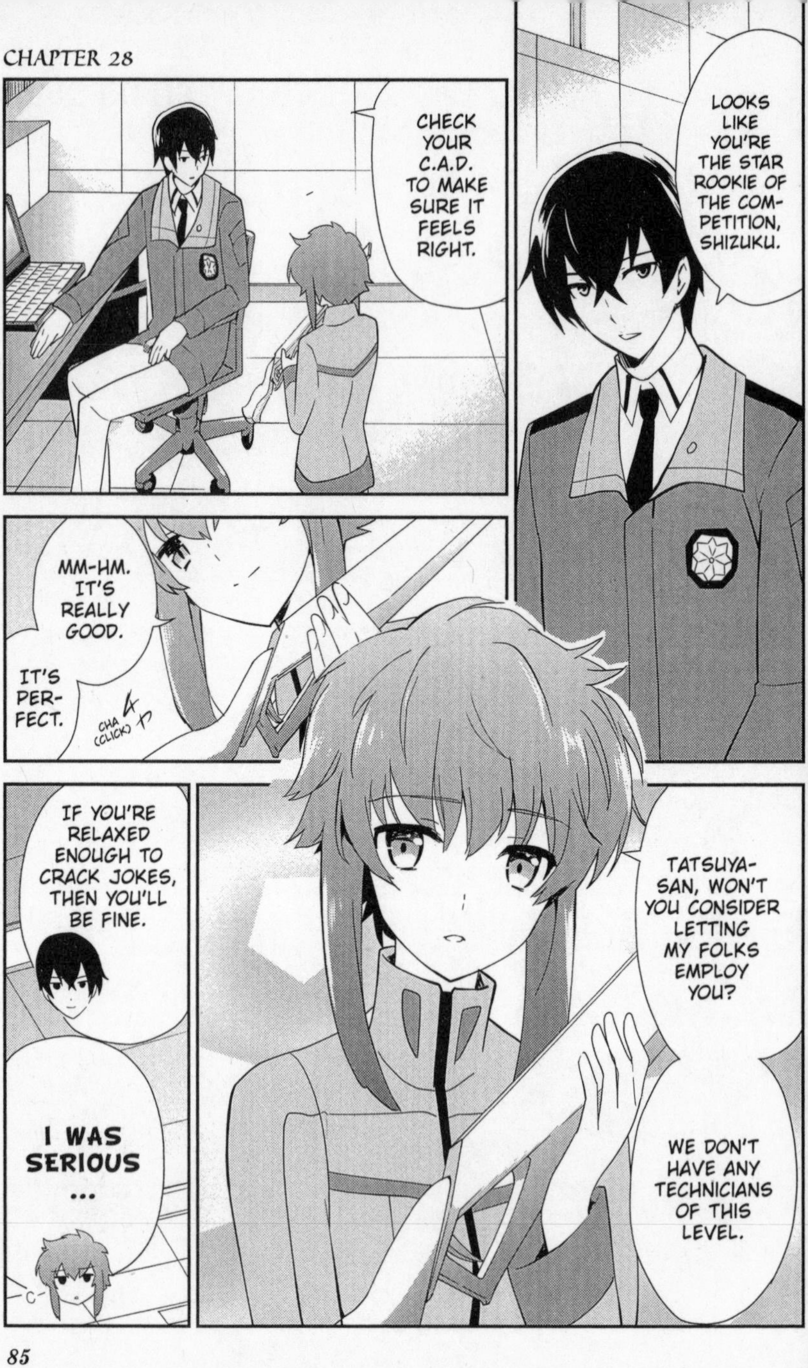
CHECK YOUR C.A.D. TO MAKE SURE IT FEELS RIGHT.
MM-HM. IT'S REALLY GOOD.
IT'S PER-FECT.
CHA (CLICK)
LOOKS LIKE YOU'RE THE STAR ROOKIE OF THE COM-PETITION, SHIZUKU.
TATSUYA-SAN, WON'T YOU CONSIDER LETTING MY FOLKS EMPLOY YOU?
WE DON'T HAVE ANY TECHNICIANS OF THIS LEVEL.
IF YOU'RE RELAXED ENOUGH TO CRACK JOKES, THEN YOU'LL BE FINE.
I WAS SERIOUS ...

# CHAPTER 28

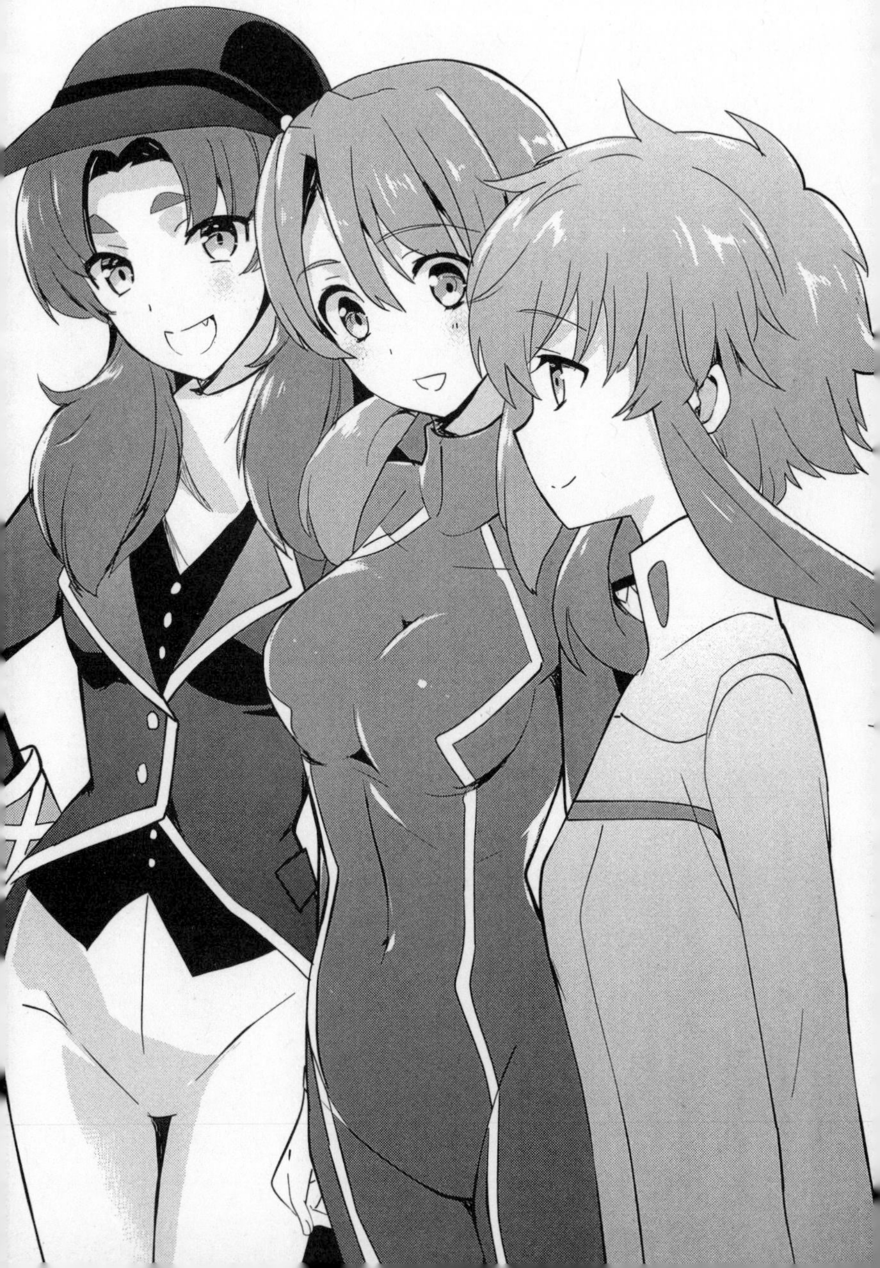

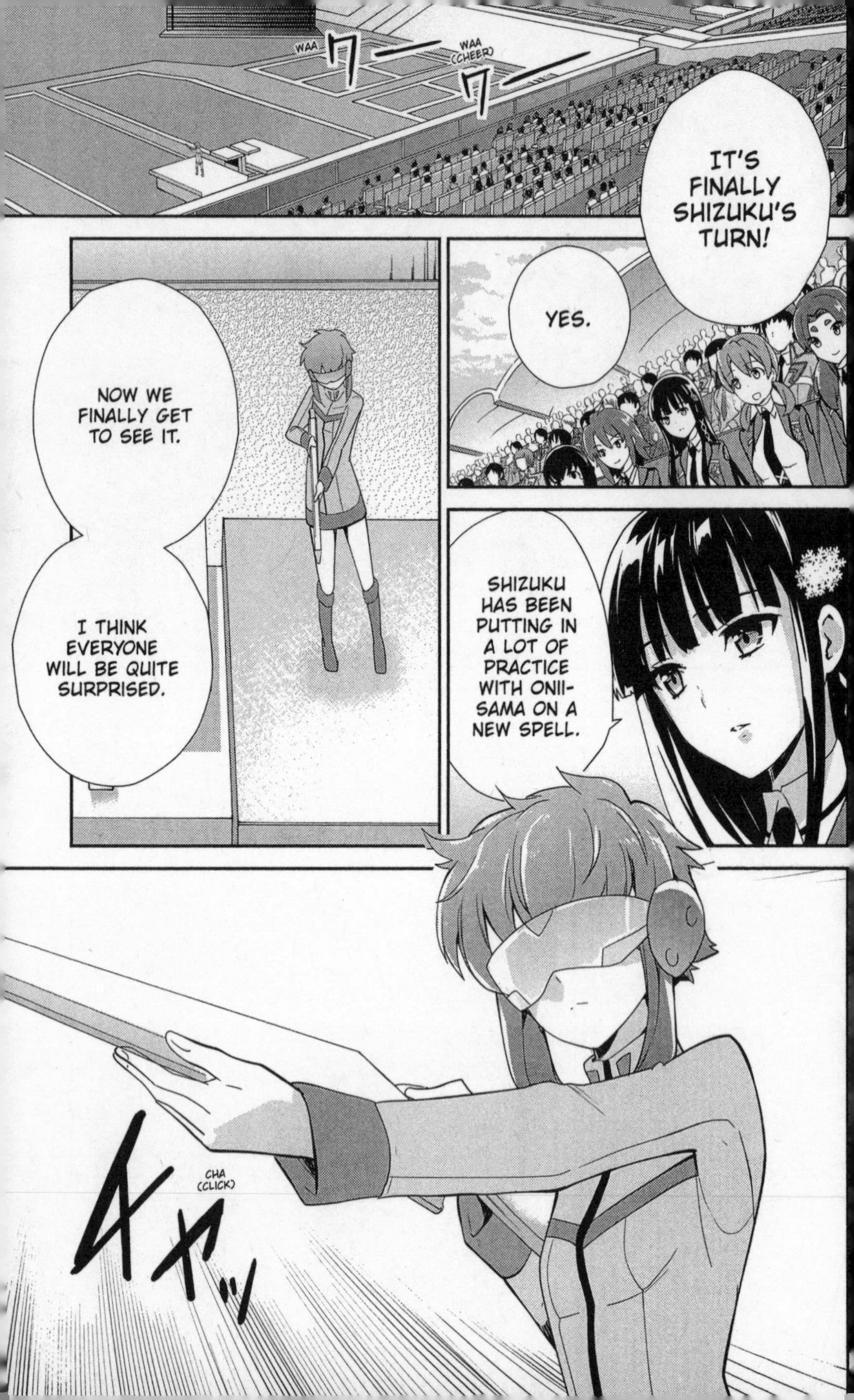
WAA
WAA (CHEER)
IT'S FINALLY SHIZUKU'S TURN!
YES.
SHIZUKU HAS BEEN PUTTING IN A LOT OF PRACTICE WITH ONII-SAMA ON A NEW SPELL.
NOW WE FINALLY GET TO SEE IT.
I THINK EVERYONE WILL BE QUITE SURPRISED.
CHA (CLICK)

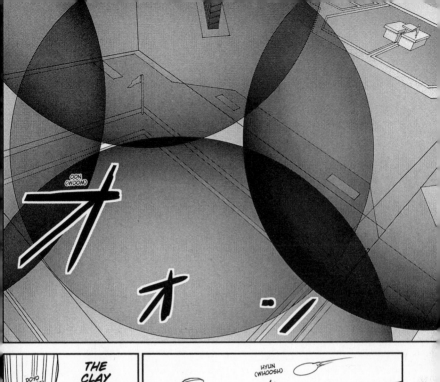

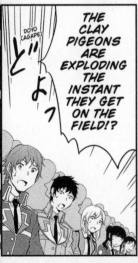

OON
(WOOM)
HYUN
(WHOOSH)
HYUN
BASHU
(BSSH)
BASHU
DOYO
(AGAPE)
THE CLAY PIGEONS ARE EXPLODING THE INSTANT THEY GET ON THE FIELD!?

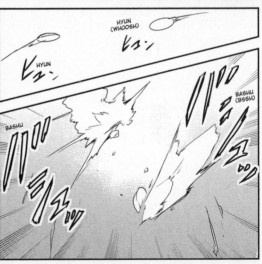

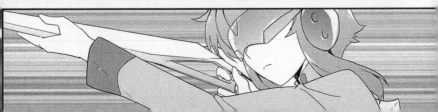

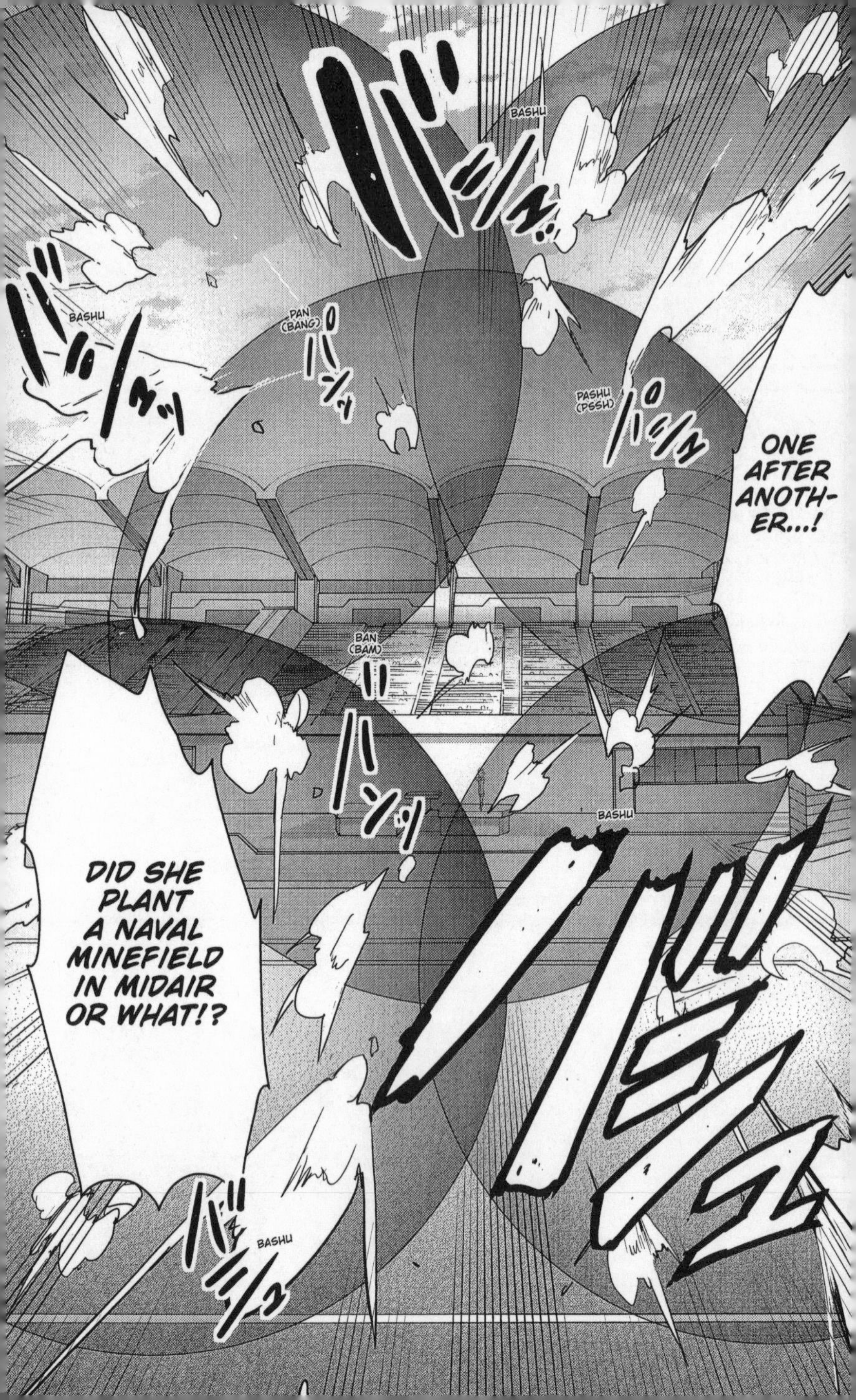
BASHU
ONE AFTER ANOTHER...!
PASHU (PSSH)
PAN (BANG)
BASHU
BAN (BAM)
BASHU
DID SHE PLANT A NAVAL MINEFIELD IN MIDAIR OR WHAT!?
BASHU

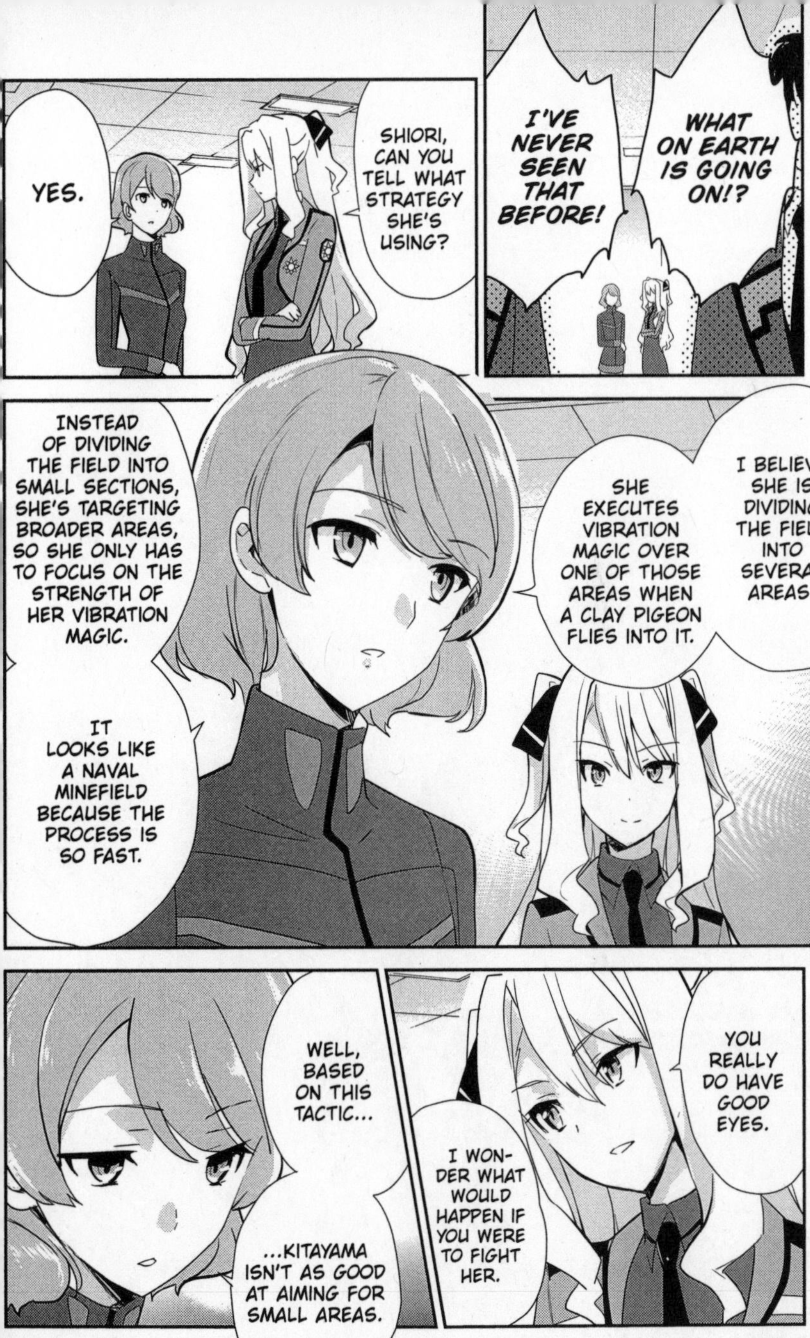
WHAT ON EARTH IS GOING ON!?
I'VE NEVER SEEN THAT BEFORE!
SHIORI, CAN YOU TELL WHAT STRATEGY SHE'S USING?
YES.
I BELIEVE SHE IS DIVIDING THE FIELD INTO SEVERAL AREAS.
SHE EXECUTES VIBRATION MAGIC OVER ONE OF THOSE AREAS WHEN A CLAY PIGEON FLIES INTO IT.
INSTEAD OF DIVIDING THE FIELD INTO SMALL SECTIONS, SHE'S TARGETING BROADER AREAS, SO SHE ONLY HAS TO FOCUS ON THE STRENGTH OF HER VIBRATION MAGIC.
IT LOOKS LIKE A NAVAL MINEFIELD BECAUSE THE PROCESS IS SO FAST.
YOU REALLY DO HAVE GOOD EYES.
I WONDER WHAT WOULD HAPPEN IF YOU WERE TO FIGHT HER.
WELL, BASED ON THIS TACTIC...
...KITAYAMA ISN'T AS GOOD AT AIMING FOR SMALL AREAS.

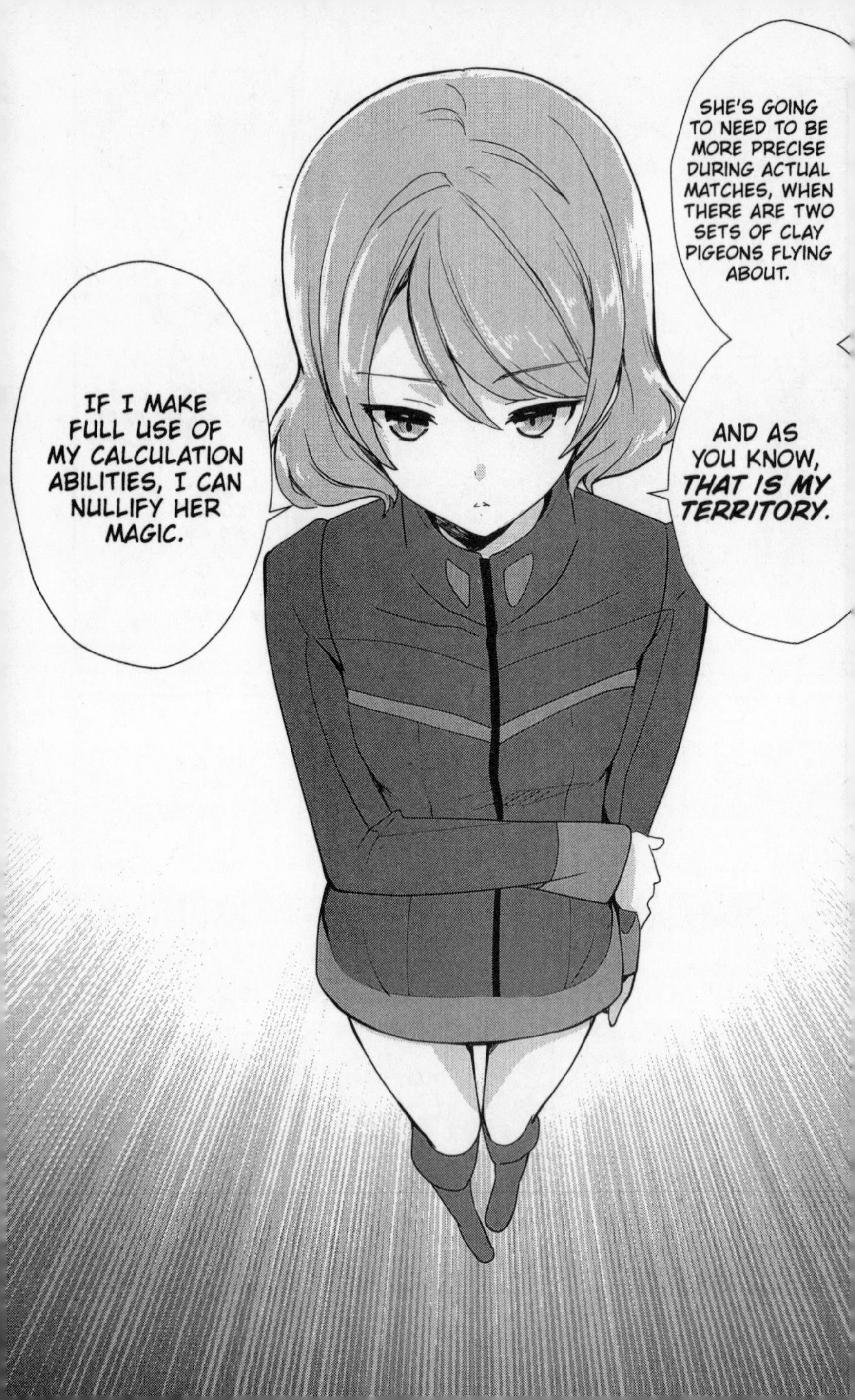
SHE'S GOING TO NEED TO BE MORE PRECISE DURING ACTUAL MATCHES, WHEN THERE ARE TWO SETS OF CLAY PIGEONS FLYING ABOUT.
AND AS YOU KNOW, *THAT IS MY TERRITORY.*
IF I MAKE FULL USE OF MY CALCULATION ABILITIES, I CAN NULLIFY HER MAGIC.

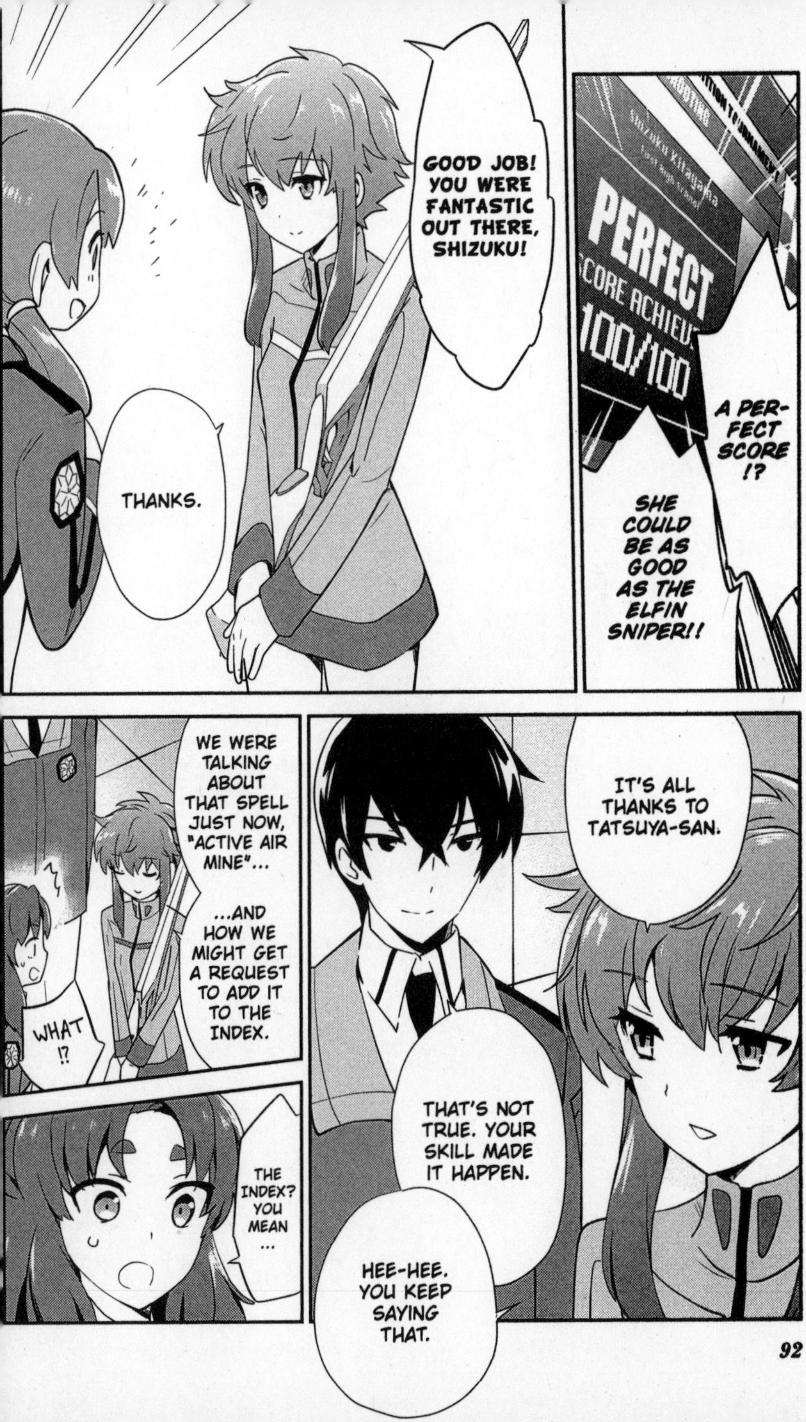
PERFECT
100/100
A PERFECT SCORE!?
SHE COULD BE AS GOOD AS THE ELFIN SNIPER!!
GOOD JOB! YOU WERE FANTASTIC OUT THERE, SHIZUKU!
THANKS.
IT'S ALL THANKS TO TATSUYA-SAN.
THAT'S NOT TRUE. YOUR SKILL MADE IT HAPPEN.
HEE-HEE. YOU KEEP SAYING THAT.
WE WERE TALKING ABOUT THAT SPELL JUST NOW, "ACTIVE AIR MINE"...
...AND HOW WE MIGHT GET A REQUEST TO ADD IT TO THE INDEX.
WHAT!?
THE INDEX? YOU MEAN...

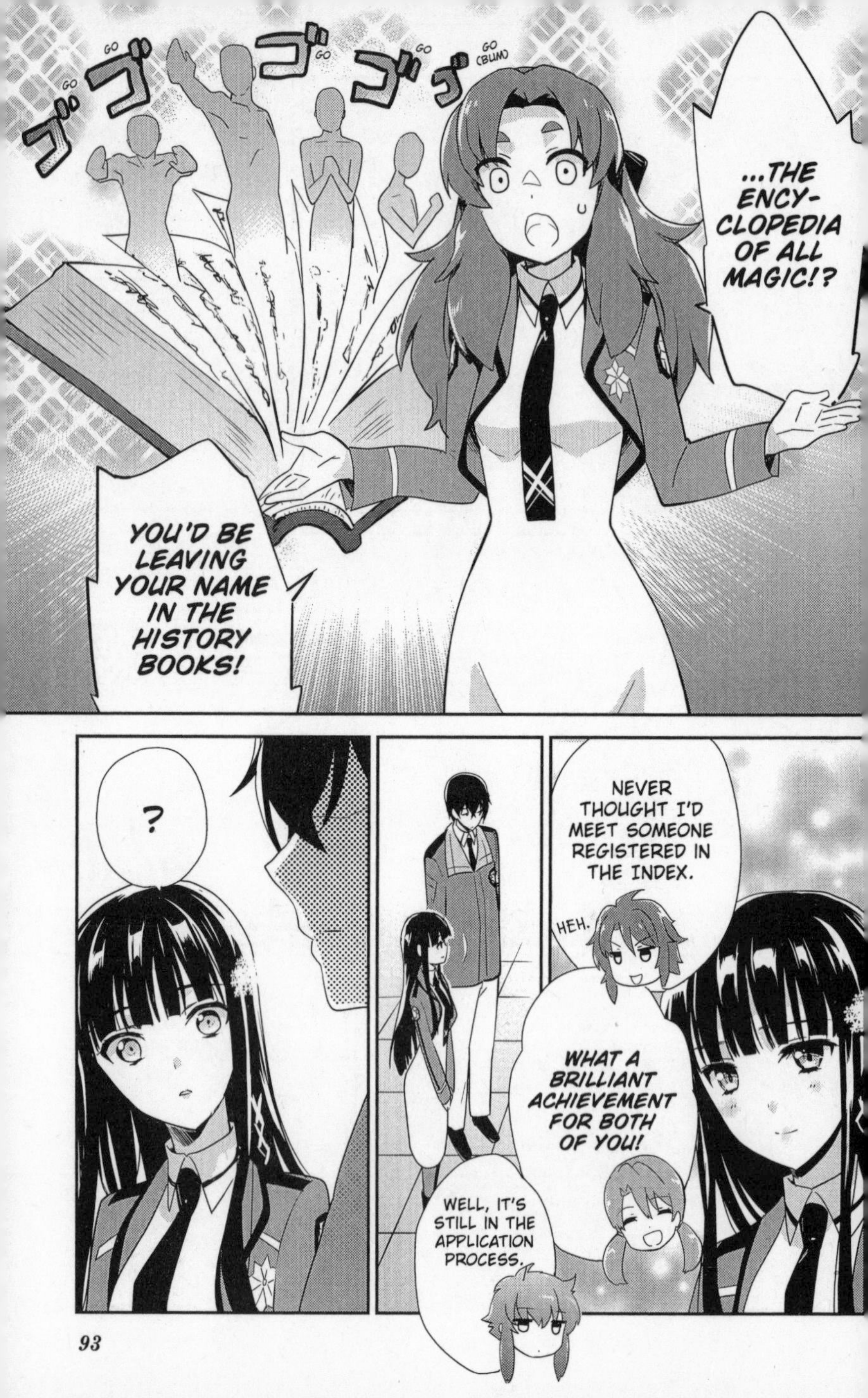
GO GO GO GO (BUM)
...THE ENCYCLOPEDIA OF ALL MAGIC!?
YOU'D BE LEAVING YOUR NAME IN THE HISTORY BOOKS!
NEVER THOUGHT I'D MEET SOMEONE REGISTERED IN THE INDEX.
HEH.
WHAT A BRILLIANT ACHIEVEMENT FOR BOTH OF YOU!
WELL, IT'S STILL IN THE APPLICATION PROCESS.
?

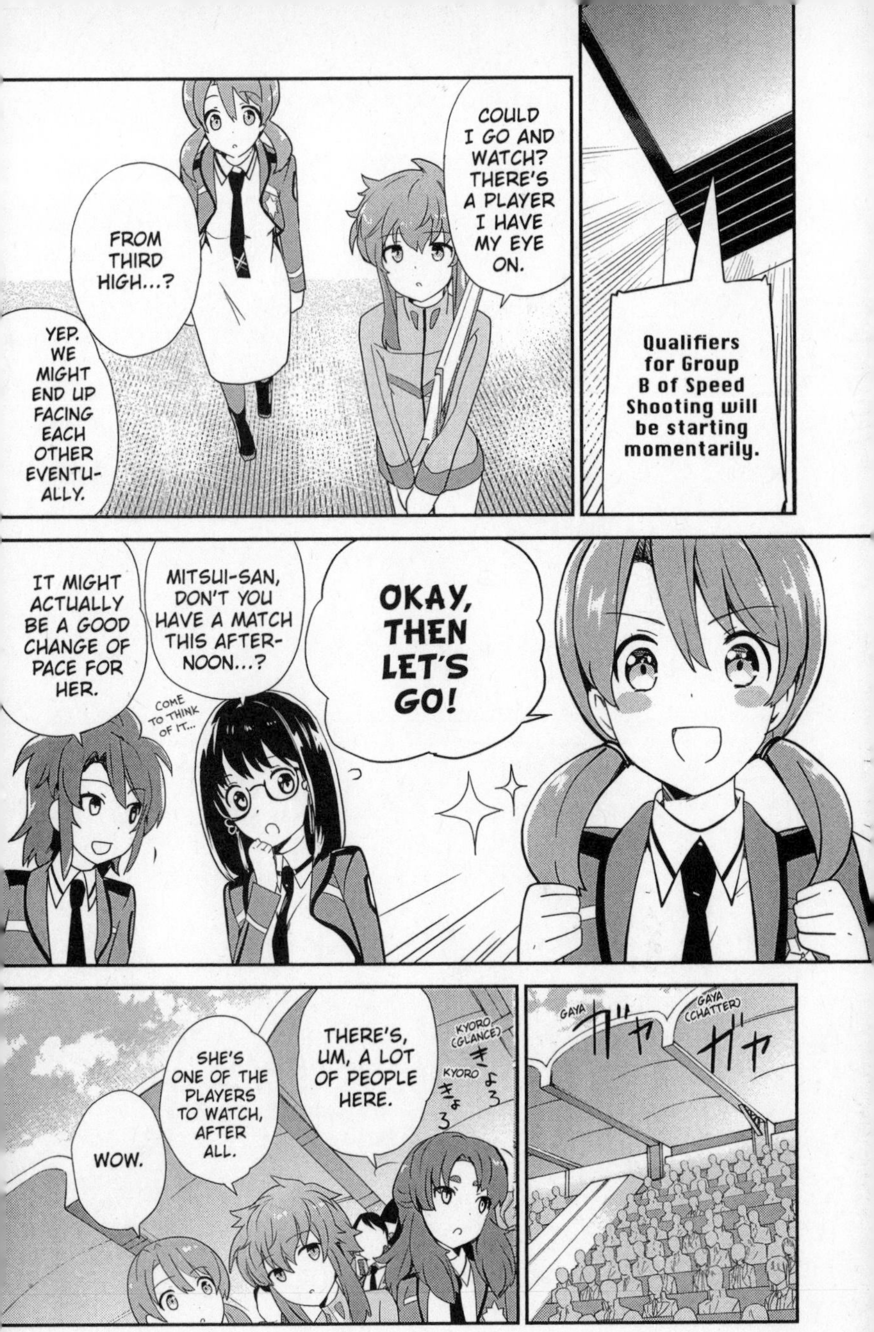
Qualifiers for Group B of Speed Shooting will be starting momentarily.
COULD I GO AND WATCH? THERE'S A PLAYER I HAVE MY EYE ON.
FROM THIRD HIGH...?
YEP. WE MIGHT END UP FACING EACH OTHER EVENTU-ALLY.
OKAY, THEN LET'S GO!
MITSUI-SAN, DON'T YOU HAVE A MATCH THIS AFTER-NOON...?
COME TO THINK OF IT...
IT MIGHT ACTUALLY BE A GOOD CHANGE OF PACE FOR HER.
GAYA (CHATTER)
GAYA
KYORO (GLANCE)
KYORO
THERE'S, UM, A LOT OF PEOPLE HERE.
SHE'S ONE OF THE PLAYERS TO WATCH, AFTER ALL.
WOW.

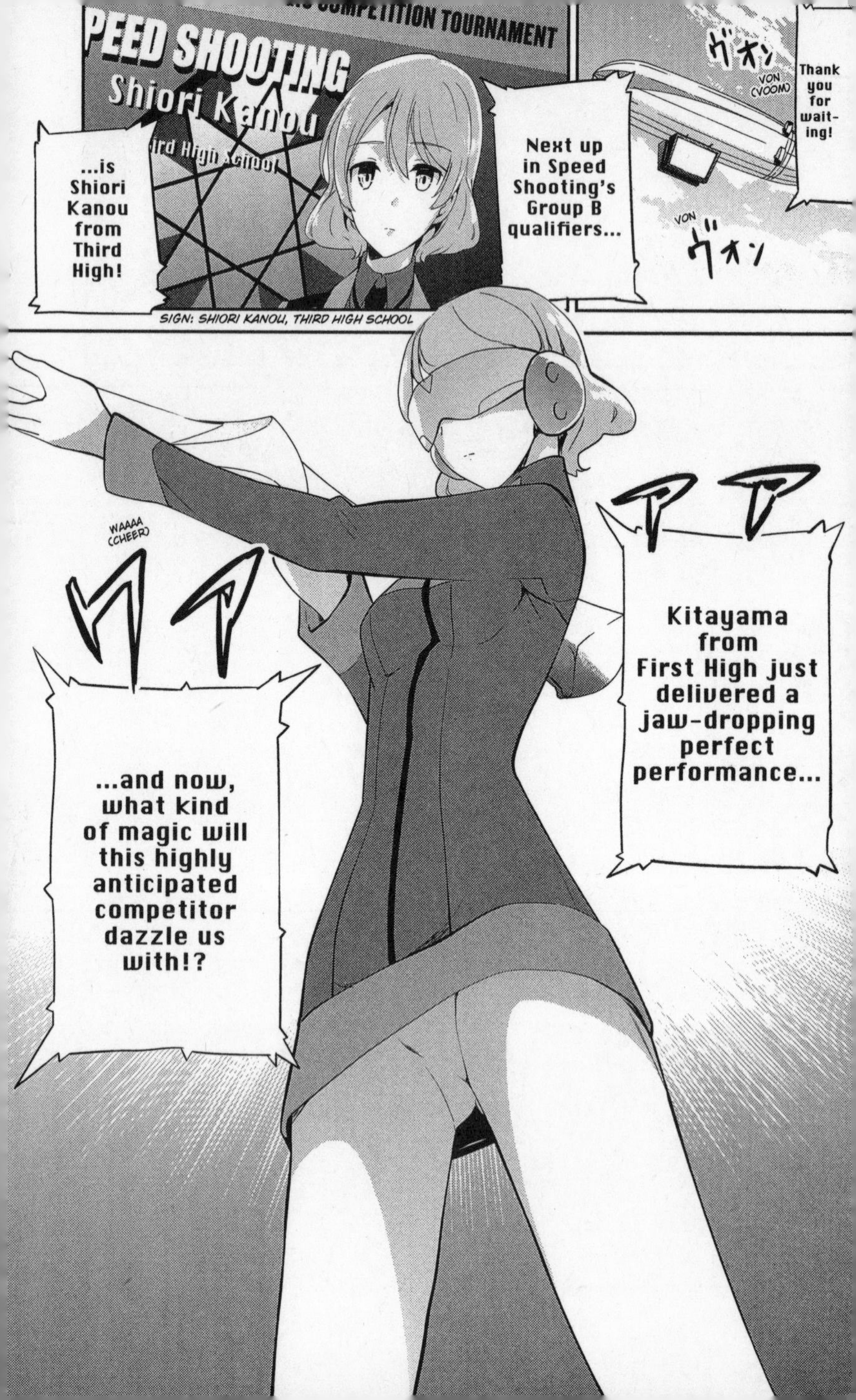
Thank you for wait-ing!
ヴォン
VON (VOOM)
ヴォン
VON
Next up in Speed Shooting's Group B qualifiers...
...is Shiori Kanou from Third High!
COMPETITION TOURNAMENT
PEED SHOOTING
Shiori Kanou
ird High School
SIGN: SHIORI KANOU, THIRD HIGH SCHOOL
アア
Kitayama from First High just delivered a jaw-dropping perfect performance...
ワア
WAAAA (CHEER)
...and now, what kind of magic will this highly anticipated competitor dazzle us with!?

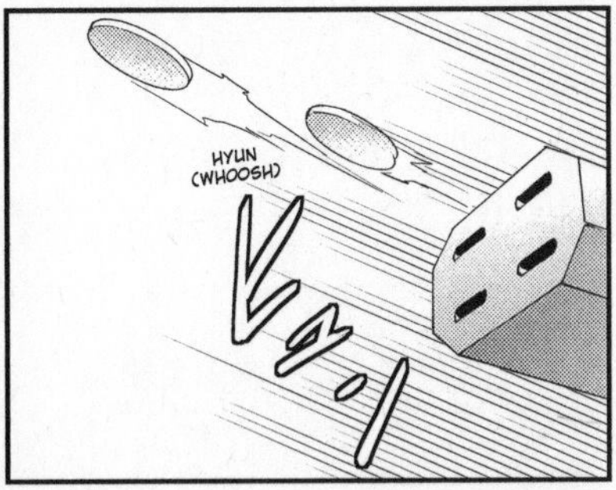
HYUN
(WHOOSH)

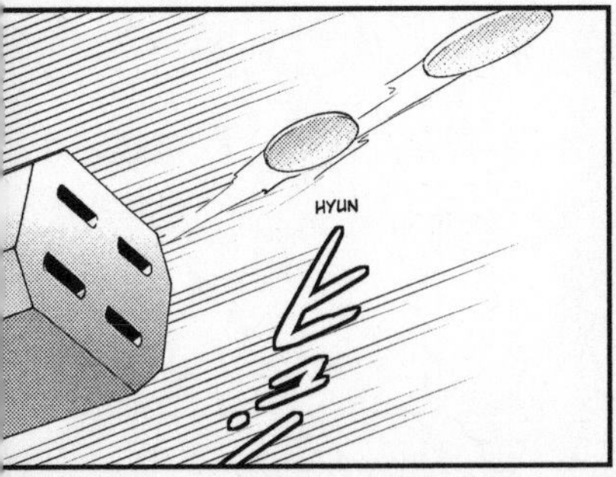
HYUN

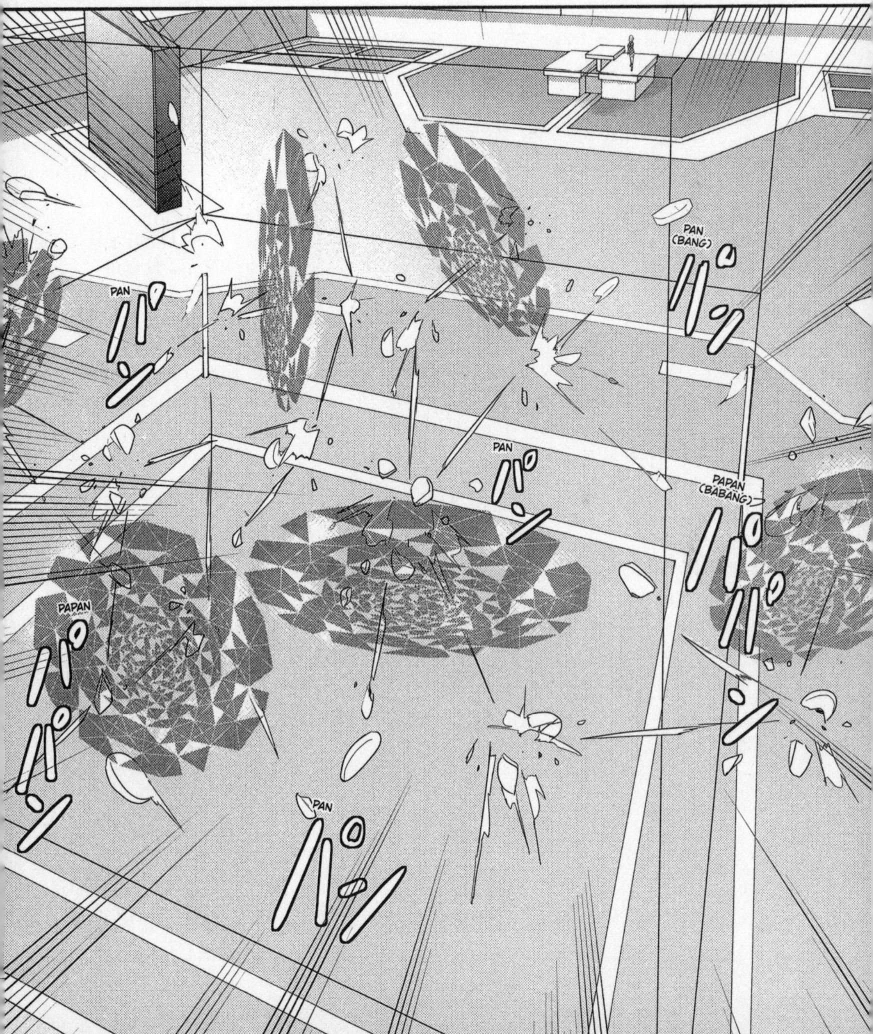
PAN
(BANG)
PAN
PAPAN
(BABANG)
PAN
PAPAN
PAN

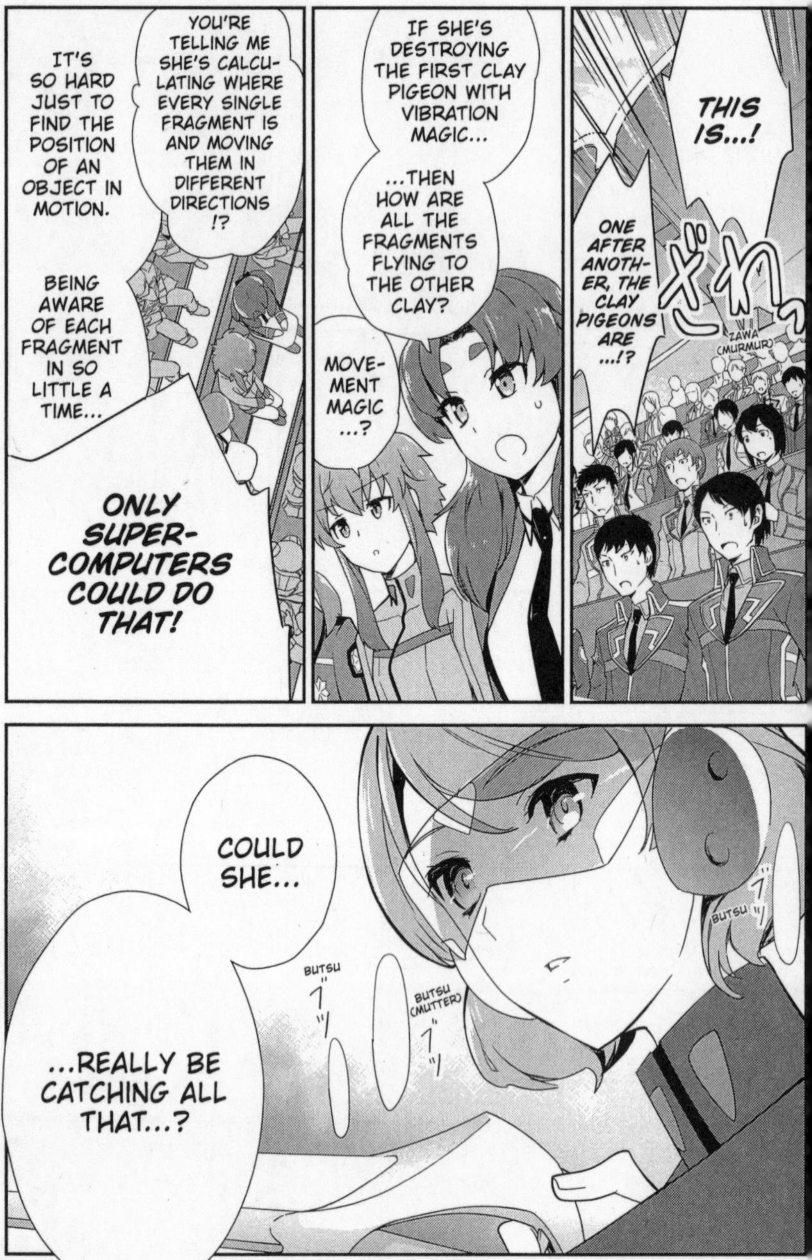
THIS IS...!
ONE AFTER ANOTHER, THE CLAY PIGEONS ARE ...!?
ZAWA (MURMUR)
IF SHE'S DESTROYING THE FIRST CLAY PIGEON WITH VIBRATION MAGIC...
...THEN HOW ARE ALL THE FRAGMENTS FLYING TO THE OTHER CLAY?
MOVEMENT MAGIC ...?
YOU'RE TELLING ME SHE'S CALCULATING WHERE EVERY SINGLE FRAGMENT IS AND MOVING THEM IN DIFFERENT DIRECTIONS !?
IT'S SO HARD JUST TO FIND THE POSITION OF AN OBJECT IN MOTION.
BEING AWARE OF EACH FRAGMENT IN SO LITTLE A TIME...
ONLY SUPER-COMPUTERS COULD DO THAT!
BUTSU
BUTSU (MUTTER)
BUTSU
COULD SHE...
...REALLY BE CATCHING ALL THAT...?

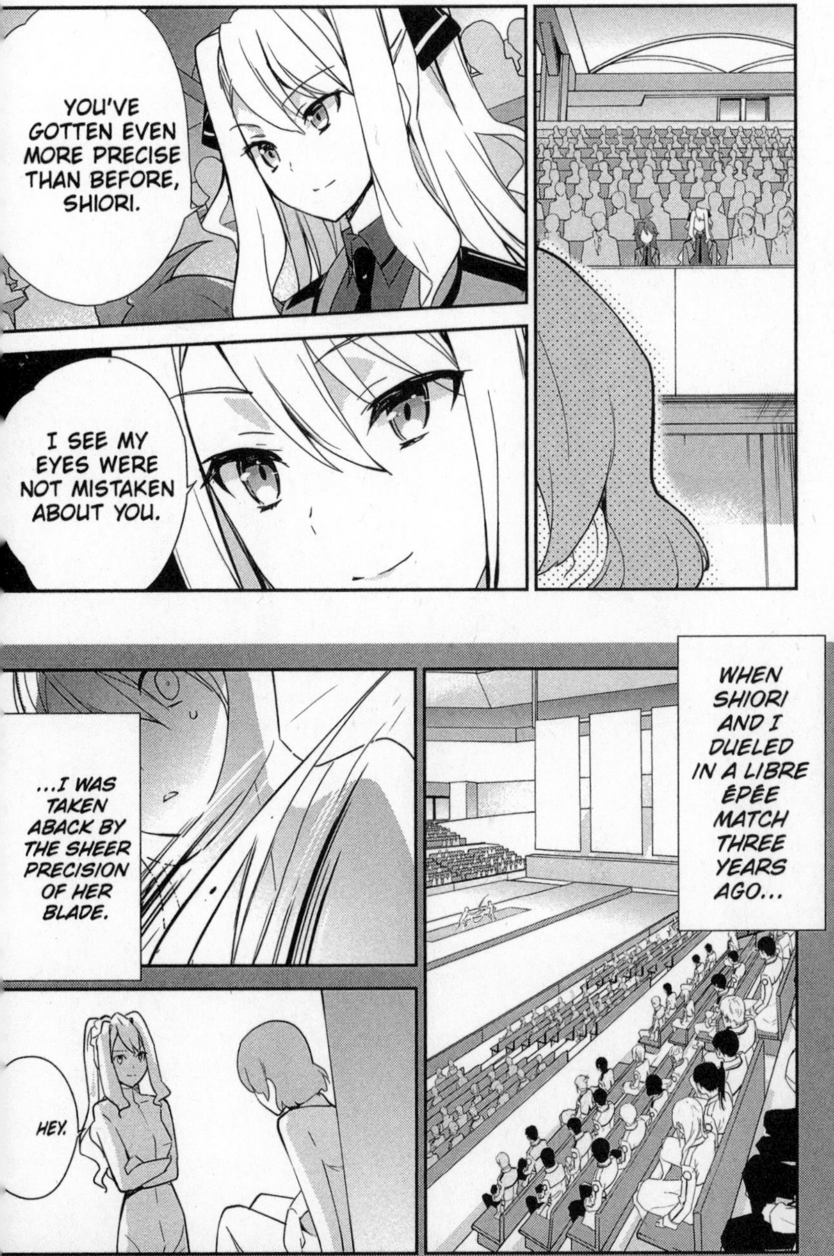
YOU'VE GOTTEN EVEN MORE PRECISE THAN BEFORE, SHIORI.
I SEE MY EYES WERE NOT MISTAKEN ABOUT YOU.
WHEN SHIORI AND I DUELED IN A LIBRE ÉPÉE MATCH THREE YEARS AGO...
...I WAS TAKEN ABACK BY THE SHEER PRECISION OF HER BLADE.
HEY.

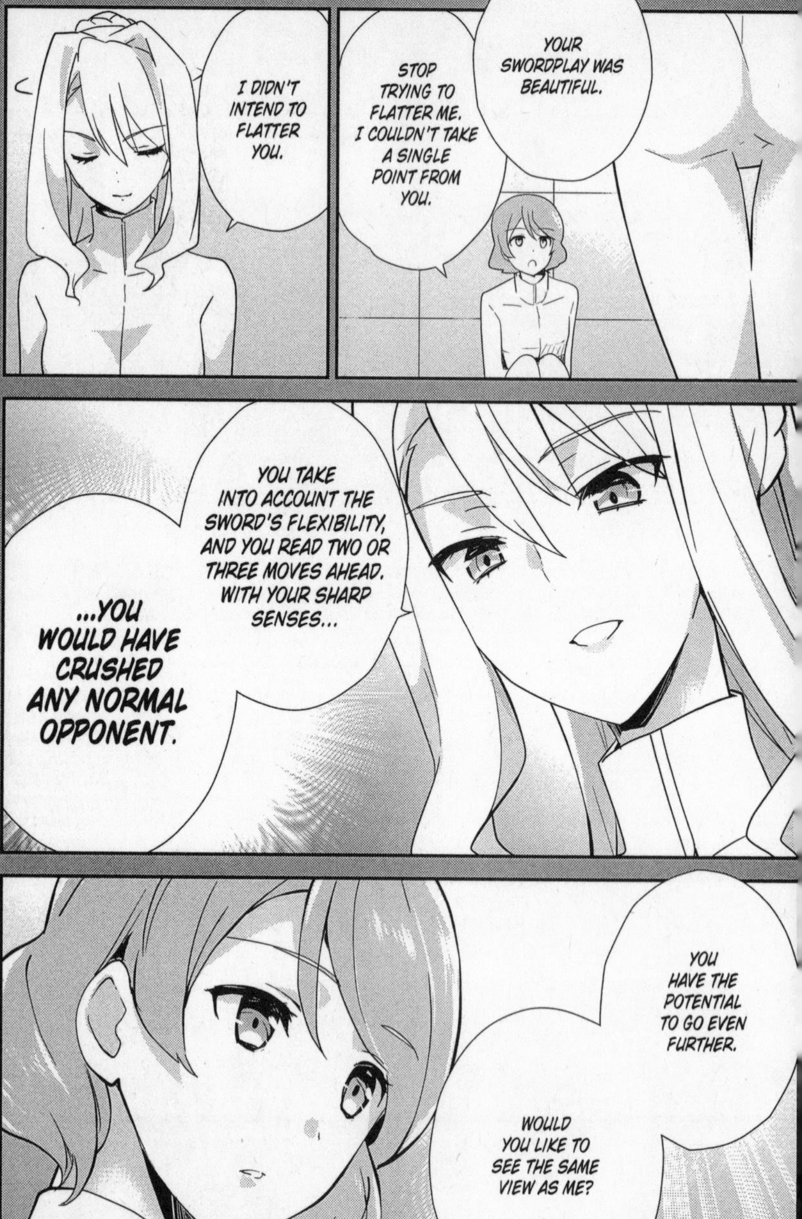
YOUR SWORDPLAY WAS BEAUTIFUL.
STOP TRYING TO FLATTER ME. I COULDN'T TAKE A SINGLE POINT FROM YOU.
I DIDN'T INTEND TO FLATTER YOU.
YOU TAKE INTO ACCOUNT THE SWORD'S FLEXIBILITY, AND YOU READ TWO OR THREE MOVES AHEAD. WITH YOUR SHARP SENSES...
...YOU WOULD HAVE CRUSHED ANY NORMAL OPPONENT.
YOU HAVE THE POTENTIAL TO GO EVEN FURTHER.
WOULD YOU LIKE TO SEE THE SAME VIEW AS ME?

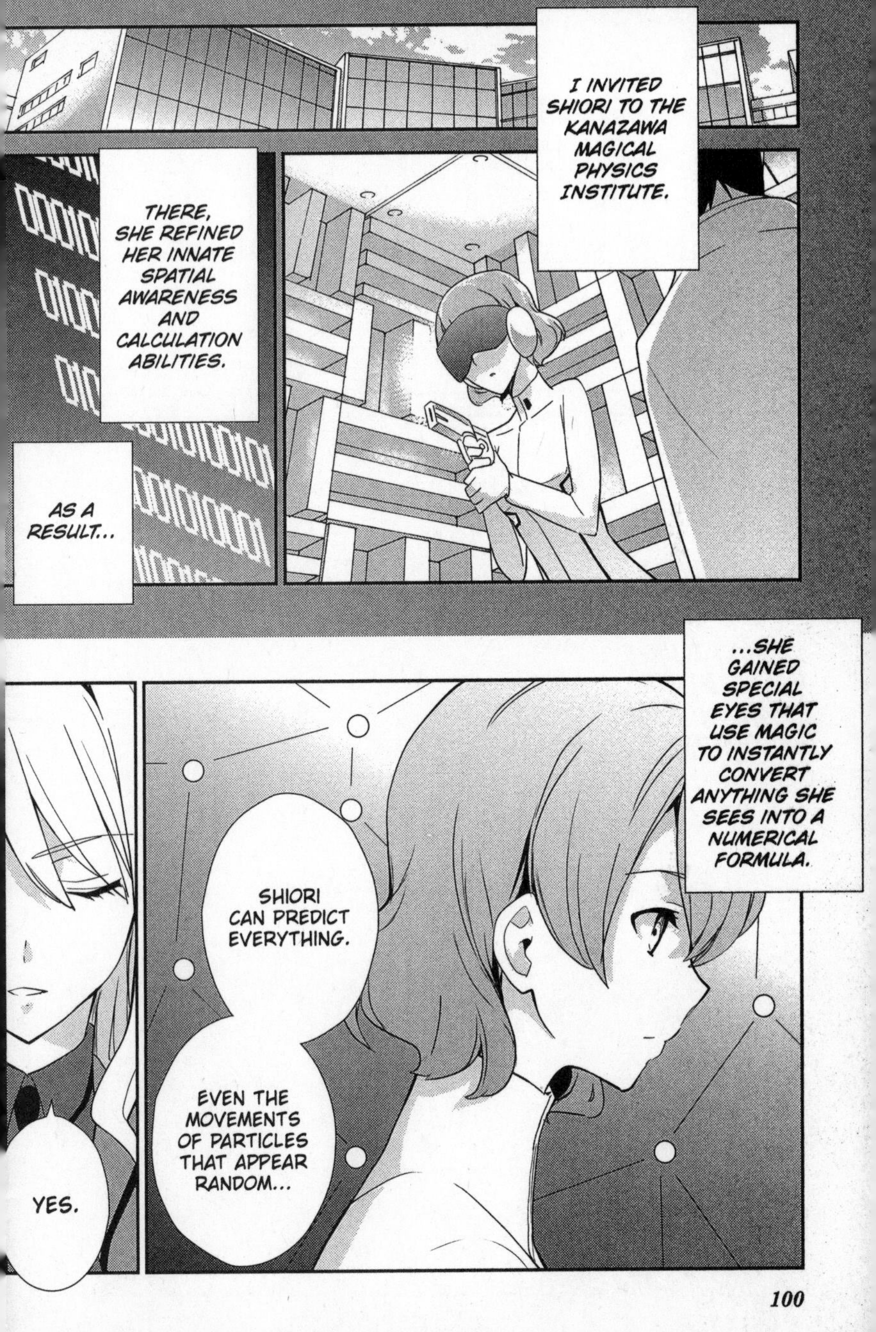
I INVITED SHIORI TO THE KANAZAWA MAGICAL PHYSICS INSTITUTE.
THERE, SHE REFINED HER INNATE SPATIAL AWARENESS AND CALCULATION ABILITIES.
AS A RESULT...
...SHE GAINED SPECIAL EYES THAT USE MAGIC TO INSTANTLY CONVERT ANYTHING SHE SEES INTO A NUMERICAL FORMULA.
SHIORI CAN PREDICT EVERYTHING.
EVEN THE MOVEMENTS OF PARTICLES THAT APPEAR RANDOM...
YES.

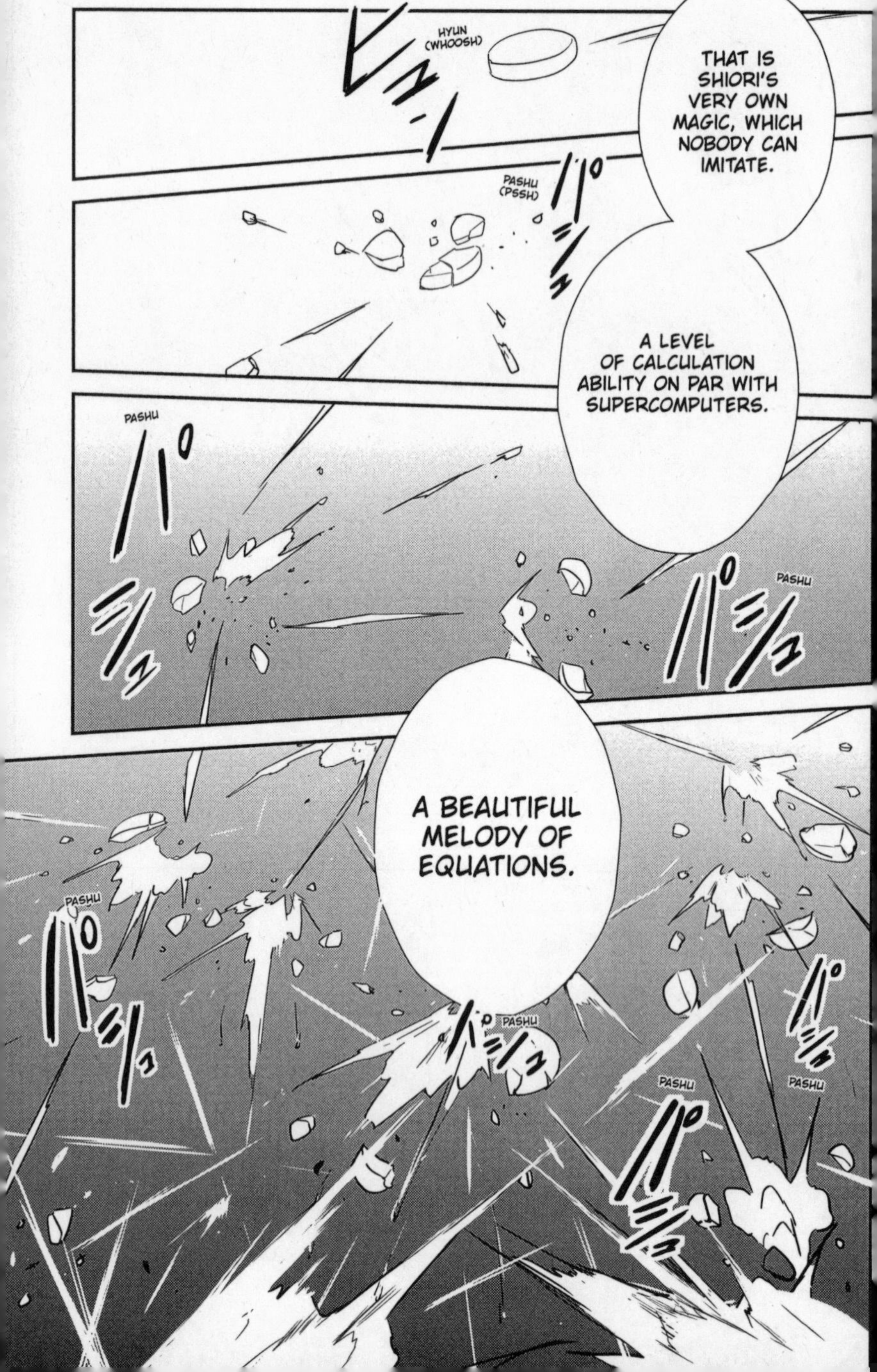
THAT IS SHIORI'S VERY OWN MAGIC, WHICH NOBODY CAN IMITATE.
HYUN (WHOOSH)
PASHU (PSSH)
A LEVEL OF CALCULATION ABILITY ON PAR WITH SUPERCOMPUTERS.
PASHU
PASHU
A BEAUTIFUL MELODY OF EQUATIONS.
PASHU
PASHU
PASHU
PASHU
PASHU

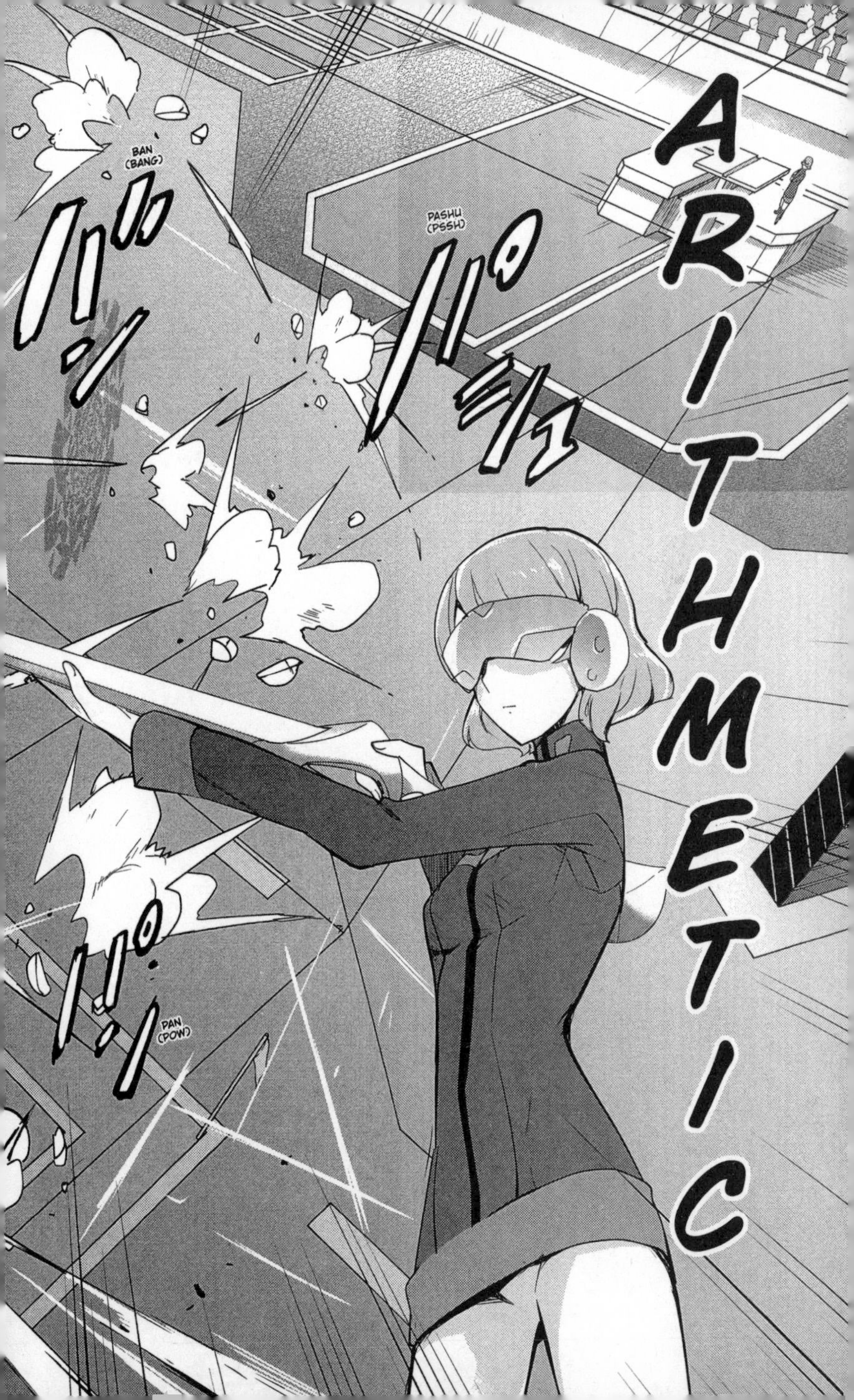
ARITHMETIC
PASHU (PSSH)
BAN (BANG)
PAN (POW)

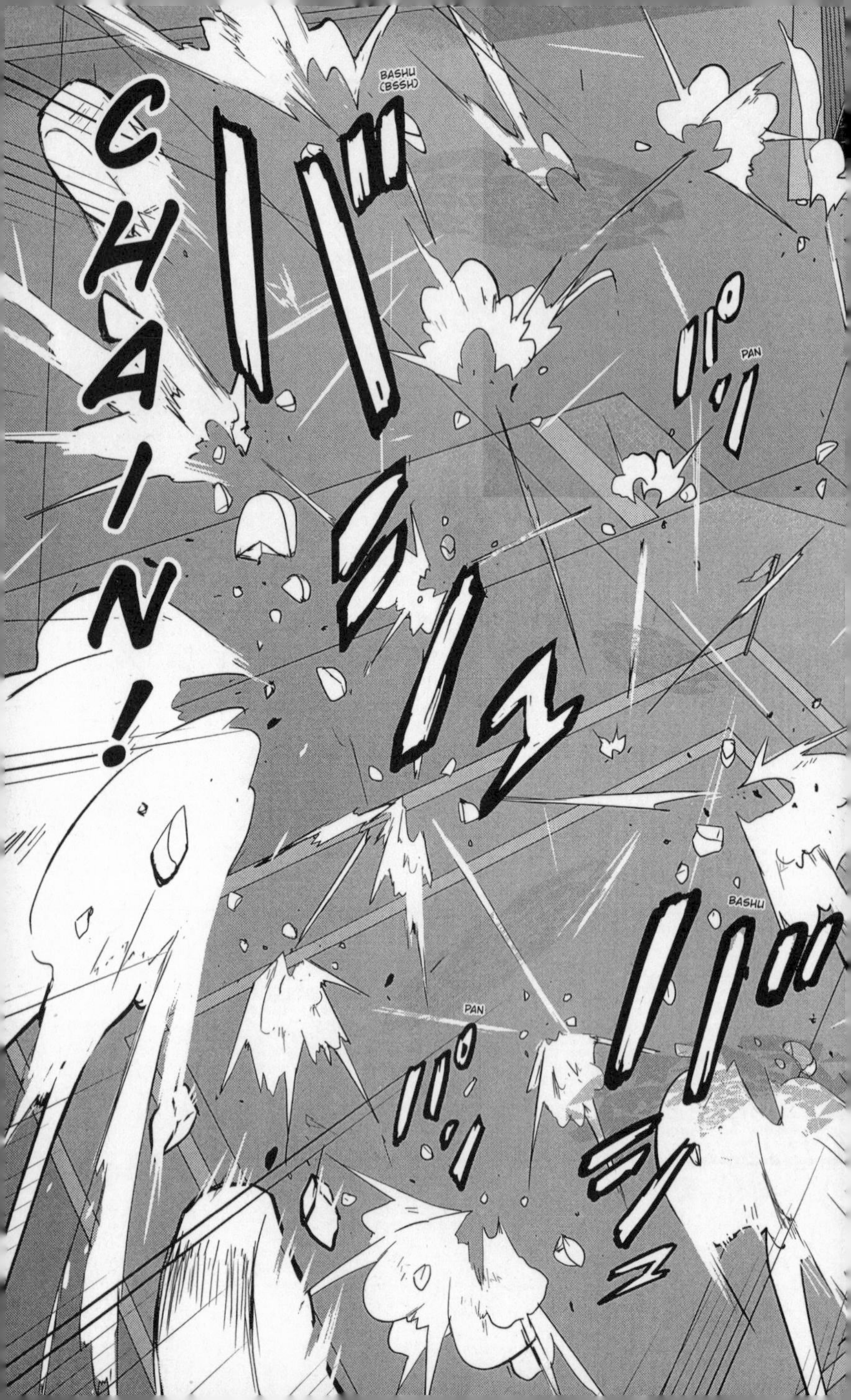
BASHU (BSSH)
PAN
CHA-I-N!
BASHU
PAN

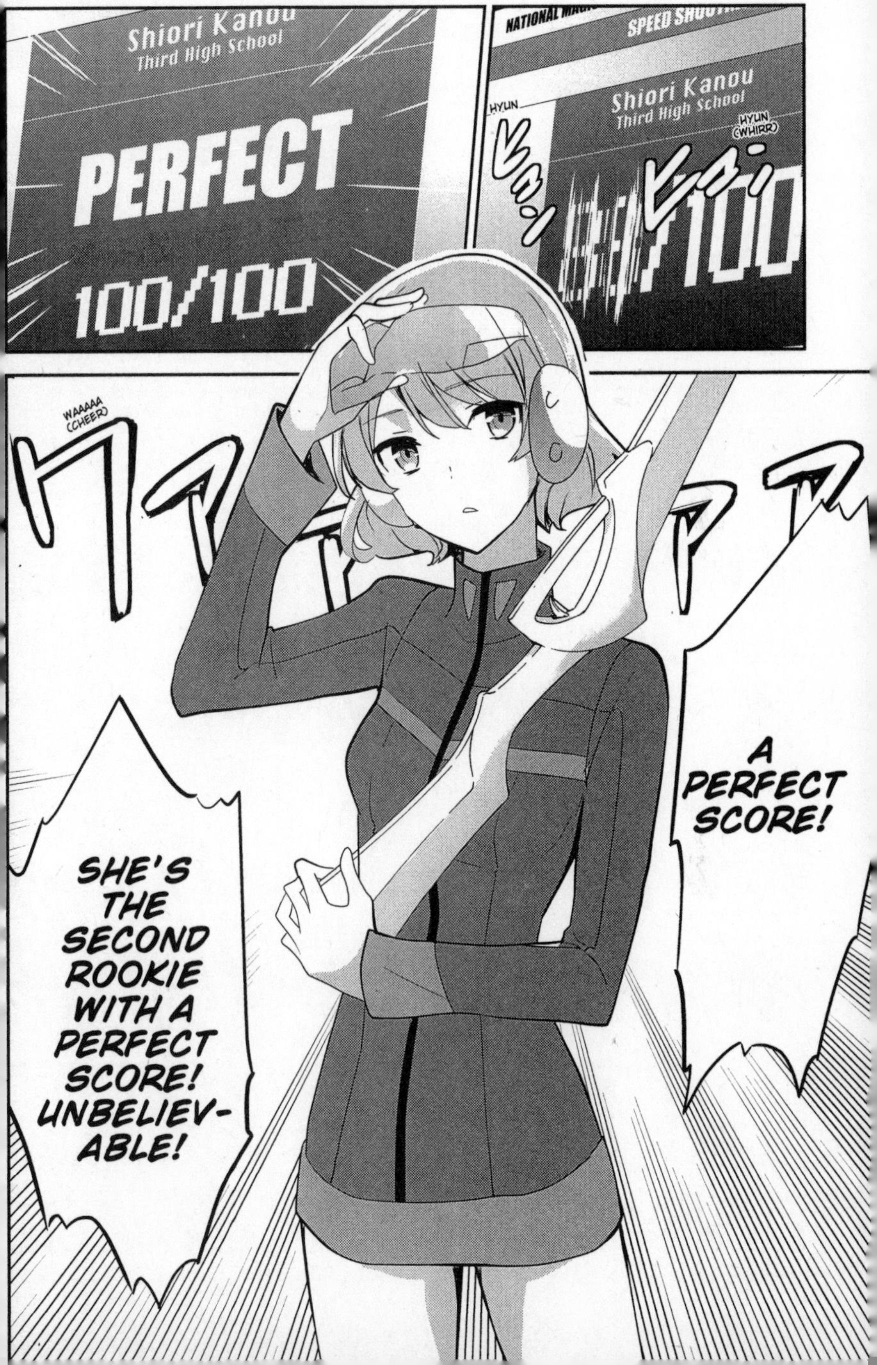
NATIONAL
Shiori Kanou
Third High School
HYUN
HYUN (WHIRR)
Shiori Kanou
Third High School
PERFECT
100/100
WAAAAA (CHEER)
A PERFECT SCORE!
SHE'S THE SECOND ROOKIE WITH A PERFECT SCORE! UNBELIEV-ABLE!

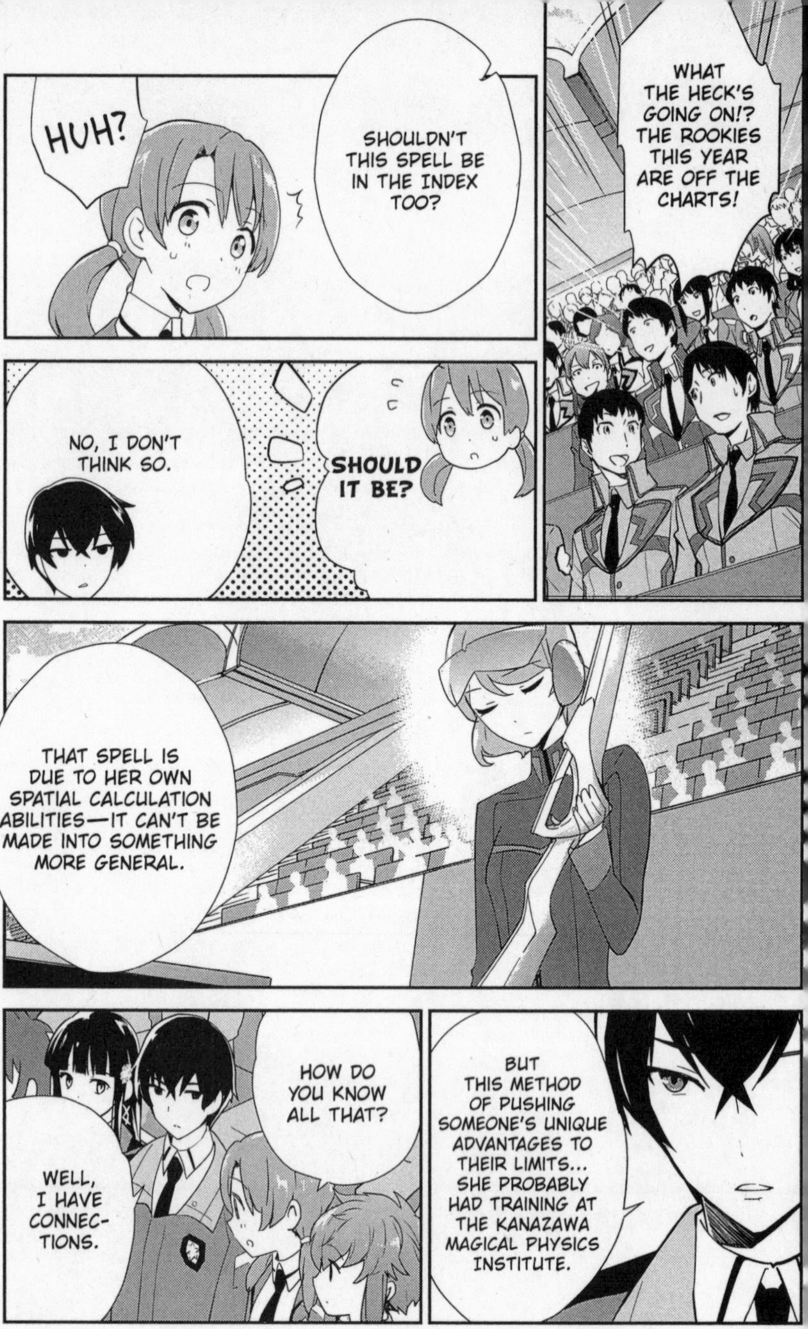
WHAT THE HECK'S GOING ON!? THE ROOKIES THIS YEAR ARE OFF THE CHARTS!
SHOULDN'T THIS SPELL BE IN THE INDEX TOO?
HUH?
SHOULD IT BE?
NO, I DON'T THINK SO.
THAT SPELL IS DUE TO HER OWN SPATIAL CALCULATION ABILITIES—IT CAN'T BE MADE INTO SOMETHING MORE GENERAL.
BUT THIS METHOD OF PUSHING SOMEONE'S UNIQUE ADVANTAGES TO THEIR LIMITS... SHE PROBABLY HAD TRAINING AT THE KANAZAWA MAGICAL PHYSICS INSTITUTE.
HOW DO YOU KNOW ALL THAT?
WELL, I HAVE CONNEC-TIONS.

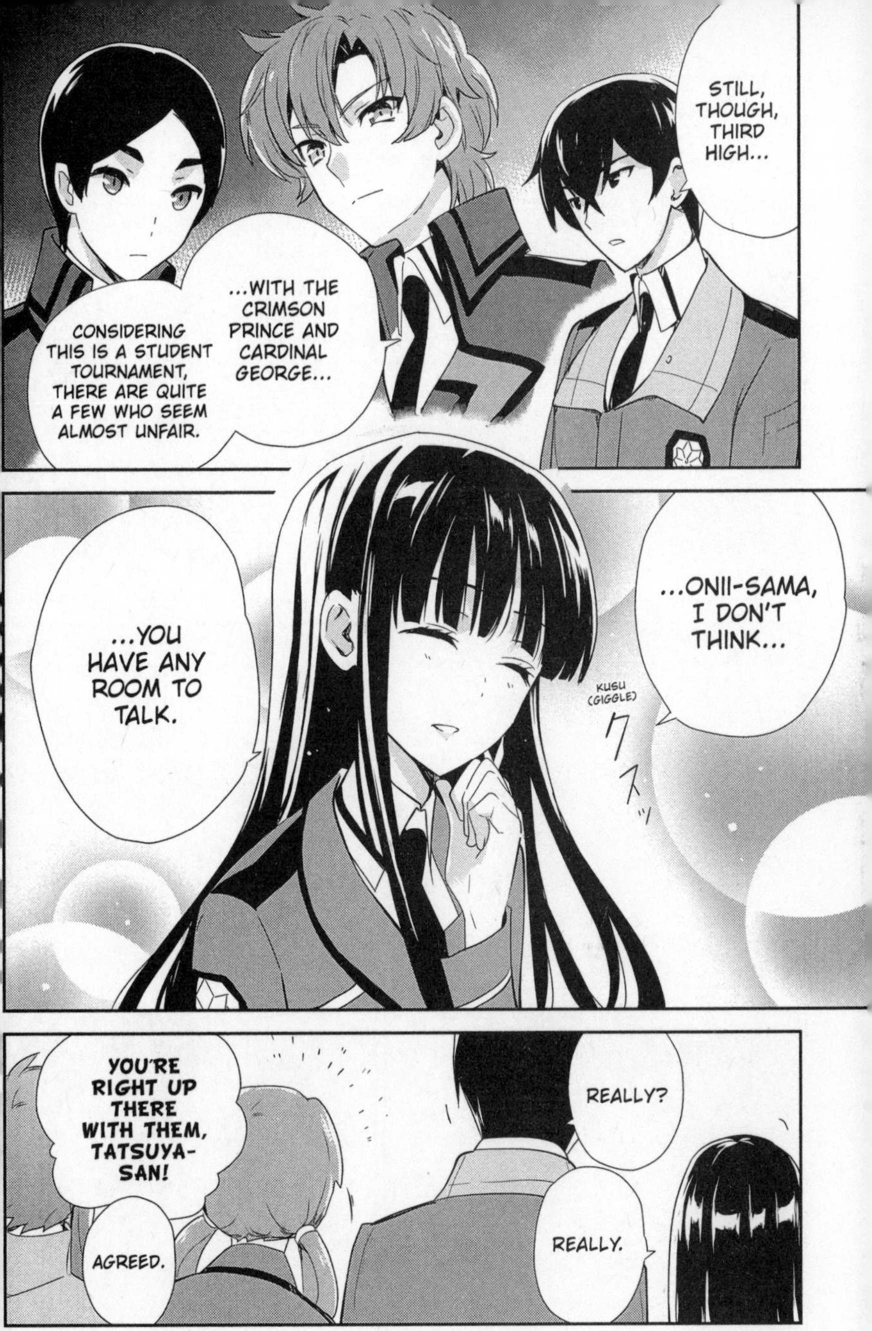
STILL, THOUGH, THIRD HIGH...
...WITH THE CRIMSON PRINCE AND CARDINAL GEORGE...
CONSIDERING THIS IS A STUDENT TOURNAMENT, THERE ARE QUITE A FEW WHO SEEM ALMOST UNFAIR.
...ONII-SAMA, I DON'T THINK...
KUSU (GIGGLE)
...YOU HAVE ANY ROOM TO TALK.
REALLY?
REALLY.
YOU'RE RIGHT UP THERE WITH THEM, TATSUYA-SAN!
AGREED.

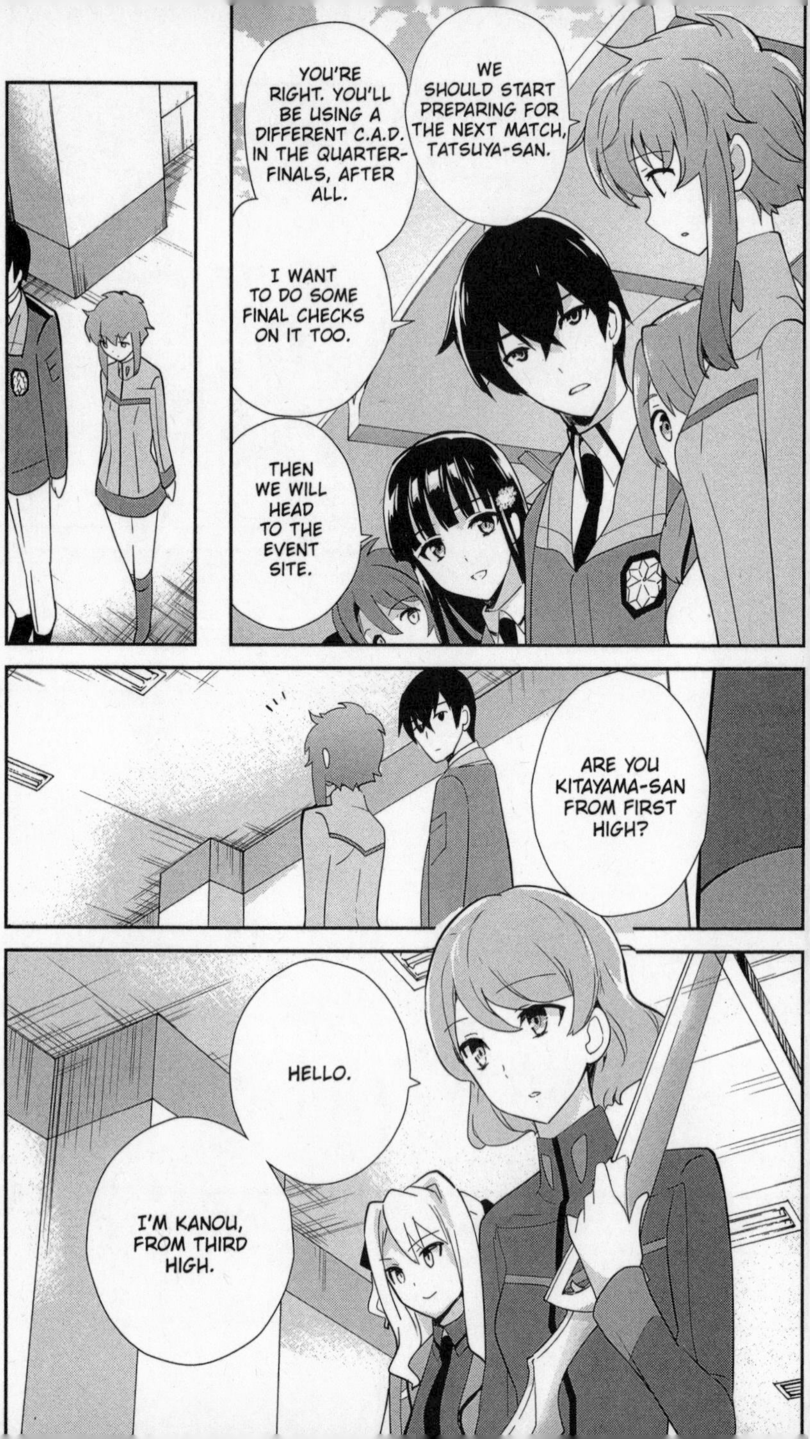
WE SHOULD START PREPARING FOR THE NEXT MATCH, TATSUYA-SAN.
YOU'RE RIGHT. YOU'LL BE USING A DIFFERENT C.A.D. IN THE QUARTER-FINALS, AFTER ALL.
I WANT TO DO SOME FINAL CHECKS ON IT TOO.
THEN WE WILL HEAD TO THE EVENT SITE.
ARE YOU KITAYAMA-SAN FROM FIRST HIGH?
HELLO.
I'M KANOU, FROM THIRD HIGH.

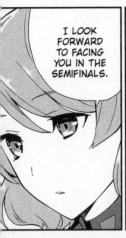

I LOOK FORWARD TO FACING YOU IN THE SEMIFINALS.

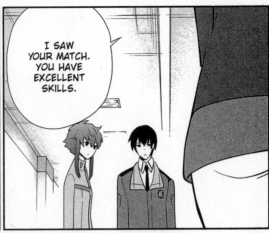

I SAW YOUR MATCH. YOU HAVE EXCELLENT SKILLS.

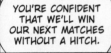

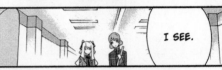

YOU'RE CONFIDENT THAT WE'LL WIN OUR NEXT MATCHES WITHOUT A HITCH.

I SEE.

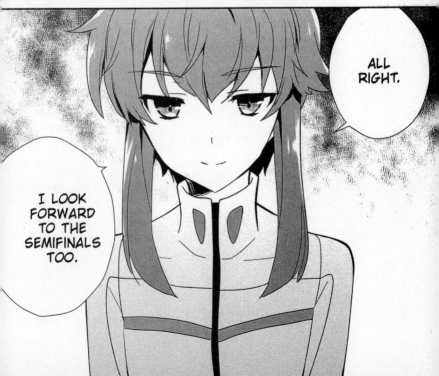

ALL RIGHT.

I LOOK FORWARD TO THE SEMIFINALS TOO.

The Honor Student at Magic High School

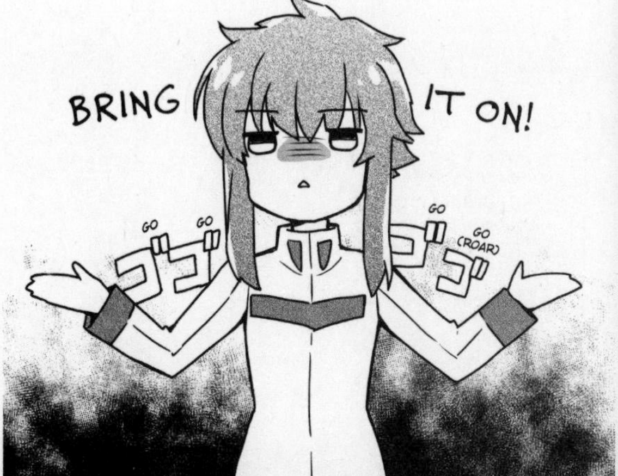
BRING IT ON!
GO GO (ROAR)
ゴゴ
GO GO
ゴゴ

## CHAPTER 29

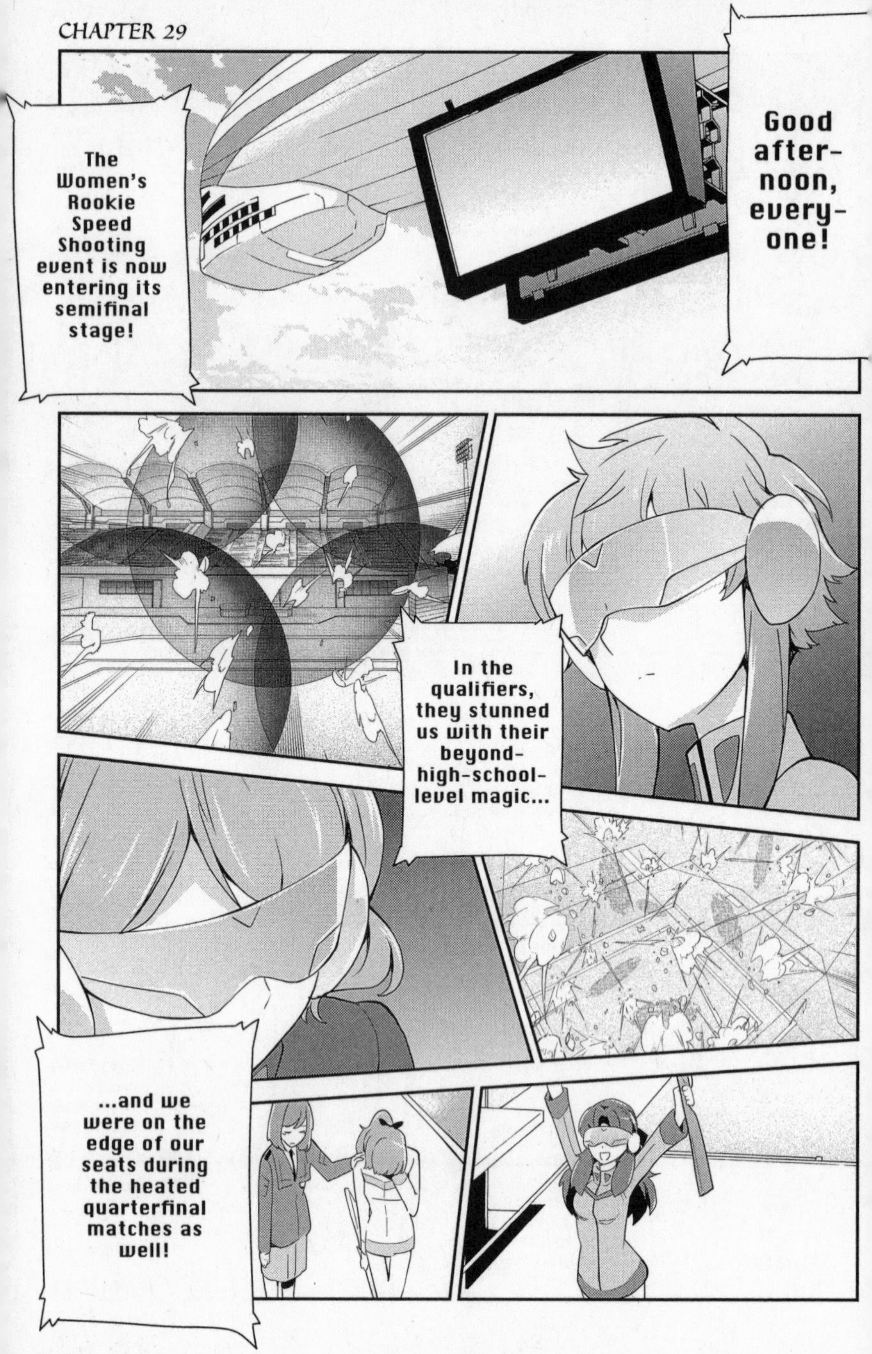
Good afternoon, everyone!
The Women's Rookie Speed Shooting event is now entering its semifinal stage!
In the qualifiers, they stunned us with their beyond-high-school-level magic...
...and we were on the edge of our seats during the heated quarterfinal matches as well!

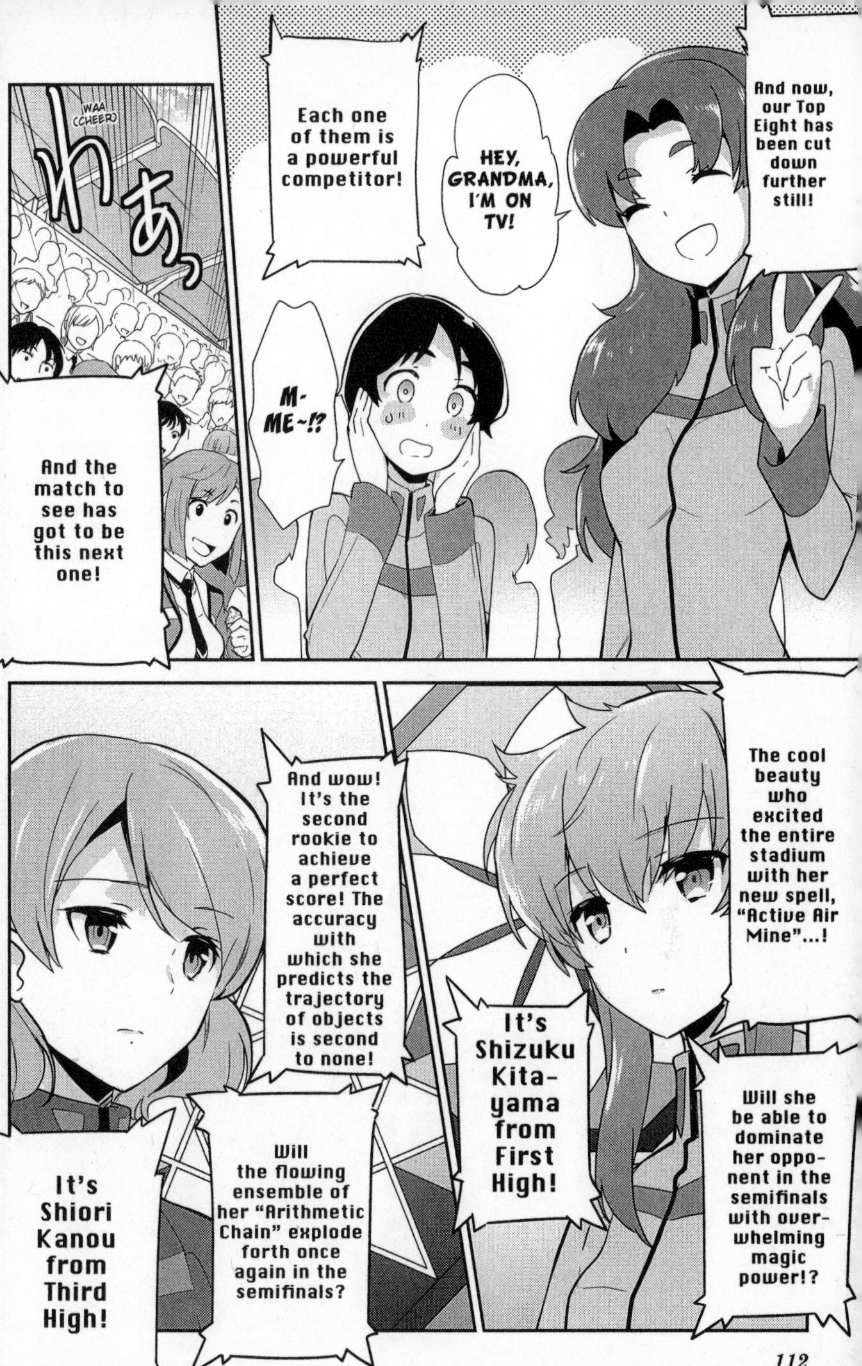
And now, our Top Eight has been cut down further still!
HEY, GRANDMA, I'M ON TV!
Each one of them is a powerful competitor!
M-ME~!?
WAA (CHEER)
わあっ
And the match to see has got to be this next one!
The cool beauty who excited the entire stadium with her new spell, "Active Air Mine"...!
It's Shizuku Kita-yama from First High!
Will she be able to dominate her oppo-nent in the semifinals with over-whelming magic power!?
And wow! It's the second rookie to achieve a perfect score! The accuracy with which she predicts the trajectory of objects is second to none!
It's Shiori Kanou from Third High!
Will the flowing ensemble of her "Arithmetic Chain" explode forth once again in the semifinals?

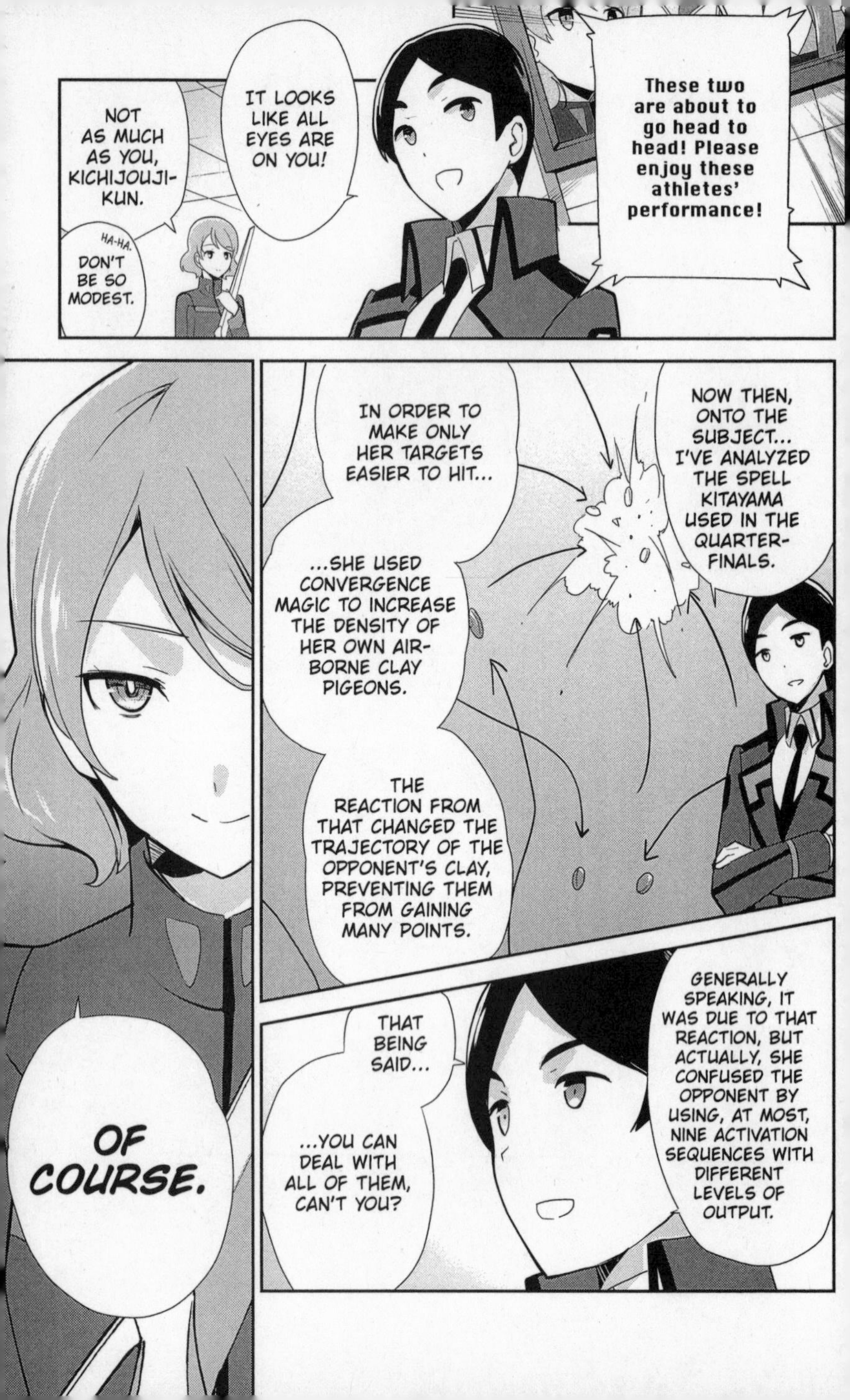
These two are about to go head to head! Please enjoy these athletes' performance!
IT LOOKS LIKE ALL EYES ARE ON YOU!
NOT AS MUCH AS YOU, KICHIJOUJI-KUN.
HA-HA. DON'T BE SO MODEST.
NOW THEN, ONTO THE SUBJECT... I'VE ANALYZED THE SPELL KITAYAMA USED IN THE QUARTER-FINALS.
IN ORDER TO MAKE ONLY HER TARGETS EASIER TO HIT...
...SHE USED CONVERGENCE MAGIC TO INCREASE THE DENSITY OF HER OWN AIR-BORNE CLAY PIGEONS.
THE REACTION FROM THAT CHANGED THE TRAJECTORY OF THE OPPONENT'S CLAY, PREVENTING THEM FROM GAINING MANY POINTS.
GENERALLY SPEAKING, IT WAS DUE TO THAT REACTION, BUT ACTUALLY, SHE CONFUSED THE OPPONENT BY USING, AT MOST, NINE ACTIVATION SEQUENCES WITH DIFFERENT LEVELS OF OUTPUT.
THAT BEING SAID...
...YOU CAN DEAL WITH ALL OF THEM, CAN'T YOU?
OF COURSE.

CHAPTER 29

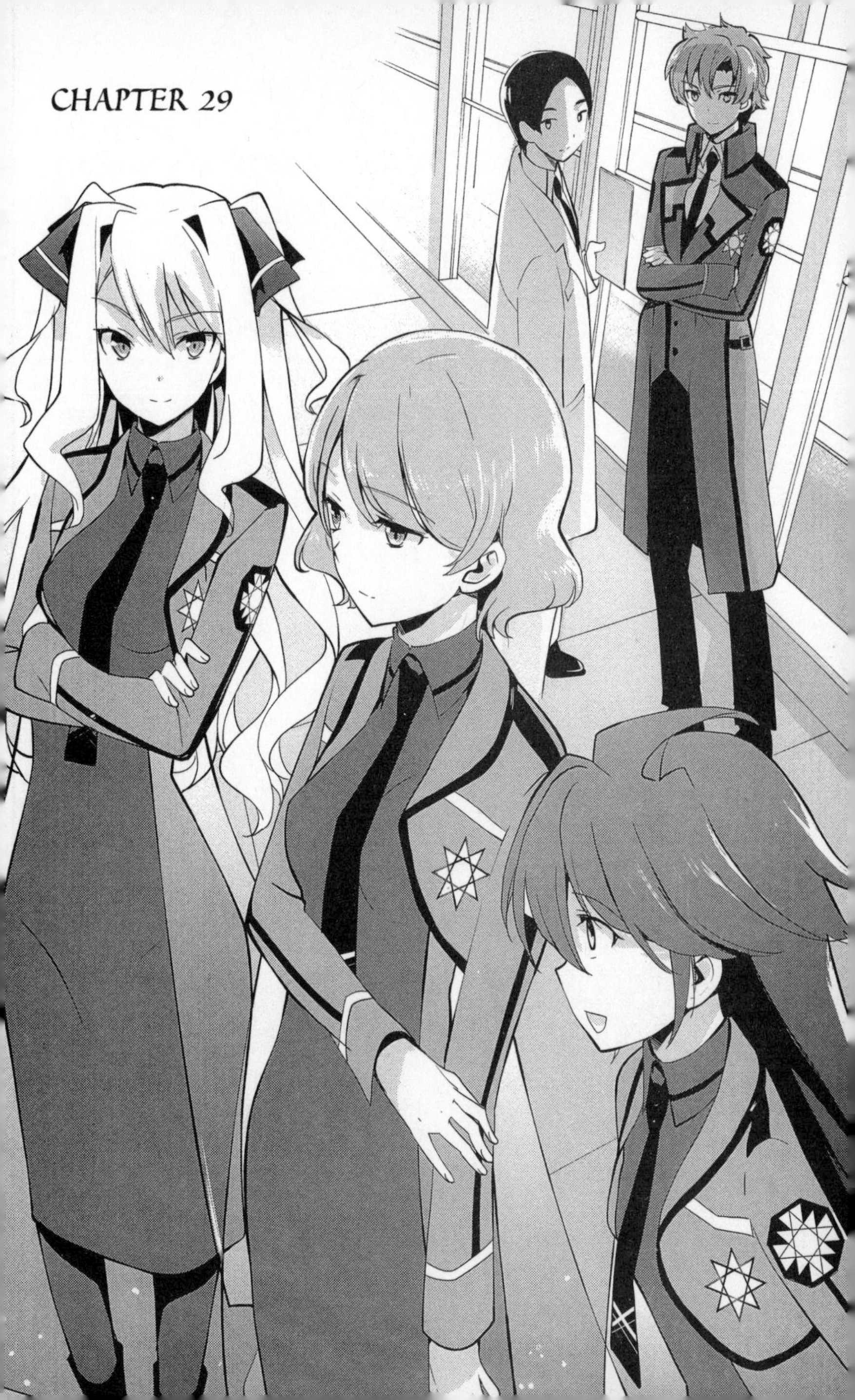

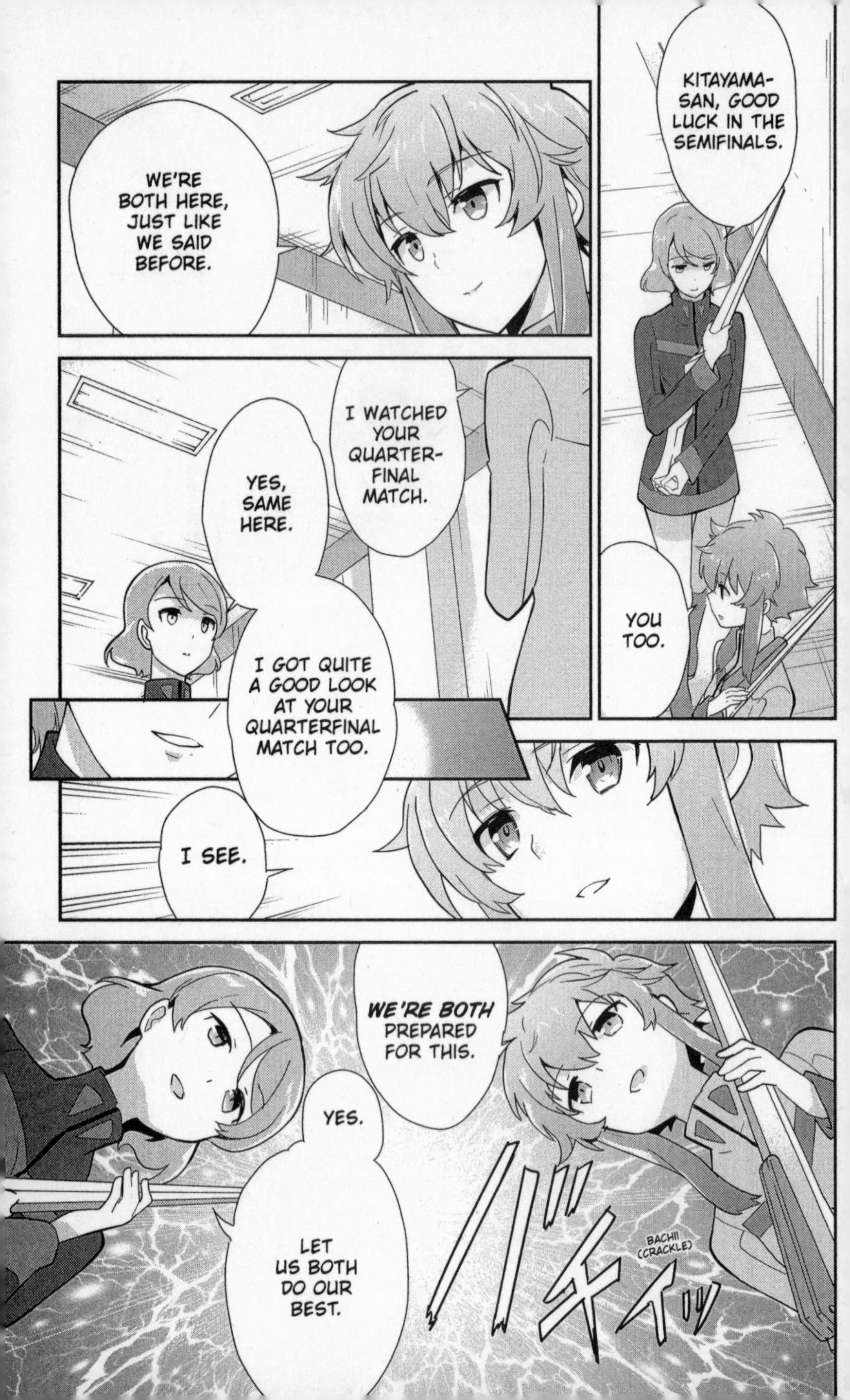
KITAYAMA-SAN, GOOD LUCK IN THE SEMIFINALS.
YOU TOO.
WE'RE BOTH HERE, JUST LIKE WE SAID BEFORE.
I WATCHED YOUR QUARTER-FINAL MATCH.
YES, SAME HERE.
I GOT QUITE A GOOD LOOK AT YOUR QUARTERFINAL MATCH TOO.
I SEE.
*WE'RE BOTH* PREPARED FOR THIS.
YES.
LET US BOTH DO OUR BEST.
BACHII (CRACKLE)

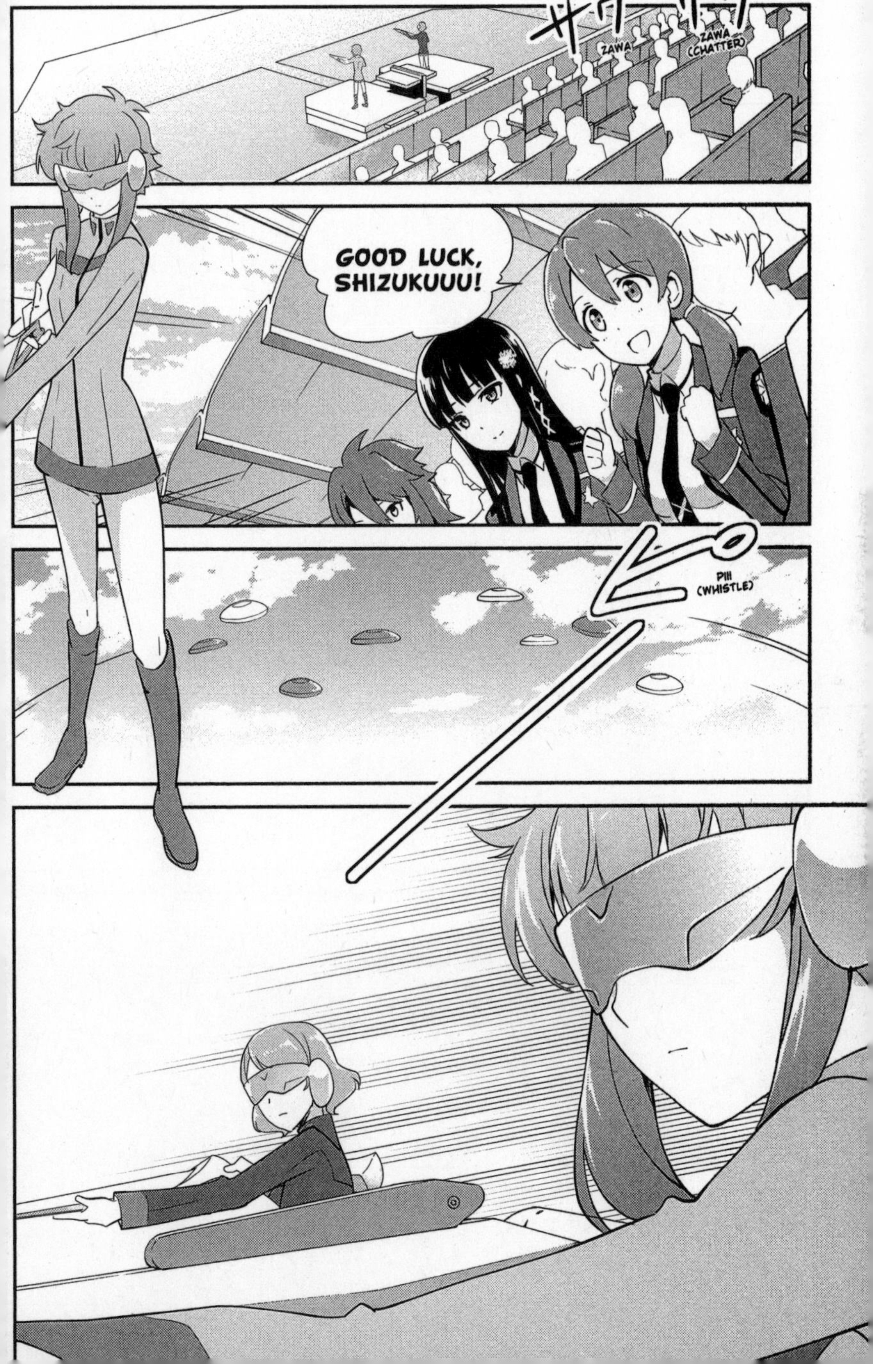
ザワ ザワ
ZAWA
(CHATTER)
ZAWA
GOOD LUCK, SHIZUKUUU!
PIII
(WHISTLE)

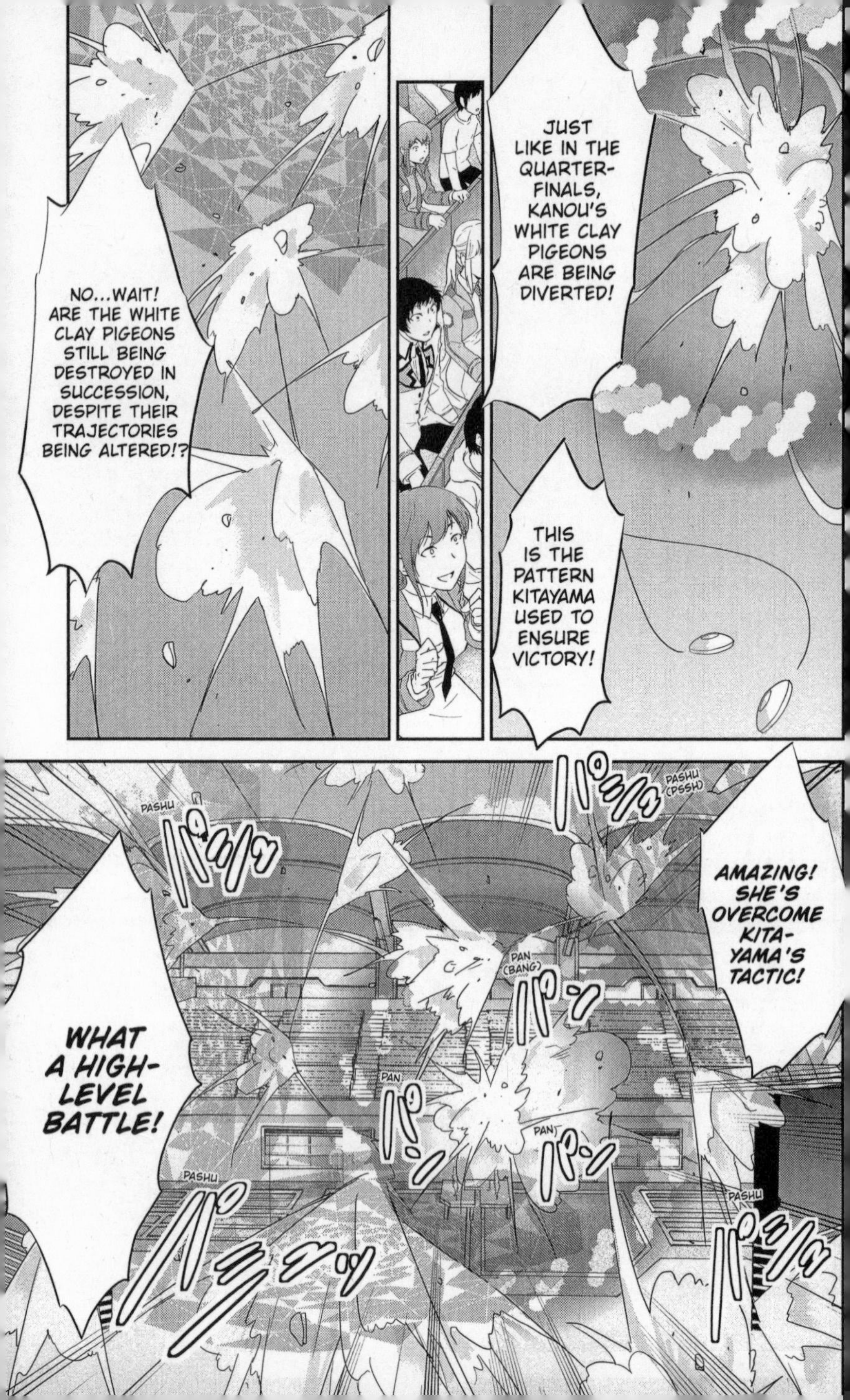
JUST LIKE IN THE QUARTER-FINALS, KANOU'S WHITE CLAY PIGEONS ARE BEING DIVERTED!
THIS IS THE PATTERN KITAYAMA USED TO ENSURE VICTORY!
NO...WAIT! ARE THE WHITE CLAY PIGEONS STILL BEING DESTROYED IN SUCCESSION, DESPITE THEIR TRAJECTORIES BEING ALTERED!?
PASHU (PSSH)
AMAZING! SHE'S OVERCOME KITA-YAMA'S TACTIC!
PAN (BANG)
PASHU
WHAT A HIGH-LEVEL BATTLE!
PAN
PAN
PASHU
PASHU

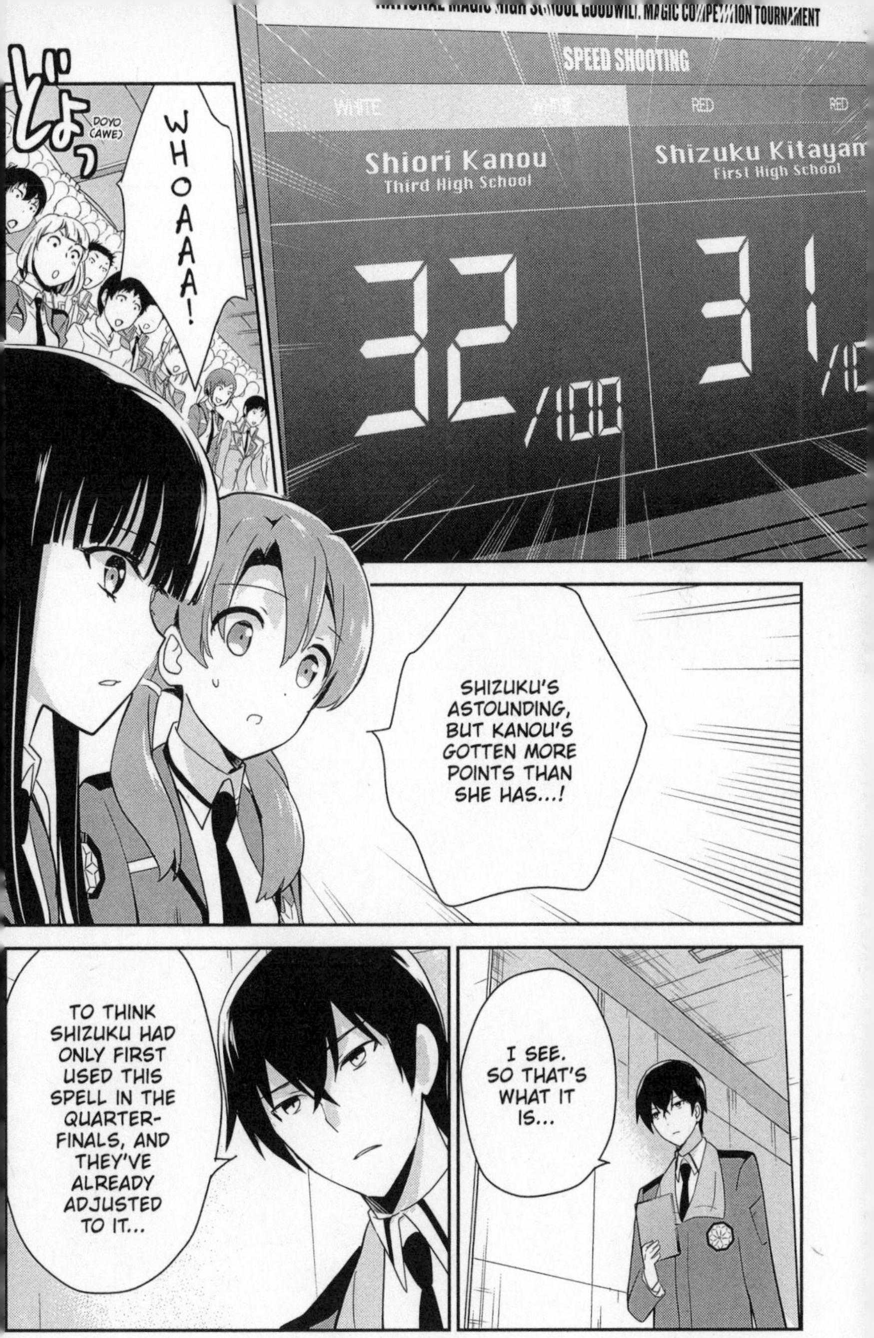
SPEED SHOOTING
WHITE
RED
RED
Shiori Kanou
Third High School
32/100
Shizuku Kitayam
First High School
31
WHOAAAA!
DOYO (AWE)
SHIZUKU'S ASTOUNDING, BUT KANOU'S GOTTEN MORE POINTS THAN SHE HAS...!
I SEE. SO THAT'S WHAT IT IS...
TO THINK SHIZUKU HAD ONLY FIRST USED THIS SPELL IN THE QUARTER-FINALS, AND THEY'VE ALREADY ADJUSTED TO IT...

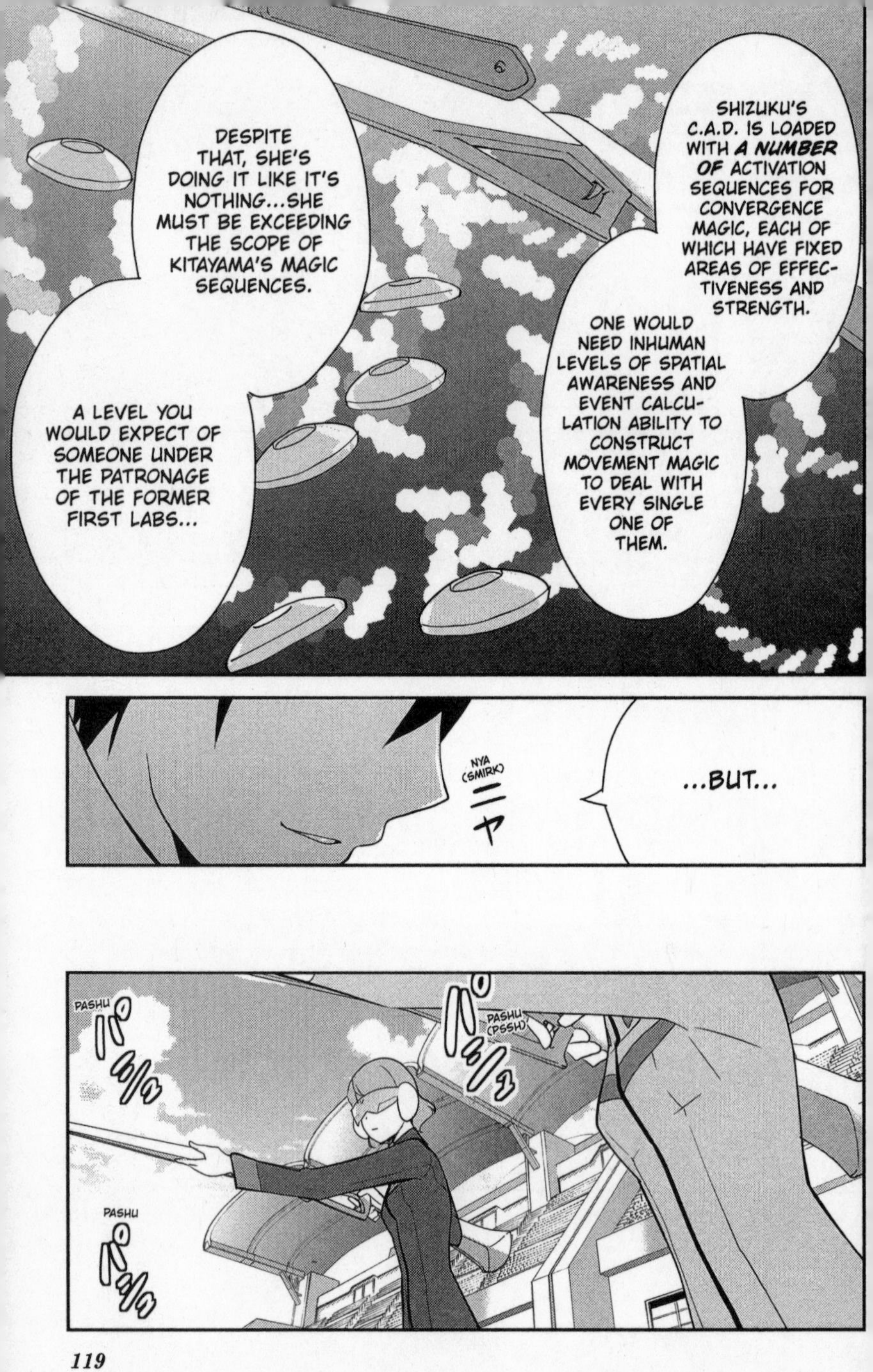
SHIZUKU'S C.A.D. IS LOADED WITH ***A NUMBER OF*** ACTIVATION SEQUENCES FOR CONVERGENCE MAGIC, EACH OF WHICH HAVE FIXED AREAS OF EFFECTIVENESS AND STRENGTH.
ONE WOULD NEED INHUMAN LEVELS OF SPATIAL AWARENESS AND EVENT CALCULATION ABILITY TO CONSTRUCT MOVEMENT MAGIC TO DEAL WITH EVERY SINGLE ONE OF THEM.
DESPITE THAT, SHE'S DOING IT LIKE IT'S NOTHING...SHE MUST BE EXCEEDING THE SCOPE OF KITAYAMA'S MAGIC SEQUENCES.
A LEVEL YOU WOULD EXPECT OF SOMEONE UNDER THE PATRONAGE OF THE FORMER FIRST LABS...
...BUT...
NYA (SMIRK)
ニヤ
PASHU (PSSH)
PASHU
PASHU

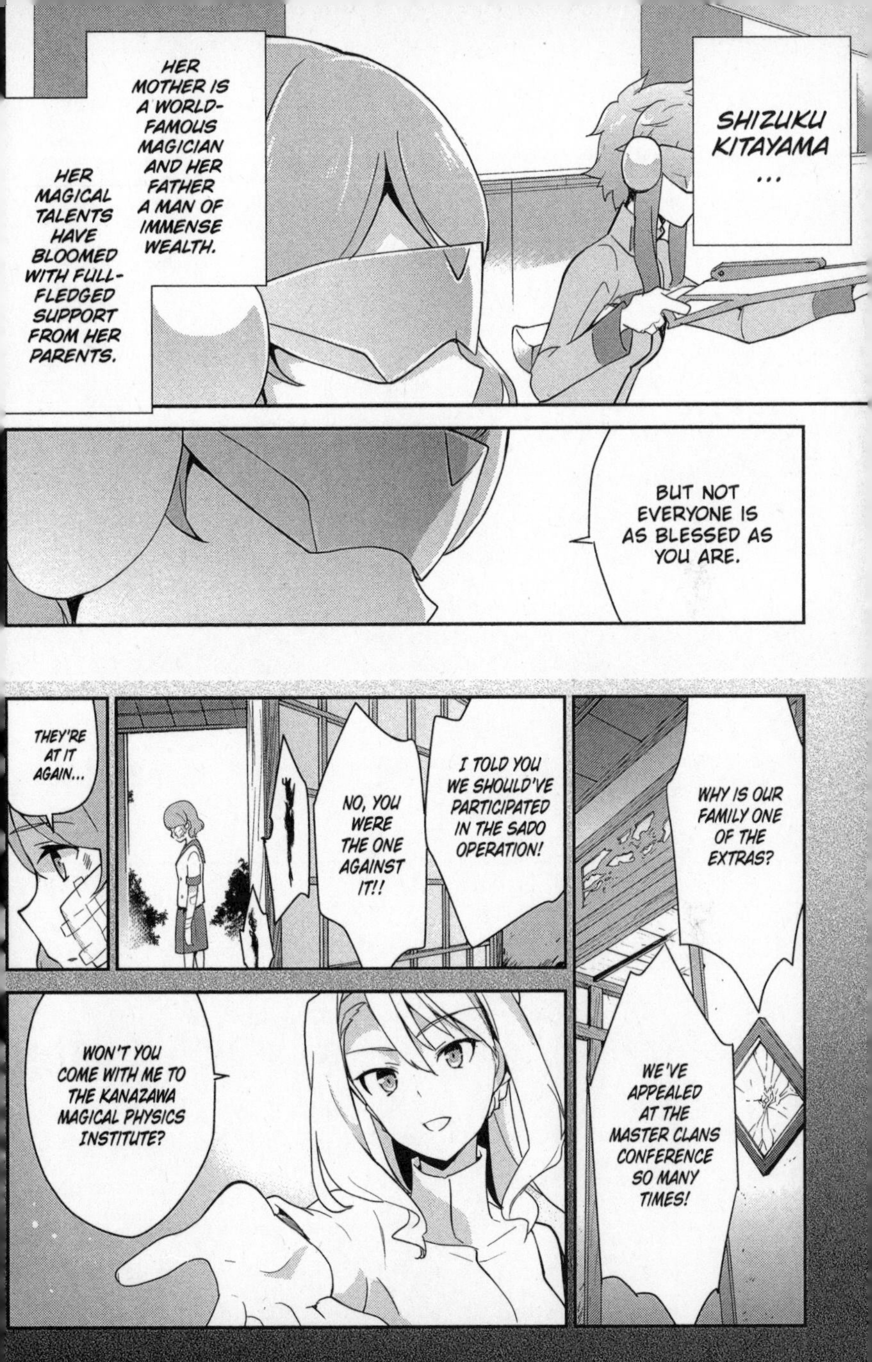
SHIZUKU KITAYAMA ...
HER MOTHER IS A WORLD-FAMOUS MAGICIAN AND HER FATHER A MAN OF IMMENSE WEALTH.
HER MAGICAL TALENTS HAVE BLOOMED WITH FULL-FLEDGED SUPPORT FROM HER PARENTS.
BUT NOT EVERYONE IS AS BLESSED AS YOU ARE.
WHY IS OUR FAMILY ONE OF THE EXTRAS?
WE'VE APPEALED AT THE MASTER CLANS CONFERENCE SO MANY TIMES!
I TOLD YOU WE SHOULD'VE PARTICIPATED IN THE SADO OPERATION!
NO, YOU WERE THE ONE AGAINST IT!!
THEY'RE AT IT AGAIN...
WON'T YOU COME WITH ME TO THE KANAZAWA MAGICAL PHYSICS INSTITUTE?

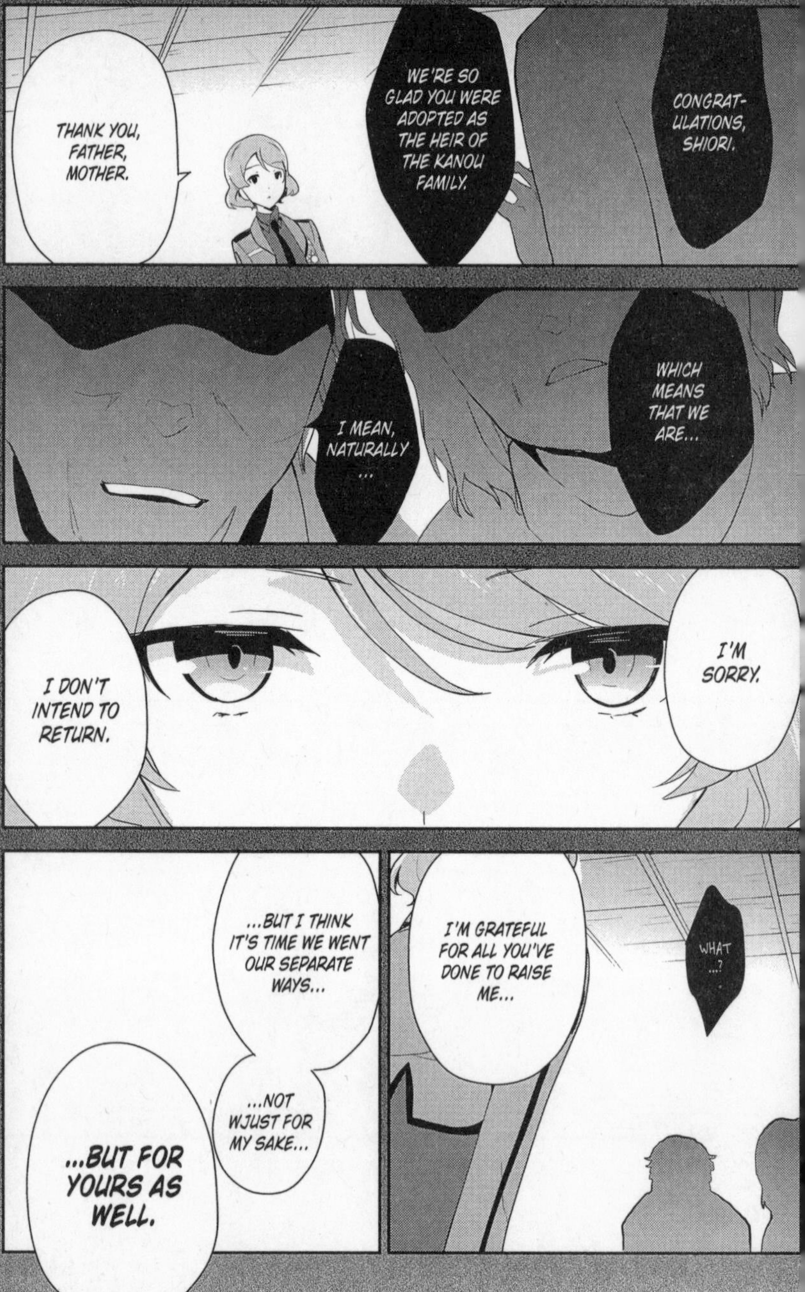
CONGRAT-ULATIONS, SHIORI.
WE'RE SO GLAD YOU WERE ADOPTED AS THE HEIR OF THE KANOU FAMILY.
THANK YOU, FATHER, MOTHER.
WHICH MEANS THAT WE ARE...
I MEAN, NATURALLY...
I'M SORRY.
I DON'T INTEND TO RETURN.
WHAT...?
I'M GRATEFUL FOR ALL YOU'VE DONE TO RAISE ME...
...BUT I THINK IT'S TIME WE WENT OUR SEPARATE WAYS...
...NOT WJUST FOR MY SAKE...
...BUT FOR YOURS AS WELL.

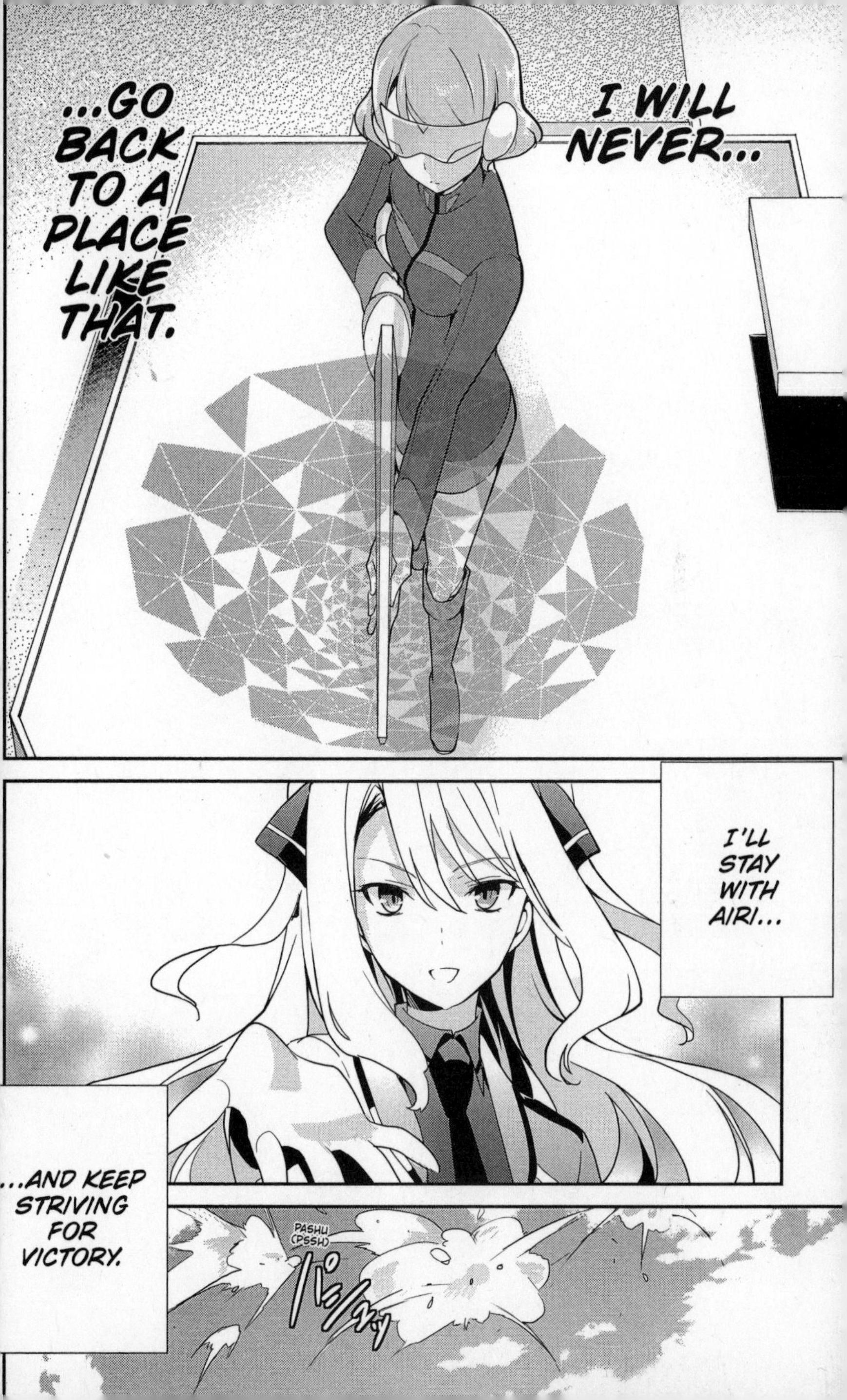
I WILL NEVER...
...GO BACK TO A PLACE LIKE THAT.
I'LL STAY WITH AIRI...
...AND KEEP STRIVING FOR VICTORY.
PASHU (PSSH)
パシュッ

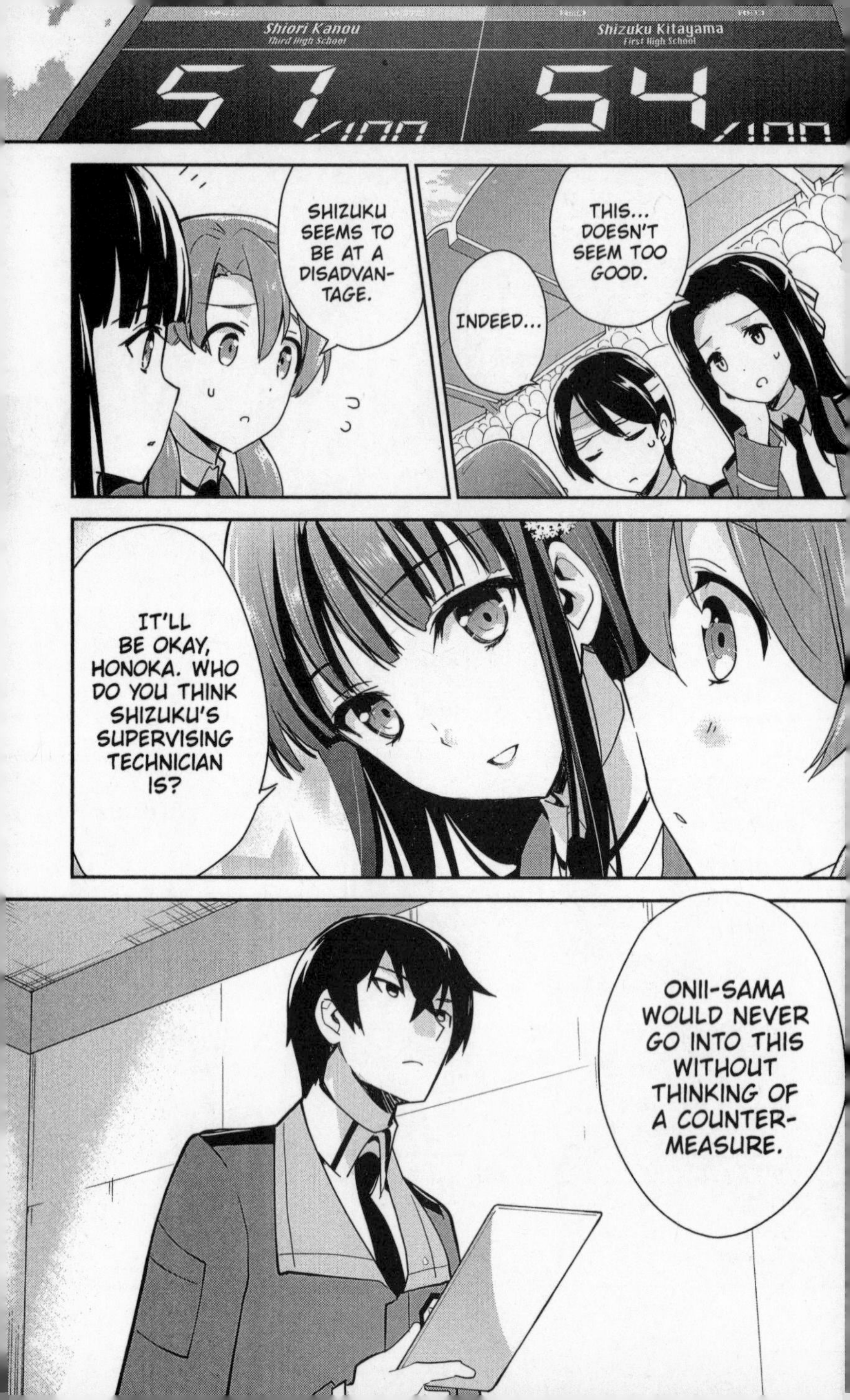
Shiori Kanou
Third High School
57/100
Shizuku Kitayama
First High School
54/100
THIS... DOESN'T SEEM TOO GOOD.
INDEED...
SHIZUKU SEEMS TO BE AT A DISADVANTAGE.
IT'LL BE OKAY, HONOKA. WHO DO YOU THINK SHIZUKU'S SUPERVISING TECHNICIAN IS?
ONII-SAMA WOULD NEVER GO INTO THIS WITHOUT THINKING OF A COUNTERMEASURE.

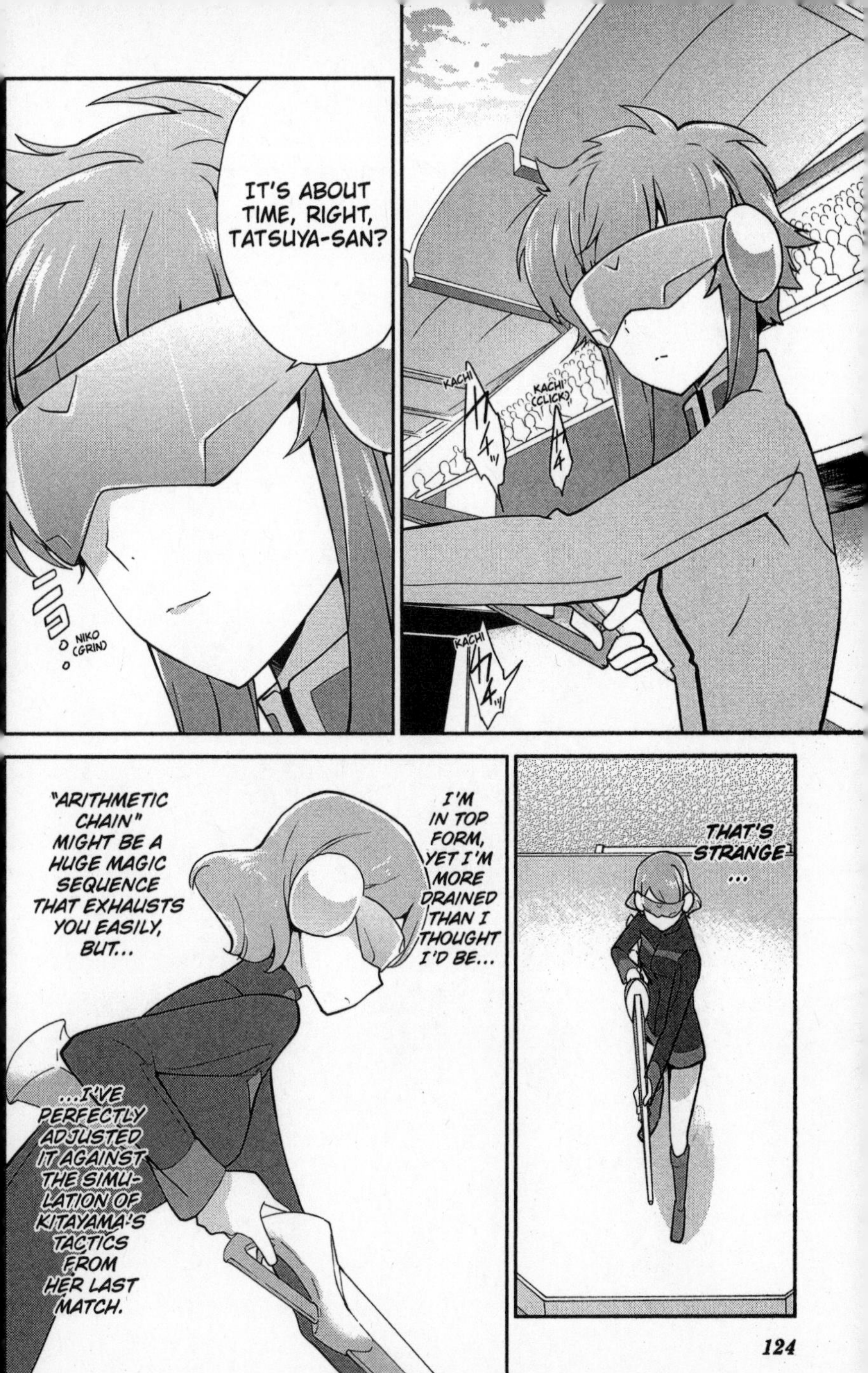
KACHI
KACHI (CLICK)
KACHI
IT'S ABOUT TIME, RIGHT, TATSUYA-SAN?
NIKO (GRIN)
THAT'S STRANGE...
I'M IN TOP FORM, YET I'M MORE DRAINED THAN I THOUGHT I'D BE...
"ARITHMETIC CHAIN" MIGHT BE A HUGE MAGIC SEQUENCE THAT EXHAUSTS YOU EASILY, BUT...
...I'VE PERFECTLY ADJUSTED IT AGAINST THE SIMU-LATION OF KITAYAMA'S TACTICS FROM HER LAST MATCH.

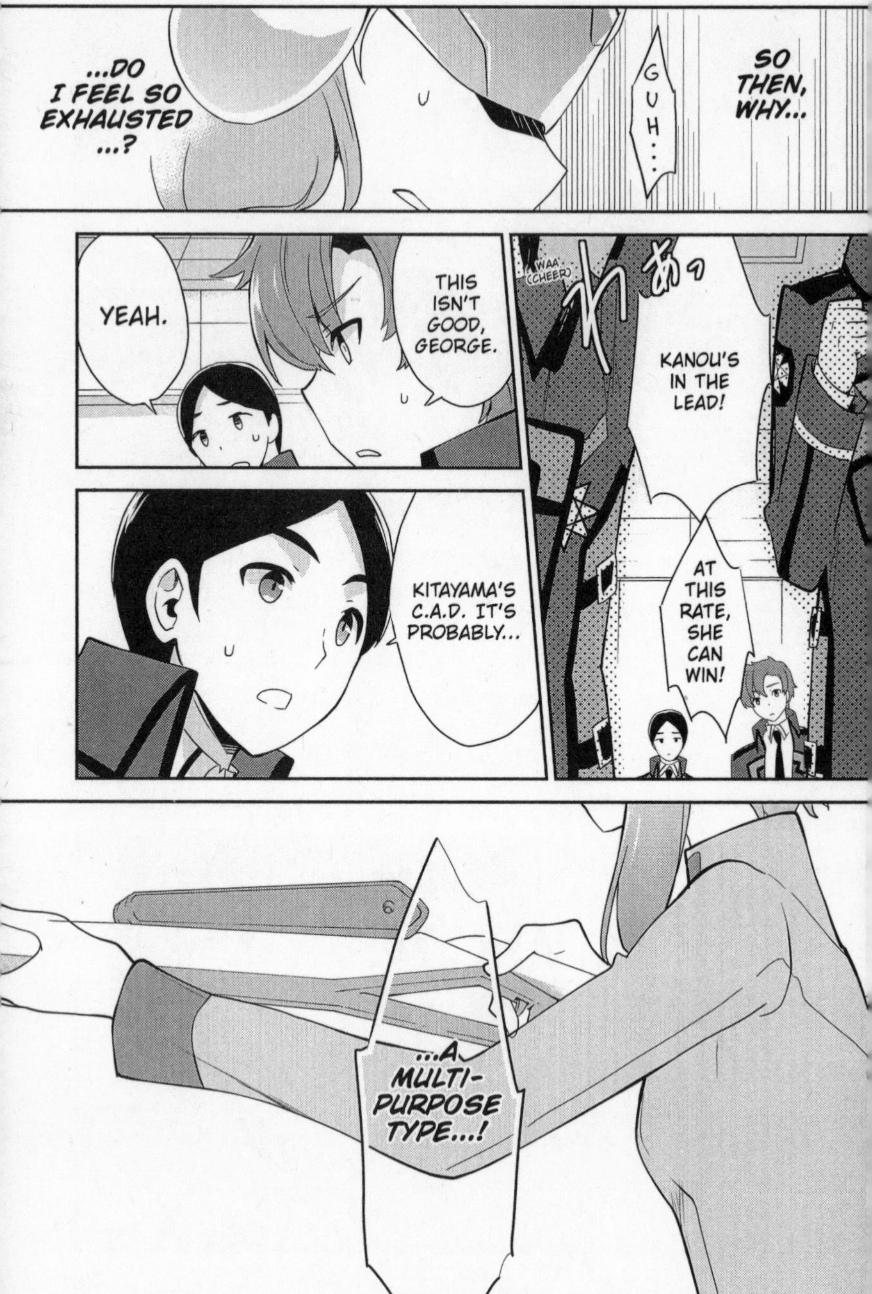
SO THEN, WHY...
GUH...
...DO I FEEL SO EXHAUSTED...?
わあっ
WAA (CHEER)
KANOU'S IN THE LEAD!
AT THIS RATE, SHE CAN WIN!
THIS ISN'T GOOD, GEORGE.
YEAH.
KITAYAMA'S C.A.D. IT'S PROBABLY...
...A MULTI-PURPOSE TYPE...!

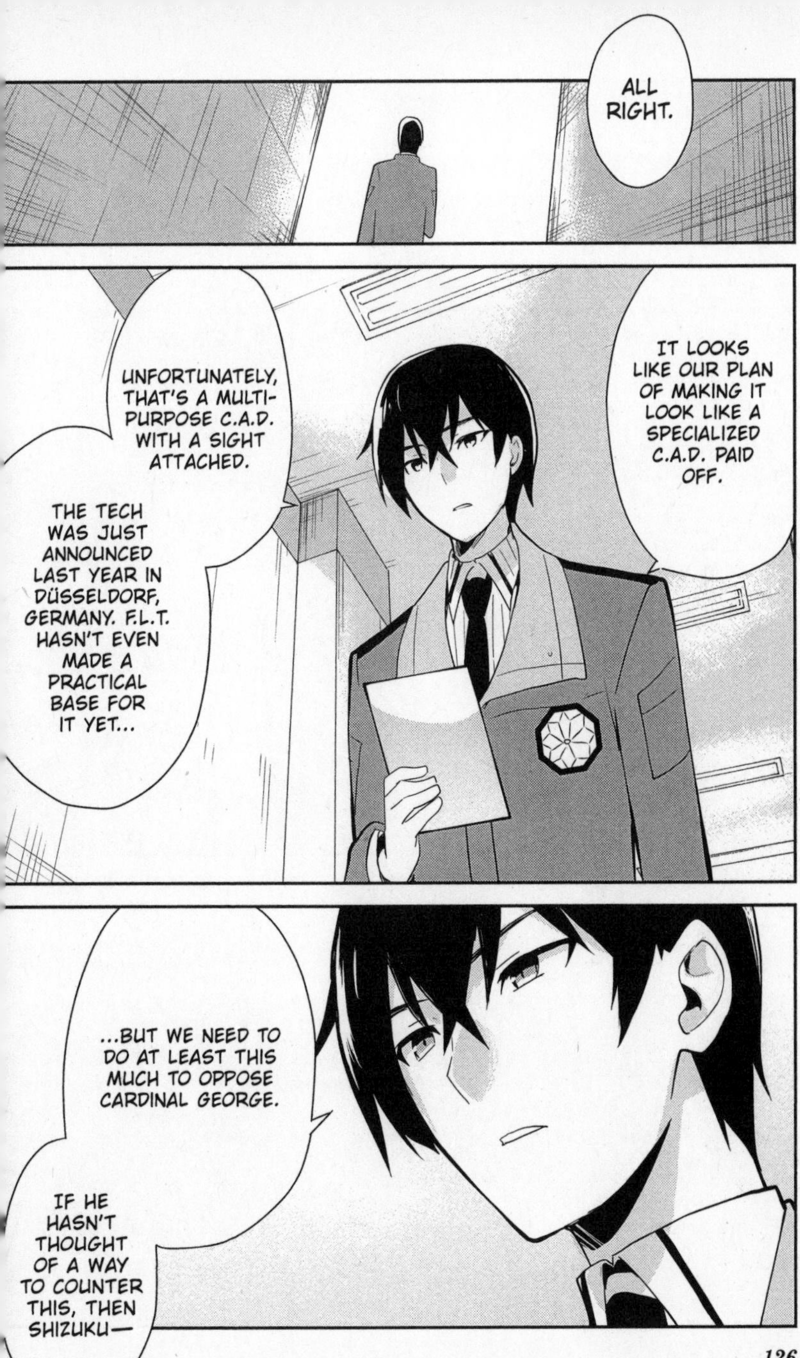
ALL RIGHT.
IT LOOKS LIKE OUR PLAN OF MAKING IT LOOK LIKE A SPECIALIZED C.A.D. PAID OFF.
UNFORTUNATELY, THAT'S A MULTI-PURPOSE C.A.D. WITH A SIGHT ATTACHED.
THE TECH WAS JUST ANNOUNCED LAST YEAR IN DÜSSELDORF, GERMANY. F.L.T. HASN'T EVEN MADE A PRACTICAL BASE FOR IT YET...
...BUT WE NEED TO DO AT LEAST THIS MUCH TO OPPOSE CARDINAL GEORGE.
IF HE HASN'T THOUGHT OF A WAY TO COUNTER THIS, THEN SHIZUKU—

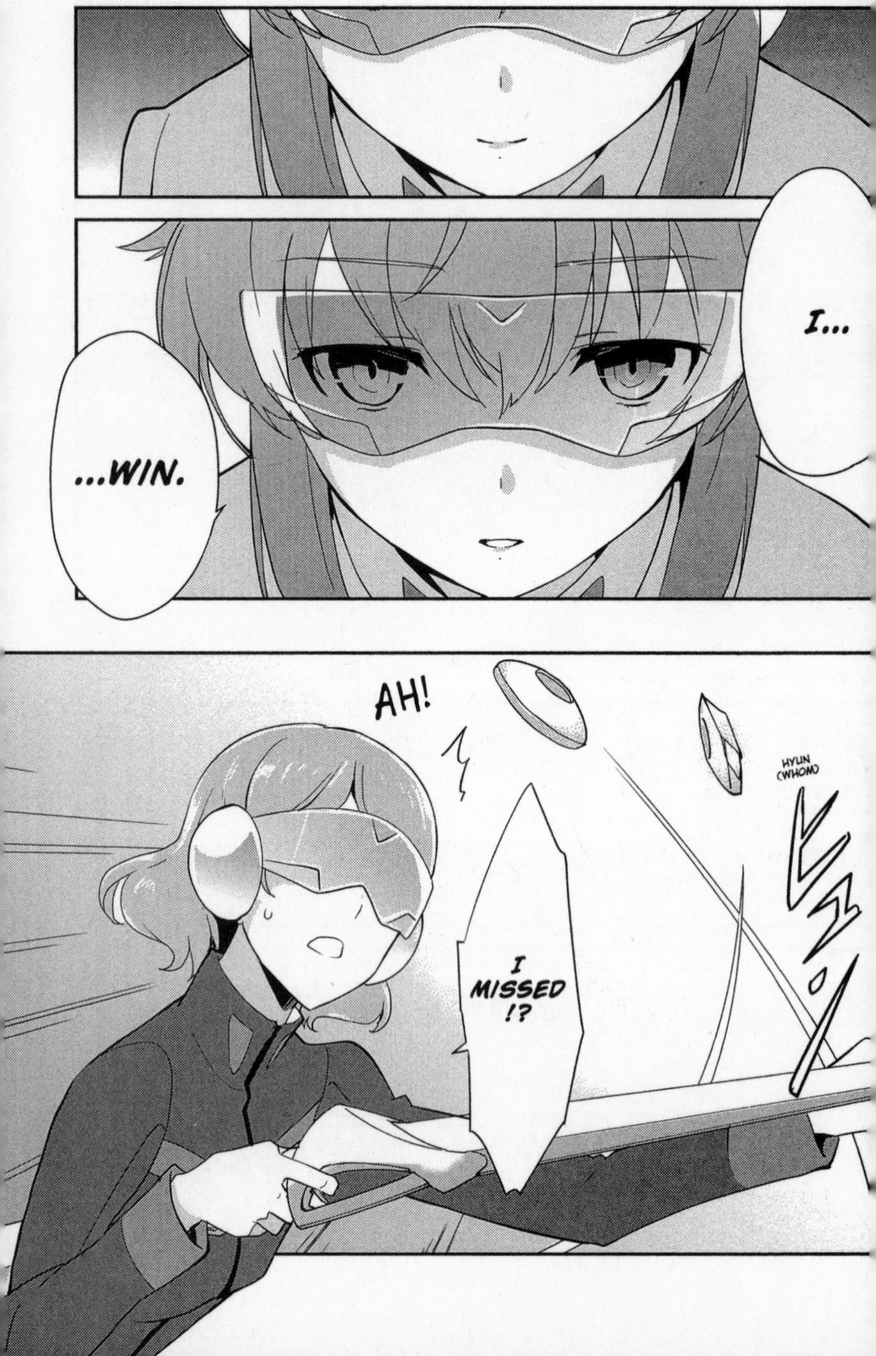
I...
...WIN.
HYUN (WHOM)
AH!
I MISSED !?

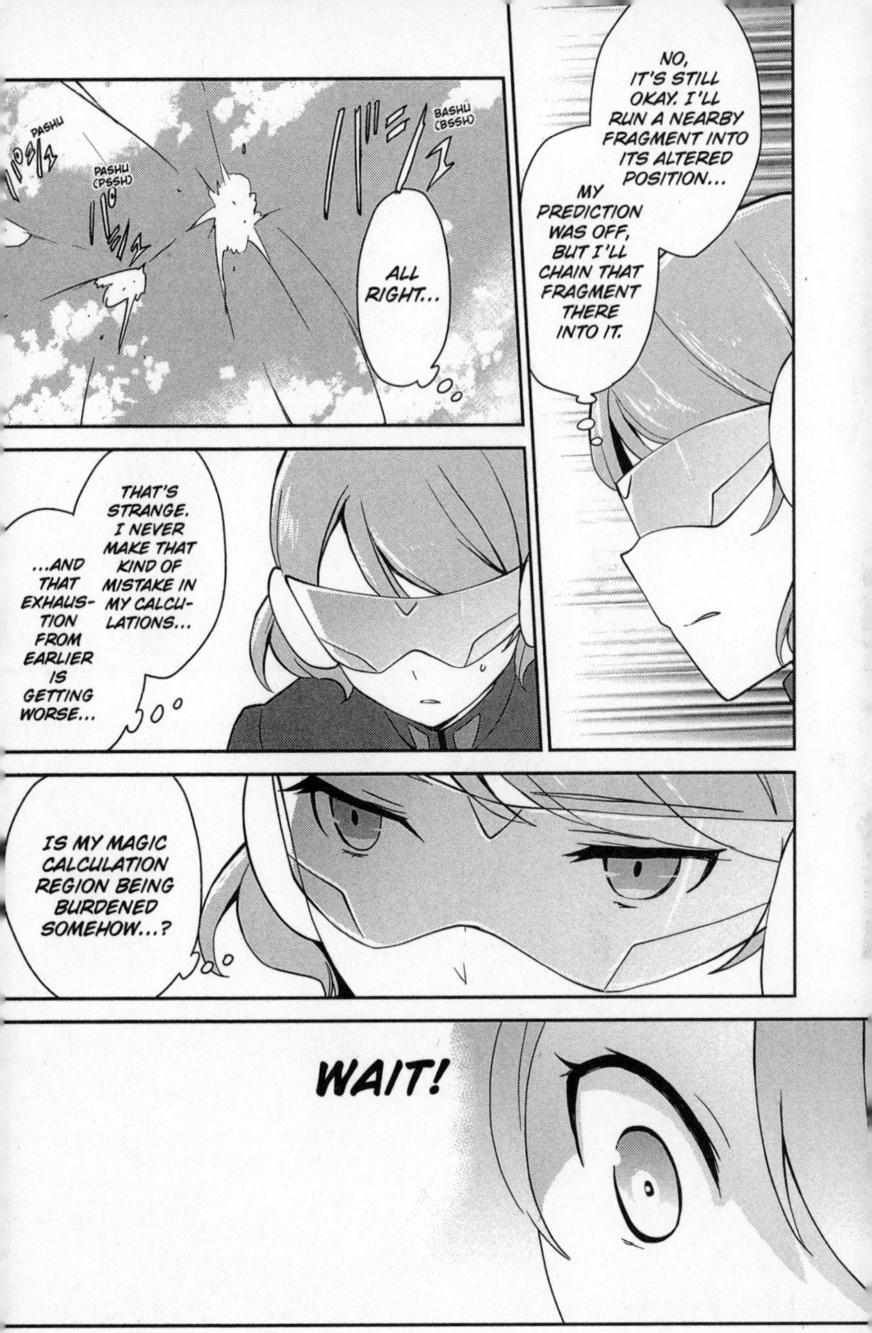
NO, IT'S STILL OKAY. I'LL RUN A NEARBY FRAGMENT INTO ITS ALTERED POSITION...
MY PREDICTION WAS OFF, BUT I'LL CHAIN THAT FRAGMENT THERE INTO IT.
BASHU (BSSH)
ALL RIGHT...
PASHU (PSSH)
PASHU
THAT'S STRANGE. I NEVER MAKE THAT KIND OF MISTAKE IN MY CALCU-LATIONS...
...AND THAT EXHAUS-TION FROM EARLIER IS GETTING WORSE...
IS MY MAGIC CALCULATION REGION BEING BURDENED SOMEHOW...?
WAIT!

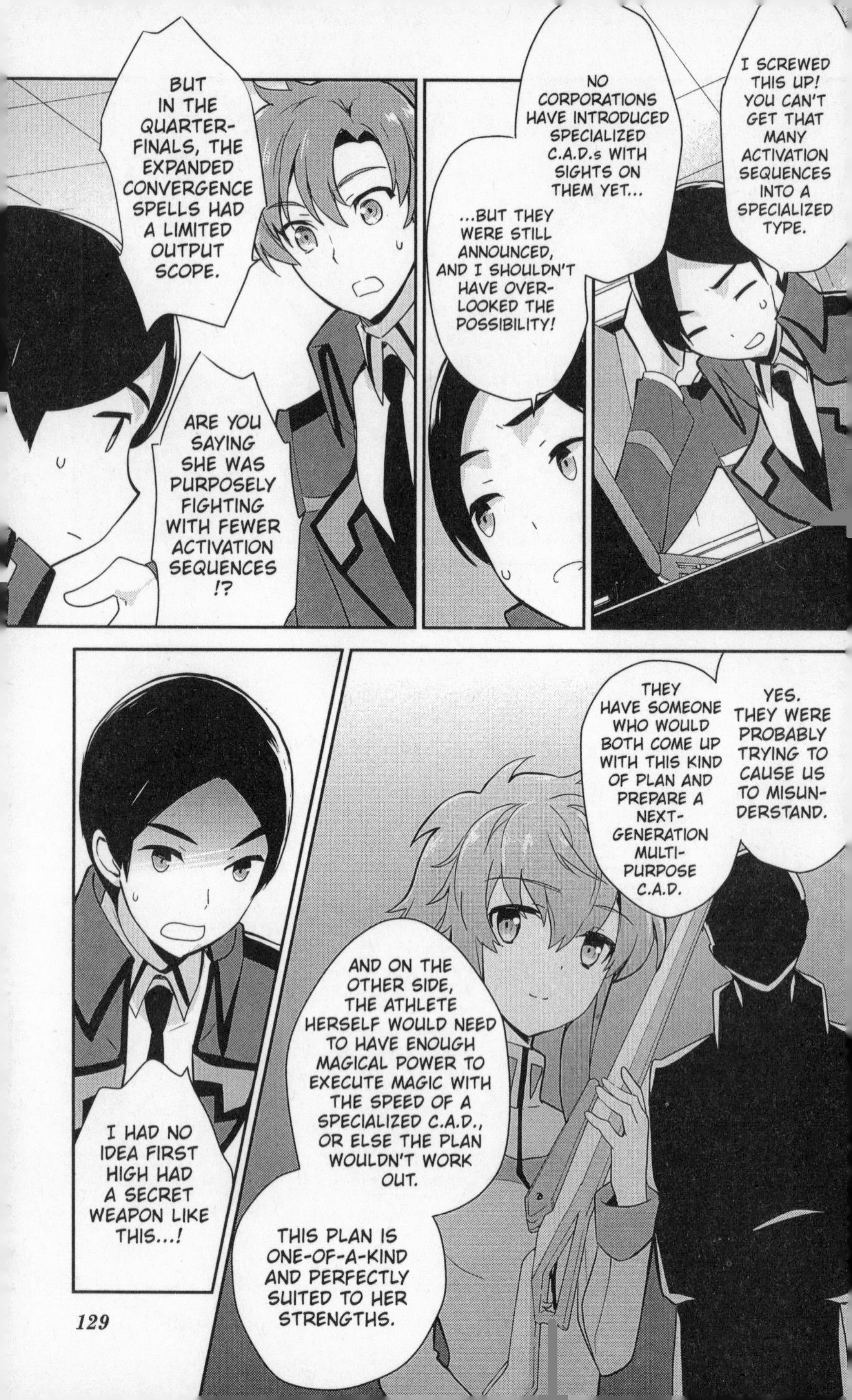
I SCREWED THIS UP! YOU CAN'T GET THAT MANY ACTIVATION SEQUENCES INTO A SPECIALIZED TYPE.
NO CORPORATIONS HAVE INTRODUCED SPECIALIZED C.A.D.s WITH SIGHTS ON THEM YET...
...BUT THEY WERE STILL ANNOUNCED, AND I SHOULDN'T HAVE OVER-LOOKED THE POSSIBILITY!
BUT IN THE QUARTER-FINALS, THE EXPANDED CONVERGENCE SPELLS HAD A LIMITED OUTPUT SCOPE.
ARE YOU SAYING SHE WAS PURPOSELY FIGHTING WITH FEWER ACTIVATION SEQUENCES!?
YES. THEY WERE PROBABLY TRYING TO CAUSE US TO MISUN-DERSTAND.
THEY HAVE SOMEONE WHO WOULD BOTH COME UP WITH THIS KIND OF PLAN AND PREPARE A NEXT-GENERATION MULTI-PURPOSE C.A.D.
AND ON THE OTHER SIDE, THE ATHLETE HERSELF WOULD NEED TO HAVE ENOUGH MAGICAL POWER TO EXECUTE MAGIC WITH THE SPEED OF A SPECIALIZED C.A.D., OR ELSE THE PLAN WOULDN'T WORK OUT.
THIS PLAN IS ONE-OF-A-KIND AND PERFECTLY SUITED TO HER STRENGTHS.
I HAD NO IDEA FIRST HIGH HAD A SECRET WEAPON LIKE THIS...!

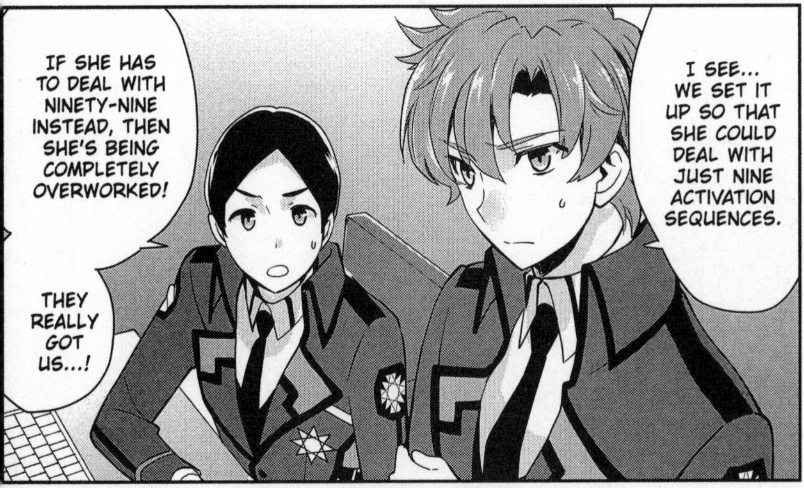
I SEE... WE SET IT UP SO THAT SHE COULD DEAL WITH JUST NINE ACTIVATION SEQUENCES.
IF SHE HAS TO DEAL WITH NINETY-NINE INSTEAD, THEN SHE'S BEING COMPLETELY OVERWORKED!
THEY REALLY GOT US...!

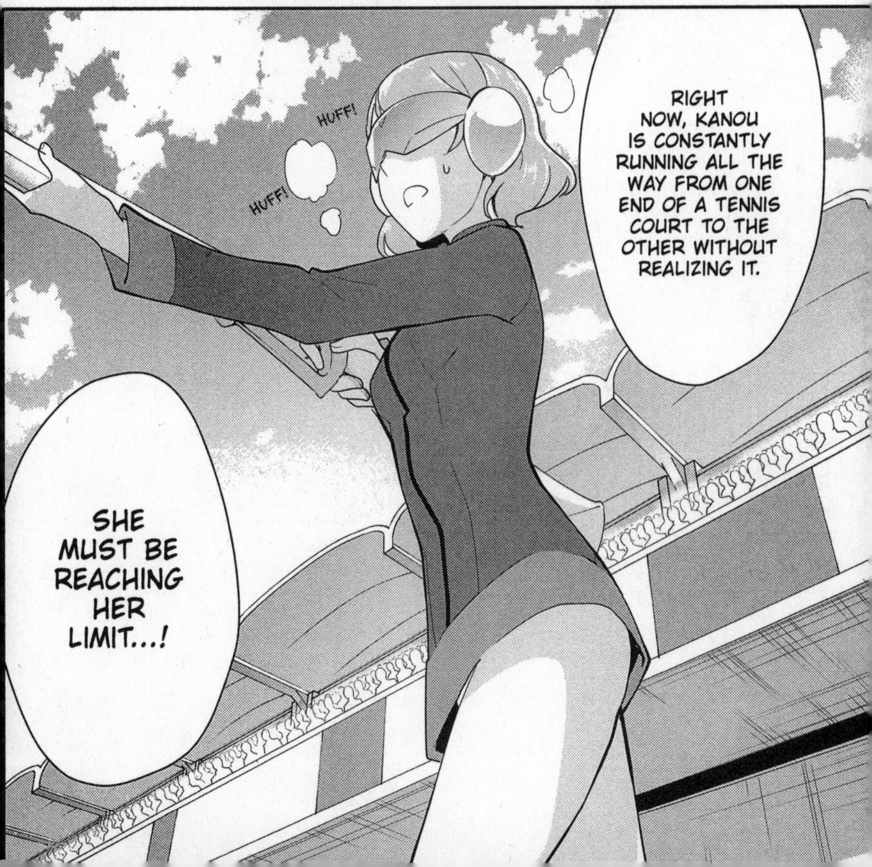
RIGHT NOW, KANOU IS CONSTANTLY RUNNING ALL THE WAY FROM ONE END OF A TENNIS COURT TO THE OTHER WITHOUT REALIZING IT.
HUFF!
HUFF!
SHE MUST BE REACHING HER LIMIT...!

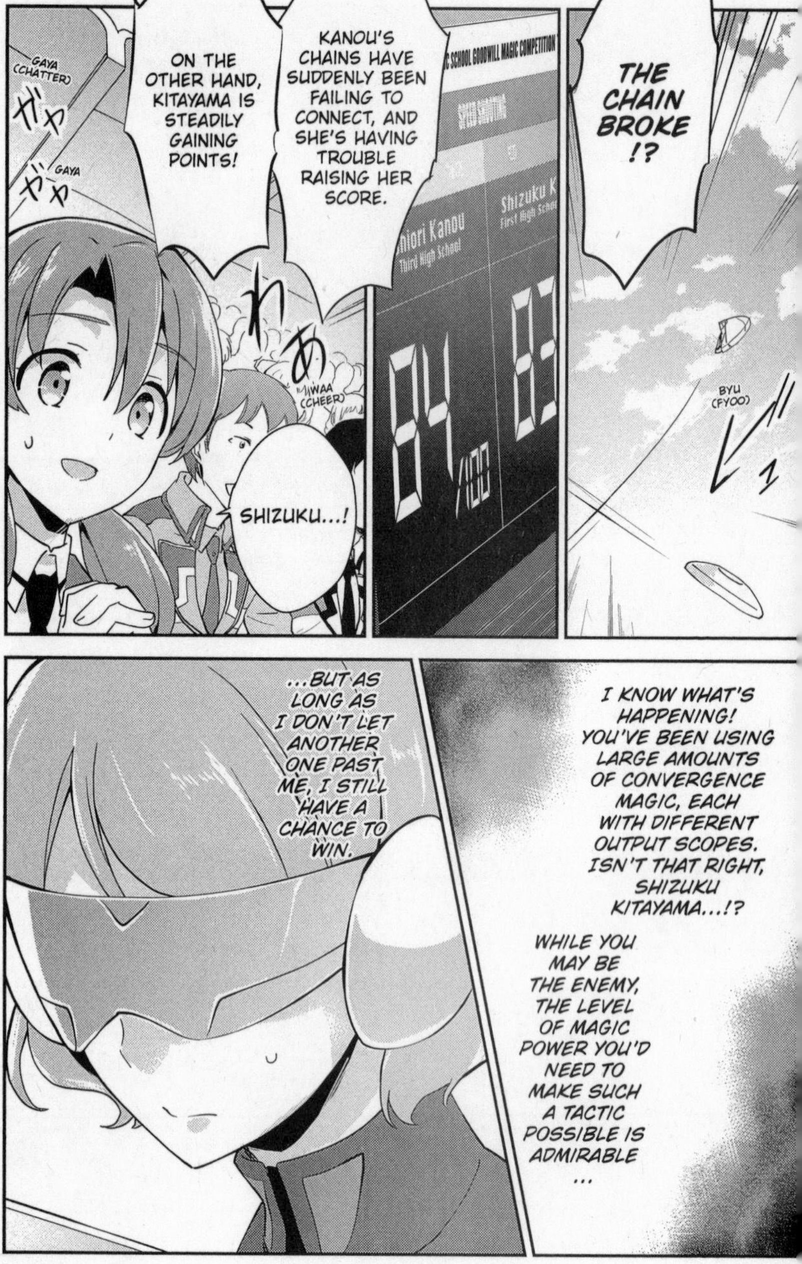
THE CHAIN BROKE !?
BYU (FYOO)
KANOU'S CHAINS HAVE SUDDENLY BEEN FAILING TO CONNECT, AND SHE'S HAVING TROUBLE RAISING HER SCORE.
ON THE OTHER HAND, KITAYAMA IS STEADILY GAINING POINTS!
C SCHOOL GOODWILL MAGIC COMPETITION
hiori Kanou
Third High School
Shizuku K
First High Schoo
84
/100
83
GAYA (CHATTER)
GAYA
WAA (CHEER)
SHIZUKU...!
I KNOW WHAT'S HAPPENING! YOU'VE BEEN USING LARGE AMOUNTS OF CONVERGENCE MAGIC, EACH WITH DIFFERENT OUTPUT SCOPES. ISN'T THAT RIGHT, SHIZUKU KITAYAMA...!?
WHILE YOU MAY BE THE ENEMY, THE LEVEL OF MAGIC POWER YOU'D NEED TO MAKE SUCH A TACTIC POSSIBLE IS ADMIRABLE ...
...BUT AS LONG AS I DON'T LET ANOTHER ONE PAST ME, I STILL HAVE A CHANCE TO WIN.

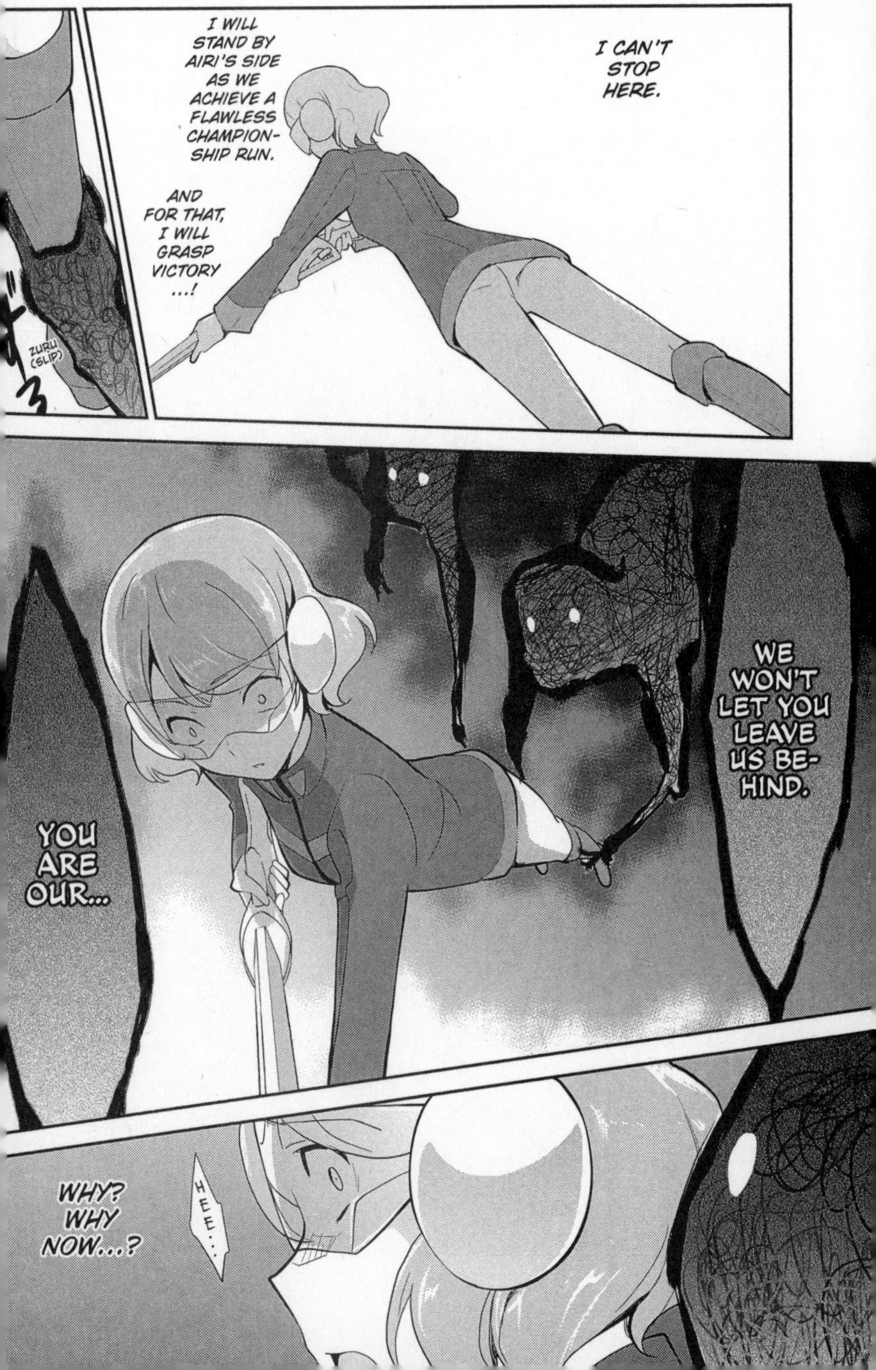
I CAN'T STOP HERE.
I WILL STAND BY AIRI'S SIDE AS WE ACHIEVE A FLAWLESS CHAMPION-SHIP RUN.
AND FOR THAT, I WILL GRASP VICTORY ...!
ZURU (SLIP)
WE WON'T LET YOU LEAVE US BE-HIND.
YOU ARE OUR...
HEE...
WHY? WHY NOW...?

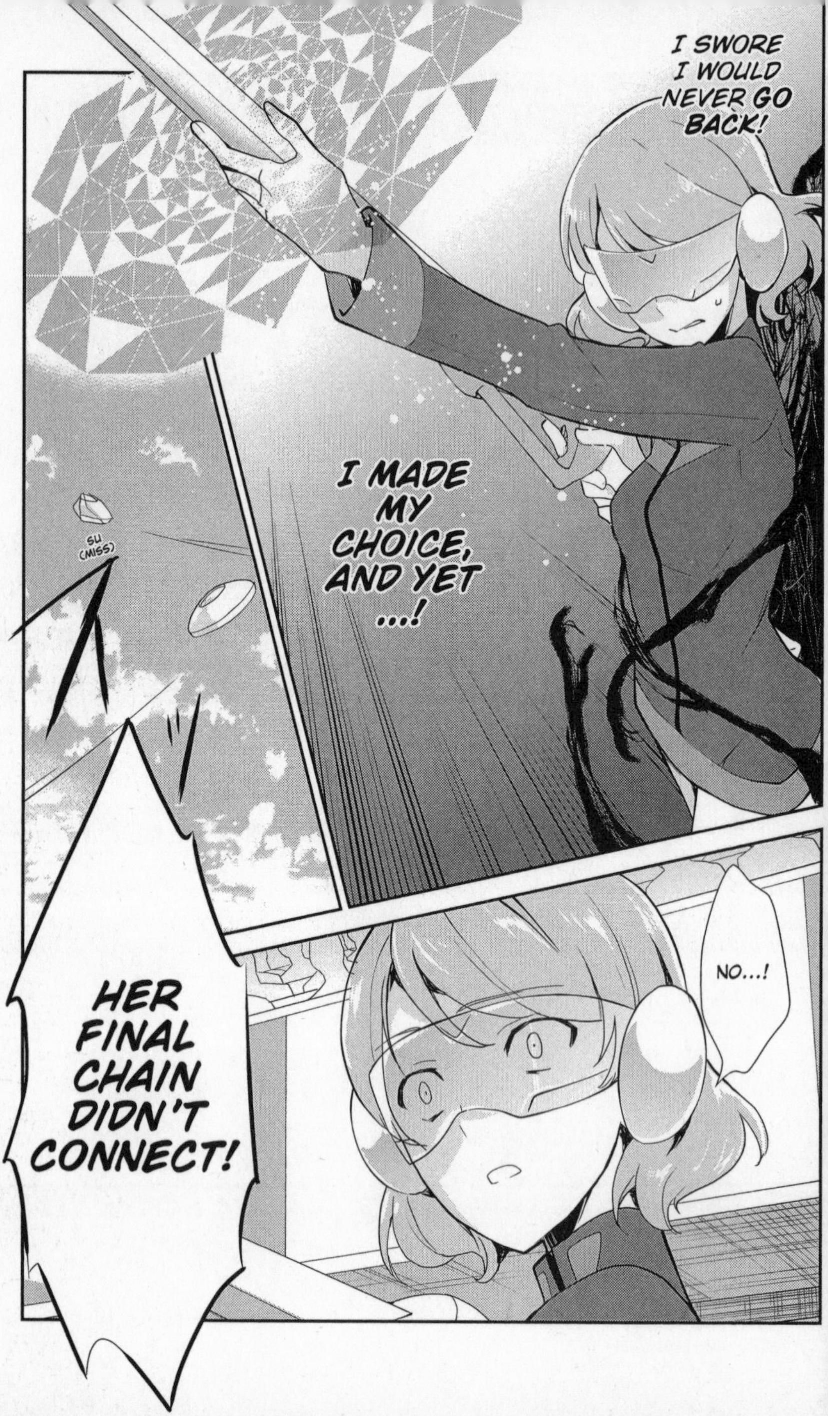
I SWORE I WOULD NEVER GO BACK!
I MADE MY CHOICE, AND YET ...!
SU (MISS)
NO...!
HER FINAL CHAIN DIDN'T CONNECT!

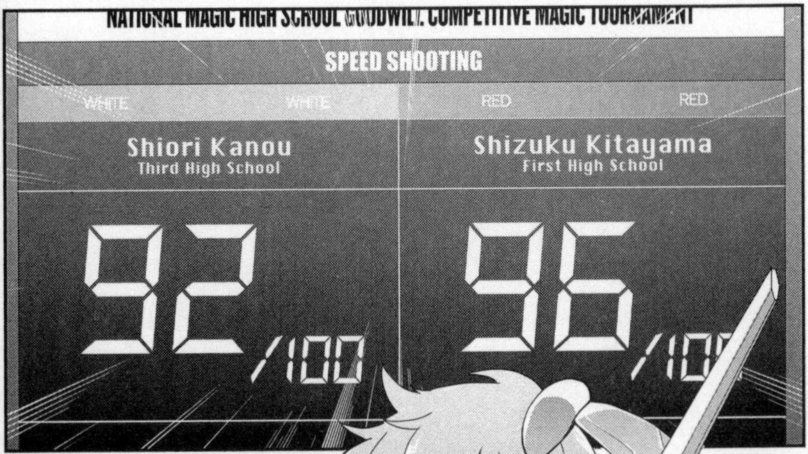
NATIONAL MAGIC HIGH SCHOOL GOODWILL COMPETITIVE MAGIC TOURNAMENT
SPEED SHOOTING
WHITE WHITE RED RED
Shiori Kanou
Third High School
Shizuku Kitayama
First High School
92 /100
96 /100

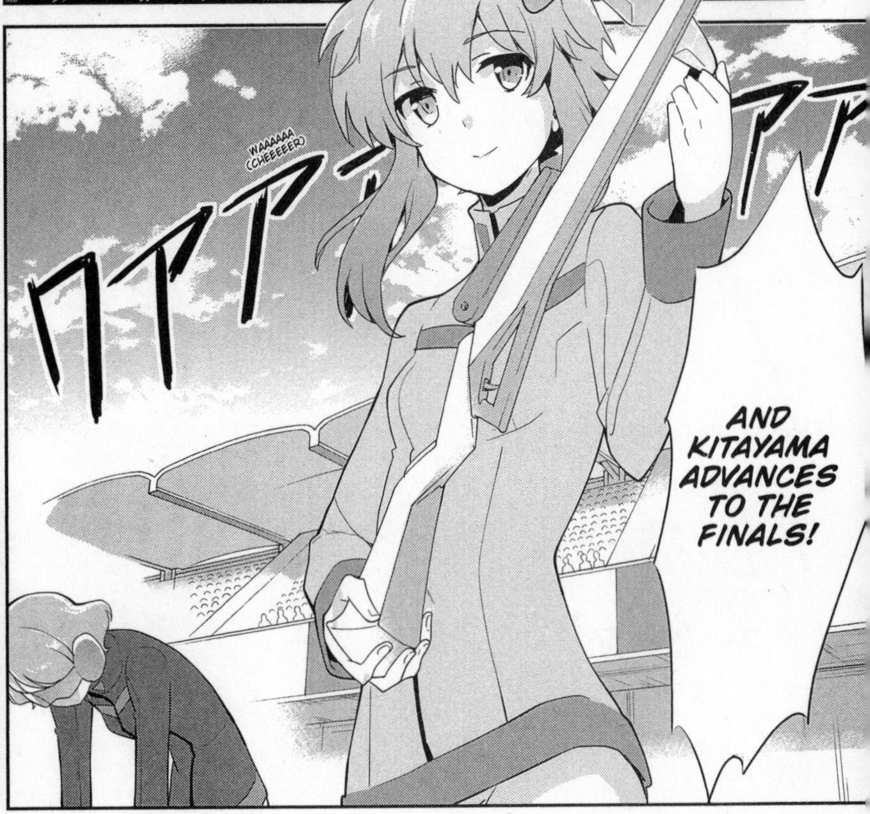
WAAAAAA (CHEEEEER)
AND KITAYAMA ADVANCES TO THE FINALS!

THE
HONOR
STUDENT
AT
Magic High
School

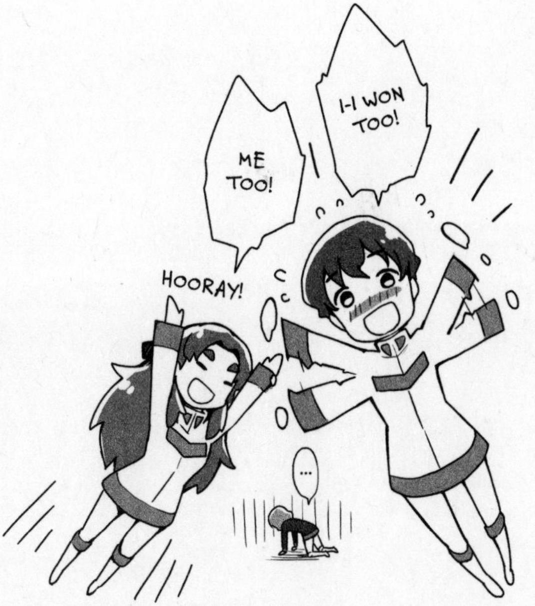
I-I WON TOO!
ME TOO!
HOORAY!
...

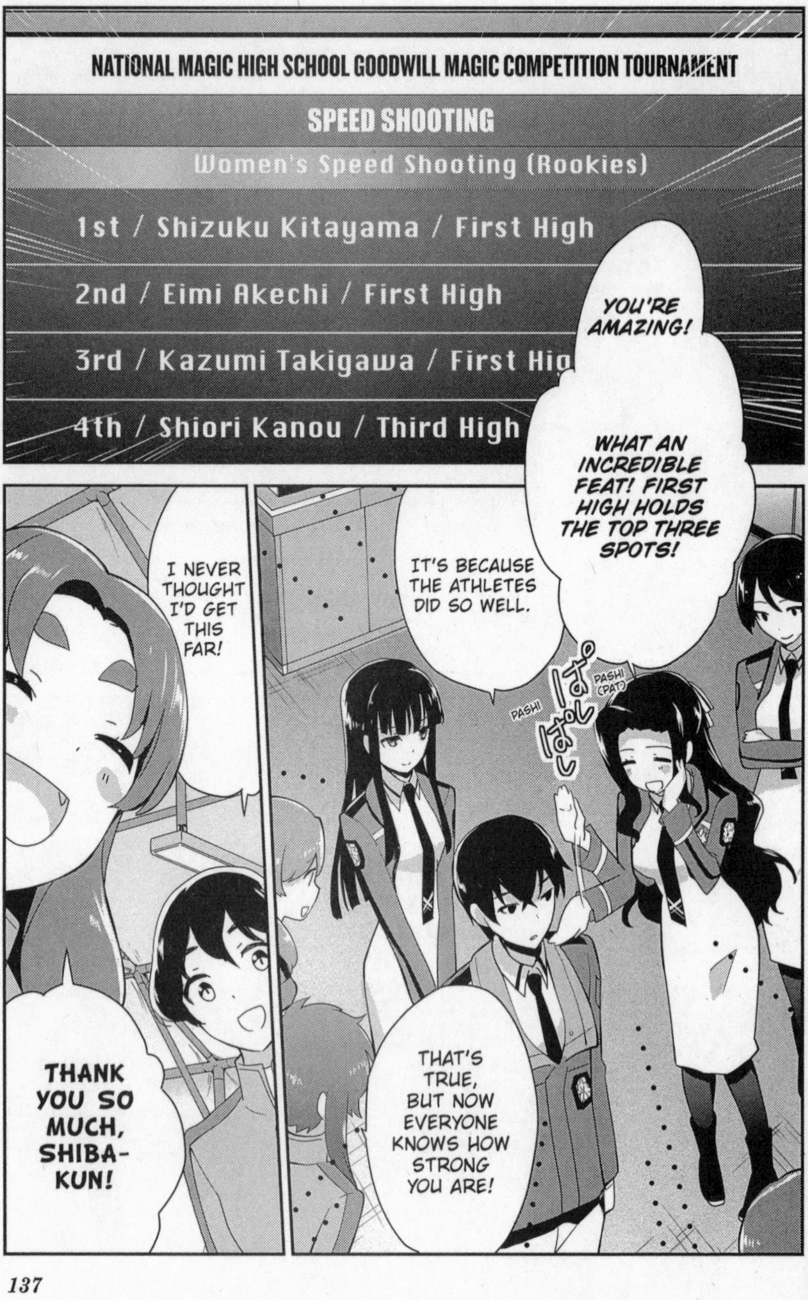
NATIONAL MAGIC HIGH SCHOOL GOODWILL MAGIC COMPETITION TOURNAMENT
SPEED SHOOTING
Women's Speed Shooting (Rookies)
1st / Shizuku Kitayama / First High
2nd / Eimi Akechi / First High
3rd / Kazumi Takigawa / First Hig
4th / Shiori Kanou / Third High
YOU'RE AMAZING!
WHAT AN INCREDIBLE FEAT! FIRST HIGH HOLDS THE TOP THREE SPOTS!
IT'S BECAUSE THE ATHLETES DID SO WELL.
PASHI (PAT)
PASHI
THAT'S TRUE, BUT NOW EVERYONE KNOWS HOW STRONG YOU ARE!
I NEVER THOUGHT I'D GET THIS FAR!
THANK YOU SO MUCH, SHIBA-KUN!

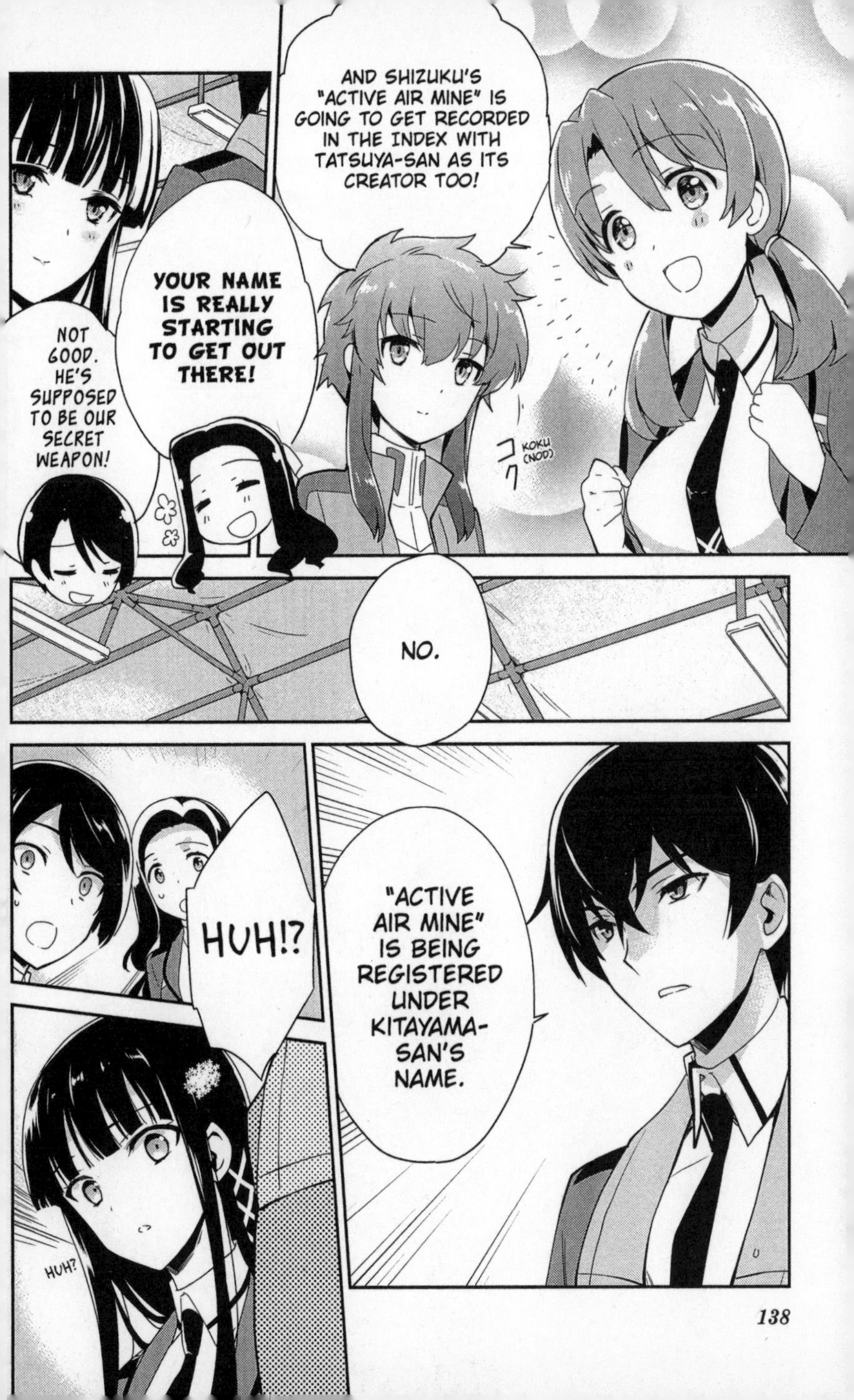
AND SHIZUKU'S "ACTIVE AIR MINE" IS GOING TO GET RECORDED IN THE INDEX WITH TATSUYA-SAN AS ITS CREATOR TOO!
KOKU (NOD)
YOUR NAME IS REALLY STARTING TO GET OUT THERE!
NOT GOOD. HE'S SUPPOSED TO BE OUR SECRET WEAPON!
NO.
"ACTIVE AIR MINE" IS BEING REGISTERED UNDER KITAYAMA-SAN'S NAME.
HUH!?
HUH?

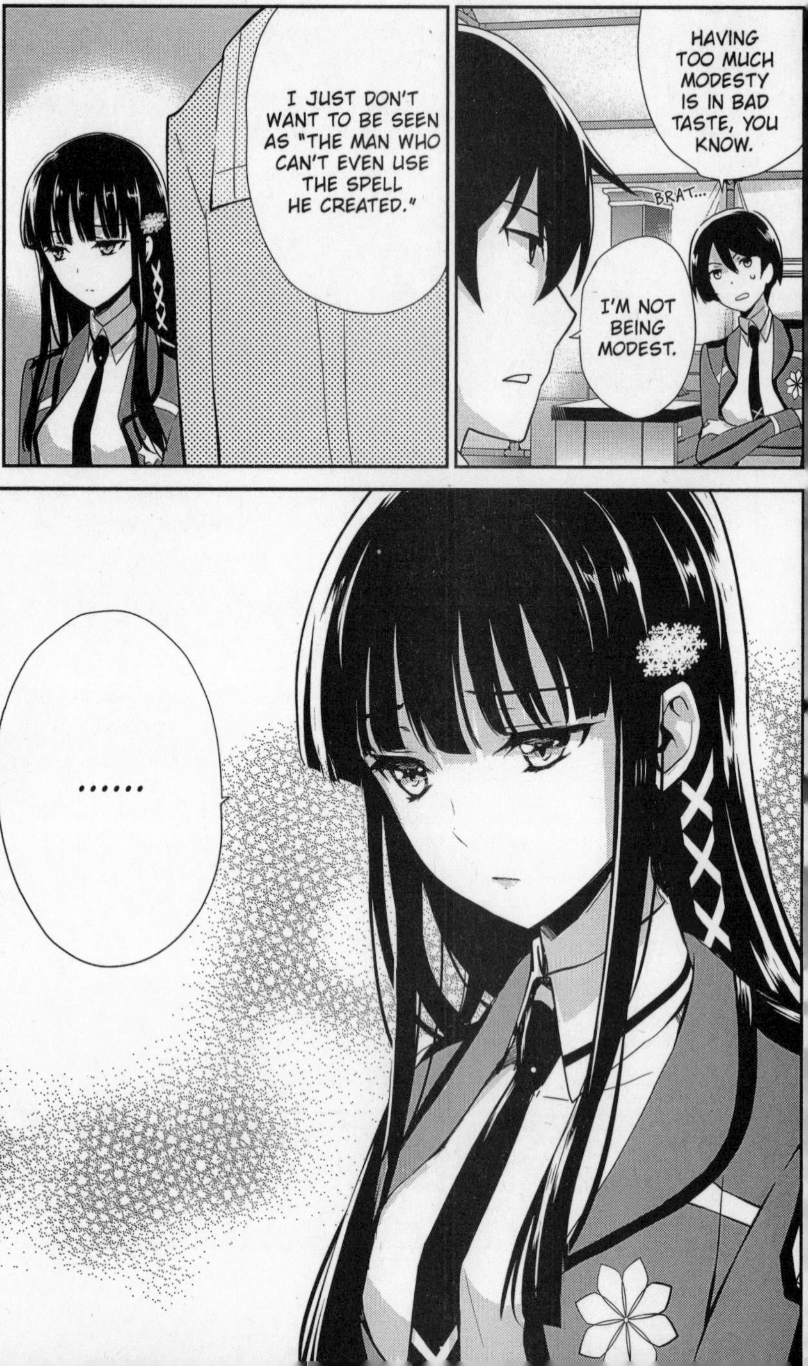
HAVING TOO MUCH MODESTY IS IN BAD TASTE, YOU KNOW.
BRAT...
I'M NOT BEING MODEST.
I JUST DON'T WANT TO BE SEEN AS "THE MAN WHO CAN'T EVEN USE THE SPELL HE CREATED."
......

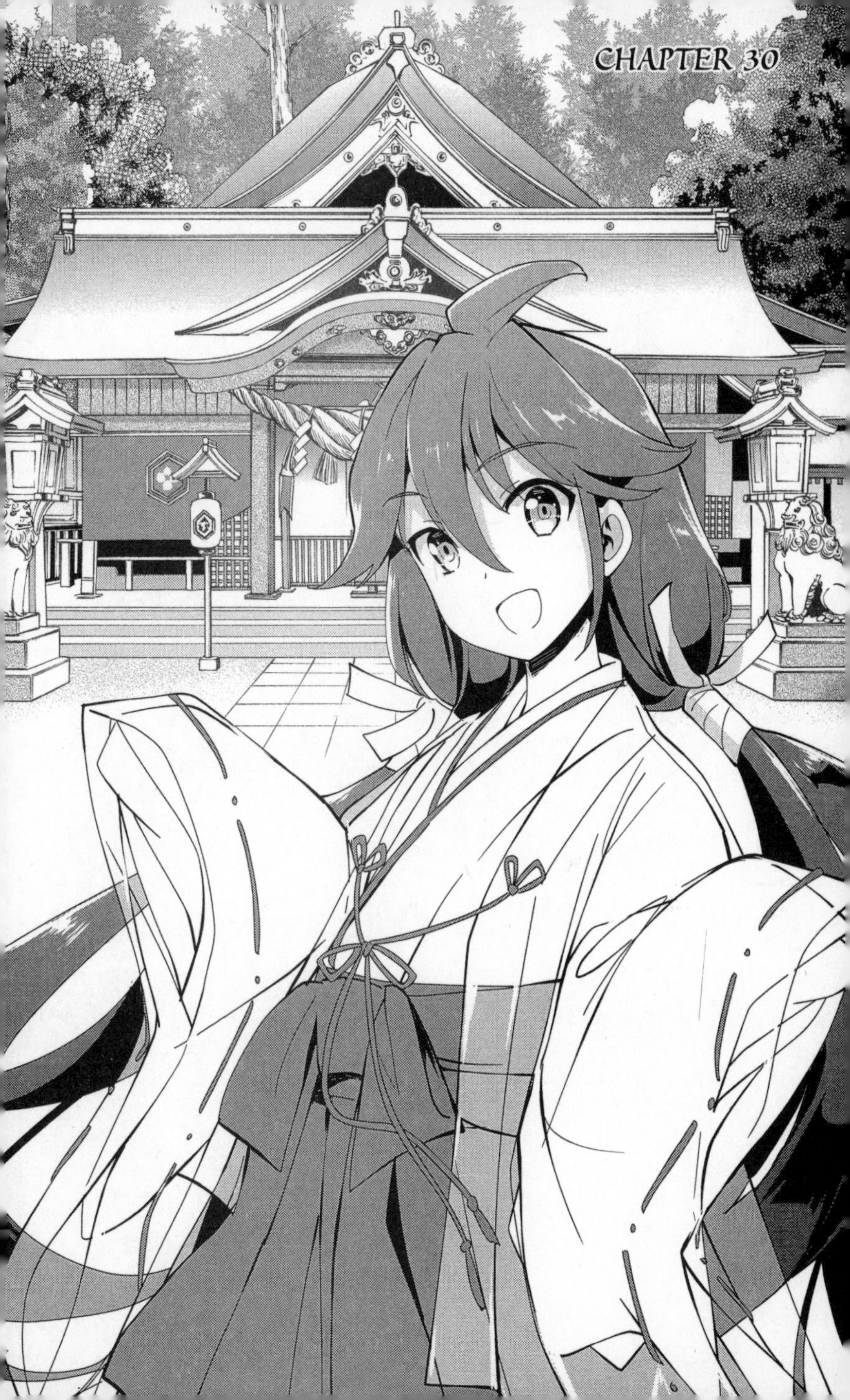
CHAPTER 30

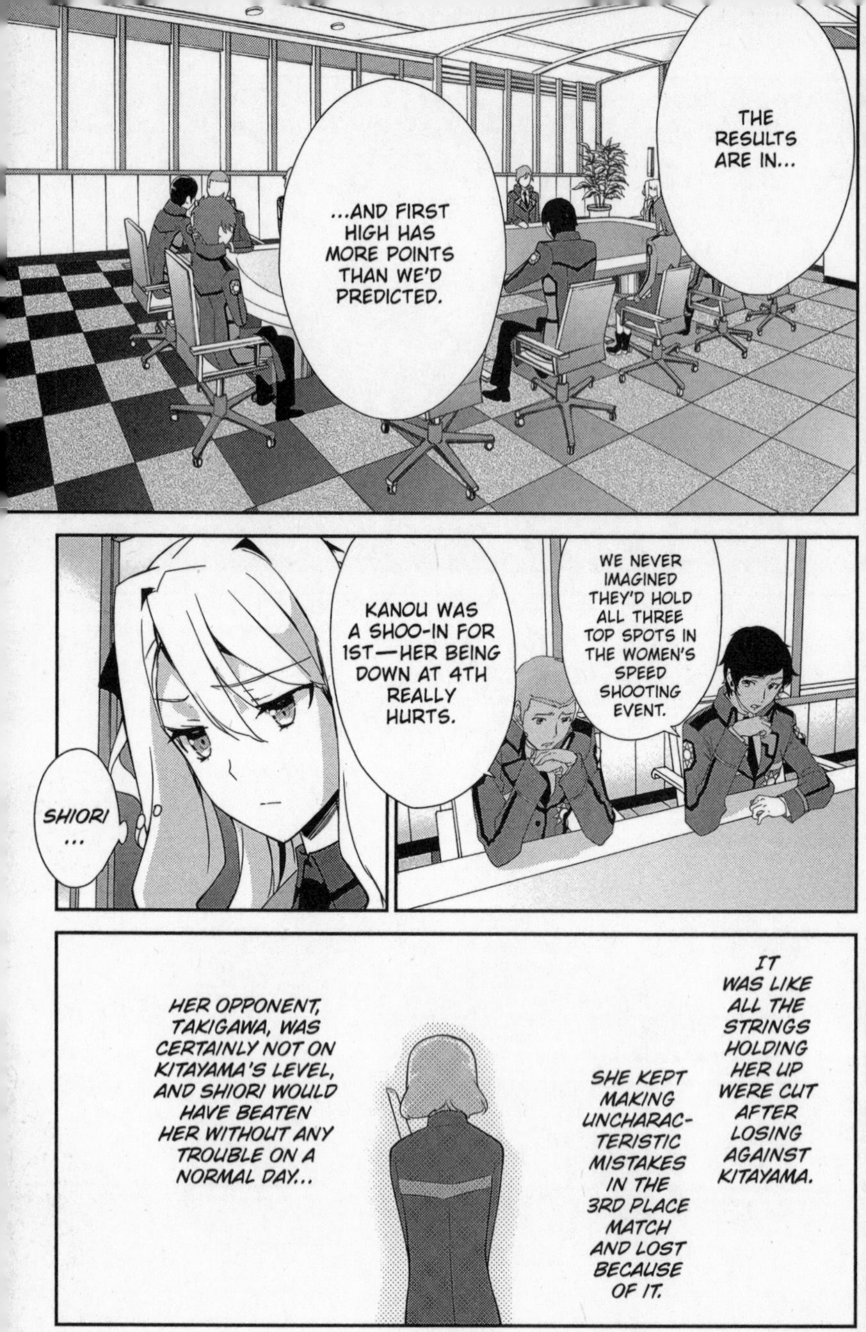
THE RESULTS ARE IN...
...AND FIRST HIGH HAS MORE POINTS THAN WE'D PREDICTED.
WE NEVER IMAGINED THEY'D HOLD ALL THREE TOP SPOTS IN THE WOMEN'S SPEED SHOOTING EVENT.
KANOU WAS A SHOO-IN FOR 1ST—HER BEING DOWN AT 4TH REALLY HURTS.
SHIORI ...
IT WAS LIKE ALL THE STRINGS HOLDING HER UP WERE CUT AFTER LOSING AGAINST KITAYAMA.
SHE KEPT MAKING UNCHARAC-TERISTIC MISTAKES IN THE 3RD PLACE MATCH AND LOST BECAUSE OF IT.
HER OPPONENT, TAKIGAWA, WAS CERTAINLY NOT ON KITAYAMA'S LEVEL, AND SHIORI WOULD HAVE BEATEN HER WITHOUT ANY TROUBLE ON A NORMAL DAY...

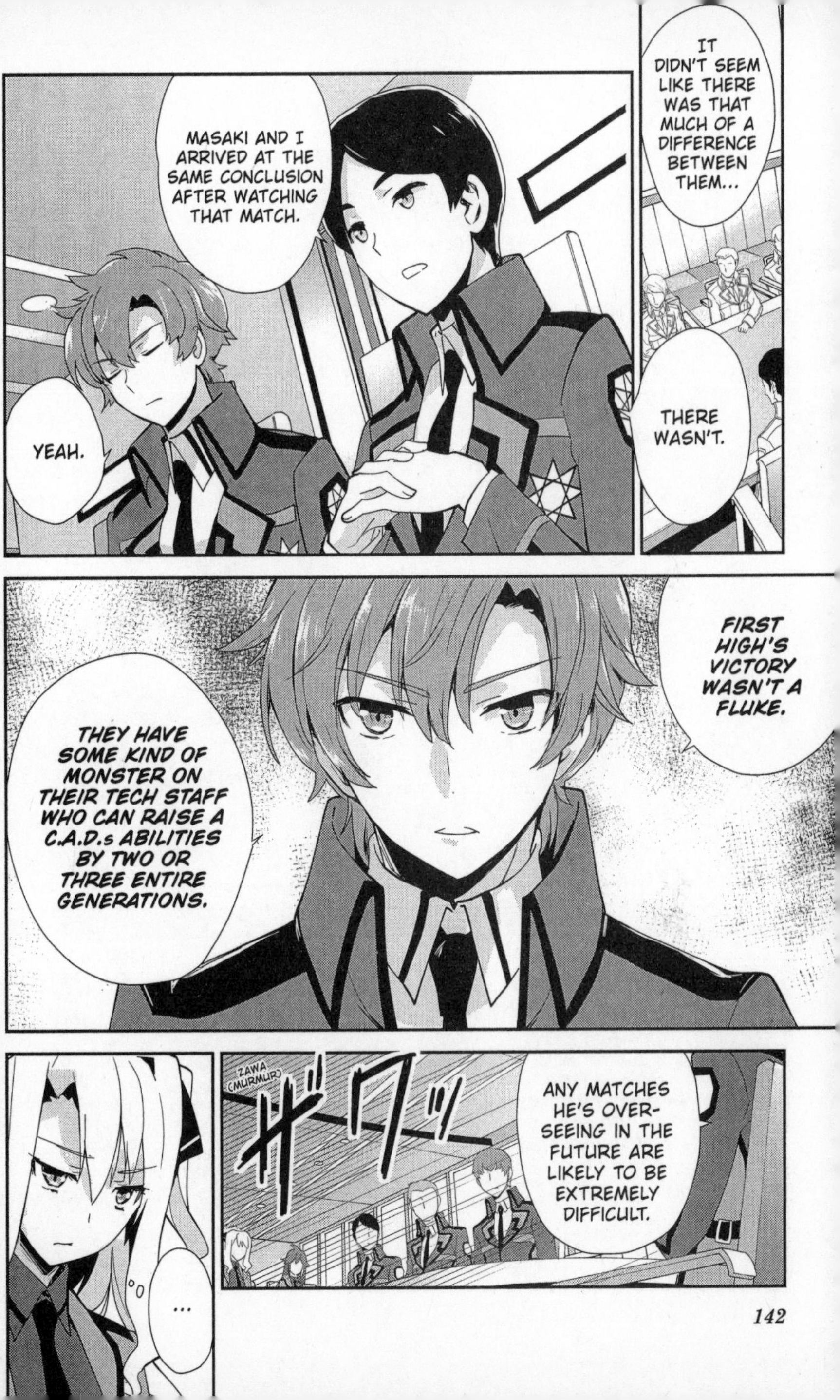
IT DIDN'T SEEM LIKE THERE WAS THAT MUCH OF A DIFFERENCE BETWEEN THEM...
THERE WASN'T.
MASAKI AND I ARRIVED AT THE SAME CONCLUSION AFTER WATCHING THAT MATCH.
YEAH.
FIRST HIGH'S VICTORY WASN'T A FLUKE.
THEY HAVE SOME KIND OF MONSTER ON THEIR TECH STAFF WHO CAN RAISE A C.A.D.s ABILITIES BY TWO OR THREE ENTIRE GENERATIONS.
ANY MATCHES HE'S OVER-SEEING IN THE FUTURE ARE LIKELY TO BE EXTREMELY DIFFICULT.
ZAWA (MURMUR)
...

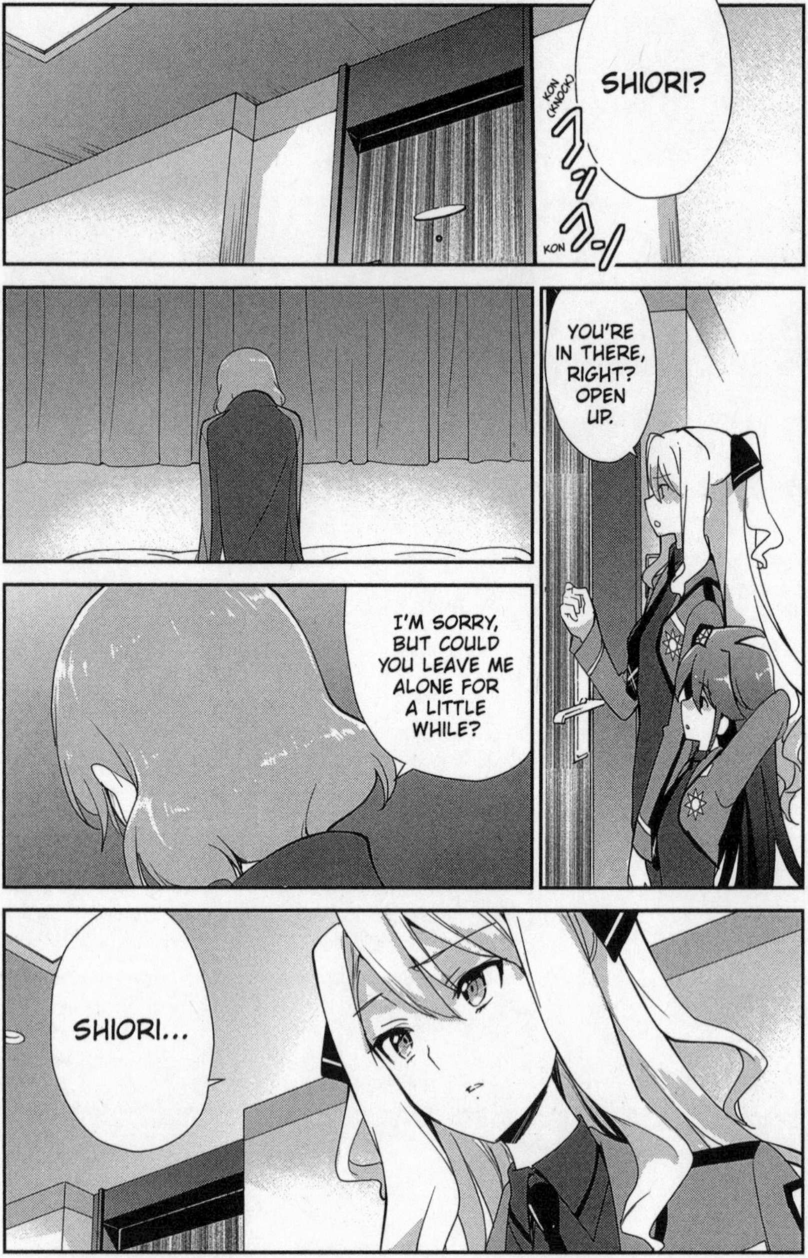
SHIORI?
KON (KNOCK)
KON
YOU'RE IN THERE, RIGHT? OPEN UP.
I'M SORRY, BUT COULD YOU LEAVE ME ALONE FOR A LITTLE WHILE?
SHIORI...

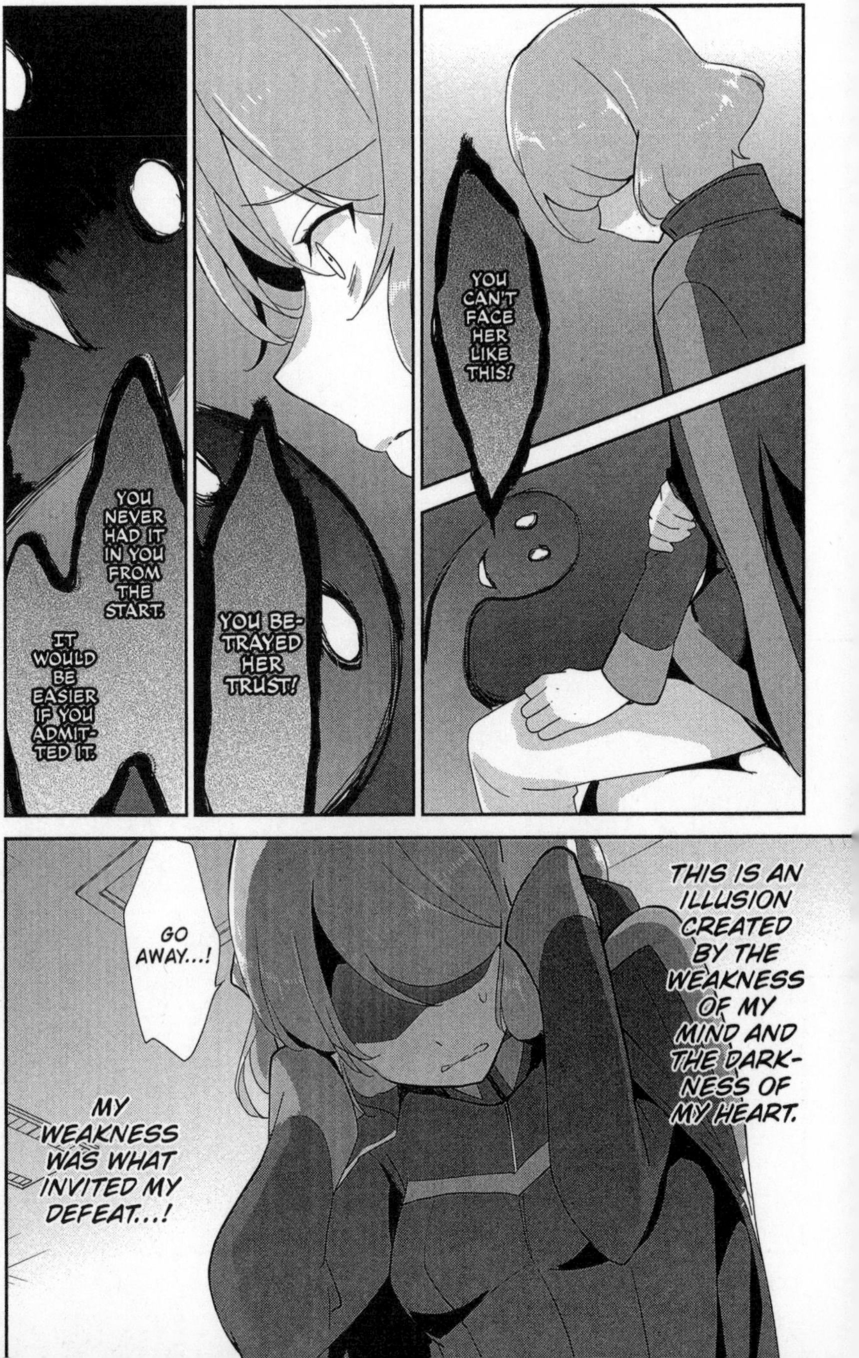
YOU CAN'T FACE HER LIKE THIS!
YOU BETRAYED HER TRUST!
YOU NEVER HAD IT IN YOU FROM THE START.
IT WOULD BE EASIER IF YOU ADMITTED IT.
THIS IS AN ILLUSION CREATED BY THE WEAKNESS OF MY MIND AND THE DARKNESS OF MY HEART.
GO AWAY...!
MY WEAKNESS WAS WHAT INVITED MY DEFEAT...!

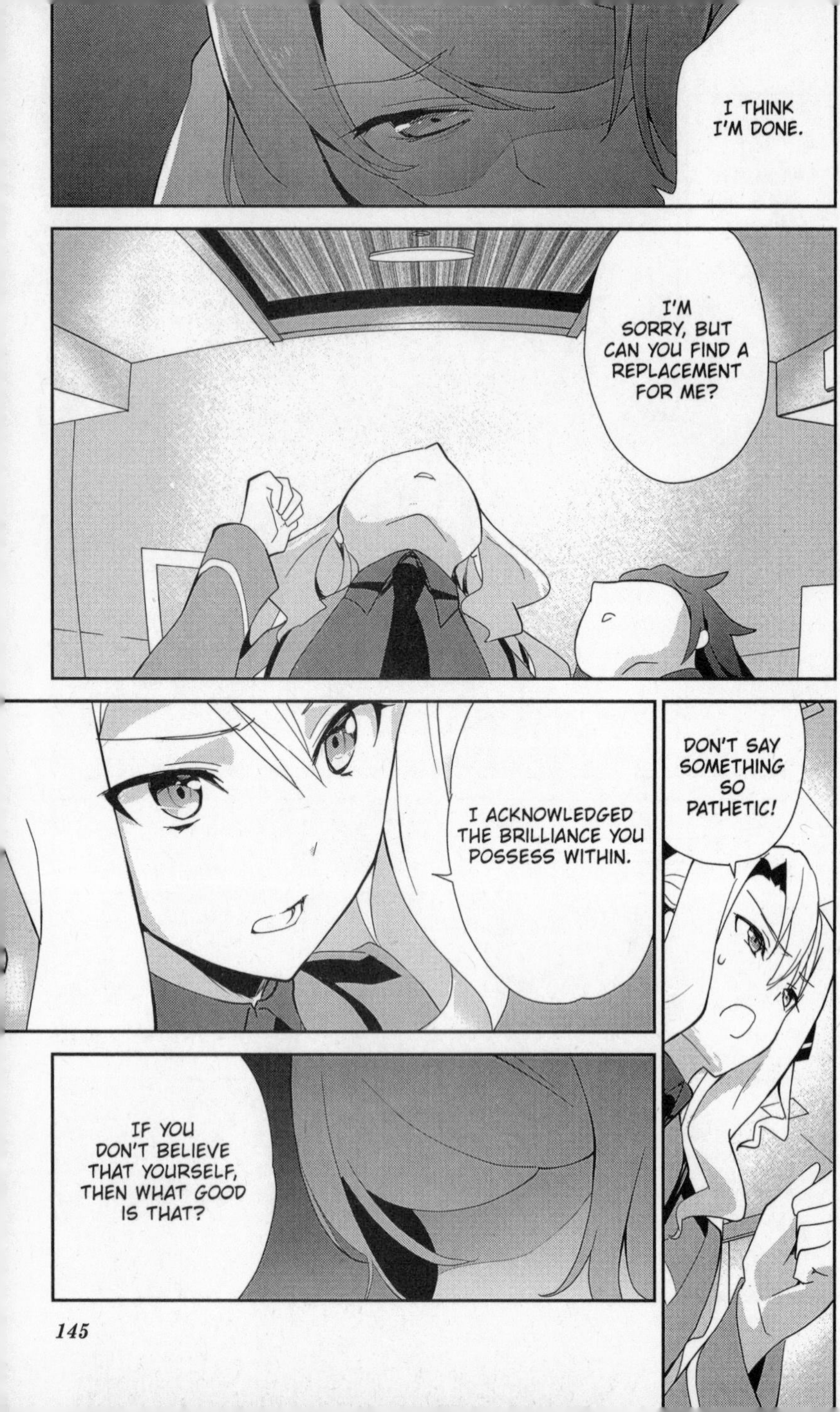
I THINK I'M DONE.
I'M SORRY, BUT CAN YOU FIND A REPLACEMENT FOR ME?
DON'T SAY SOMETHING SO PATHETIC!
I ACKNOWLEDGED THE BRILLIANCE YOU POSSESS WITHIN.
IF YOU DON'T BELIEVE THAT YOURSELF, THEN WHAT GOOD IS THAT?

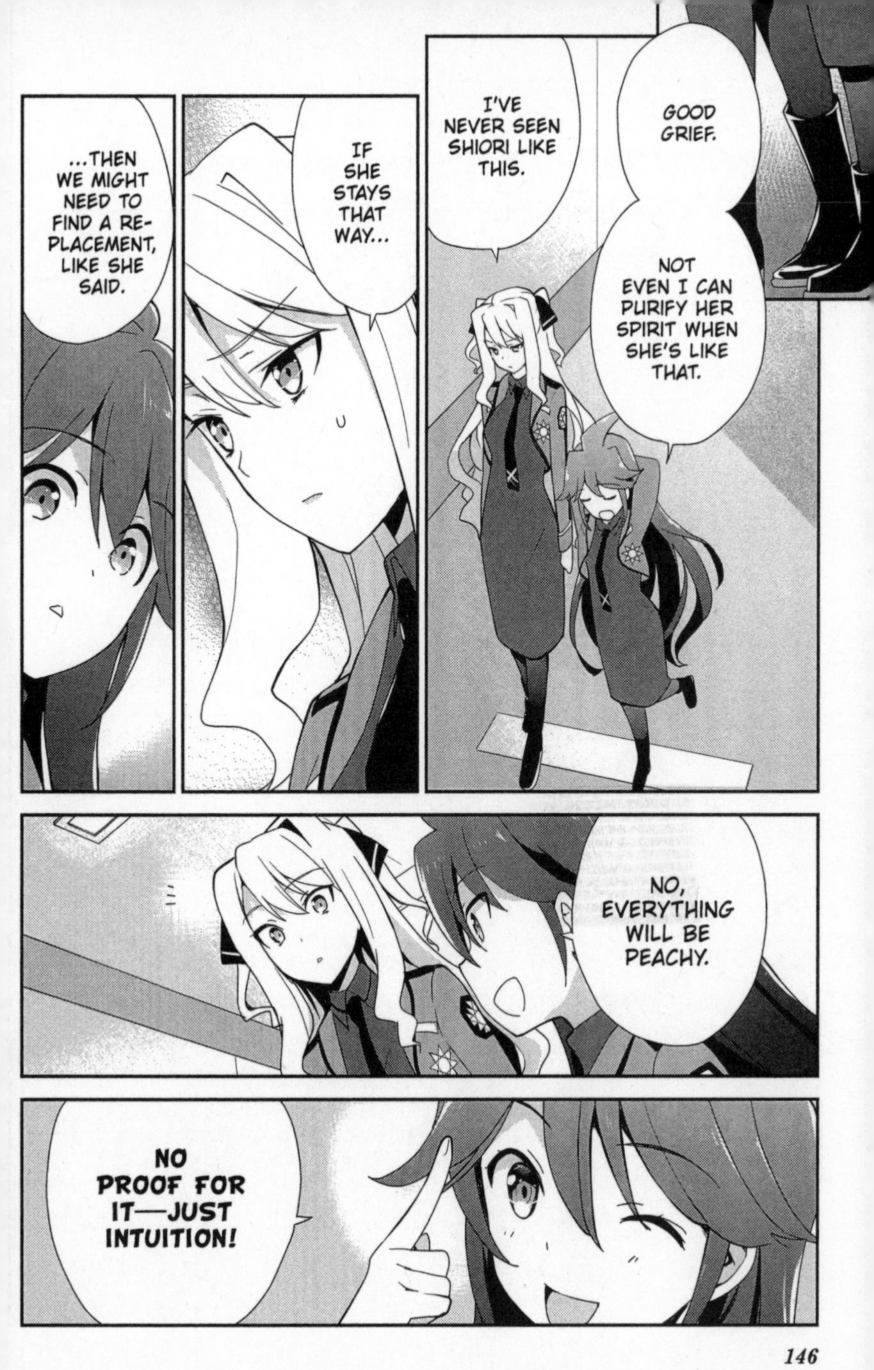
GOOD GRIEF.
NOT EVEN I CAN PURIFY HER SPIRIT WHEN SHE'S LIKE THAT.
I'VE NEVER SEEN SHIORI LIKE THIS.
IF SHE STAYS THAT WAY...
...THEN WE MIGHT NEED TO FIND A RE-PLACEMENT, LIKE SHE SAID.
NO, EVERYTHING WILL BE PEACHY.
NO PROOF FOR IT—JUST INTUITION!

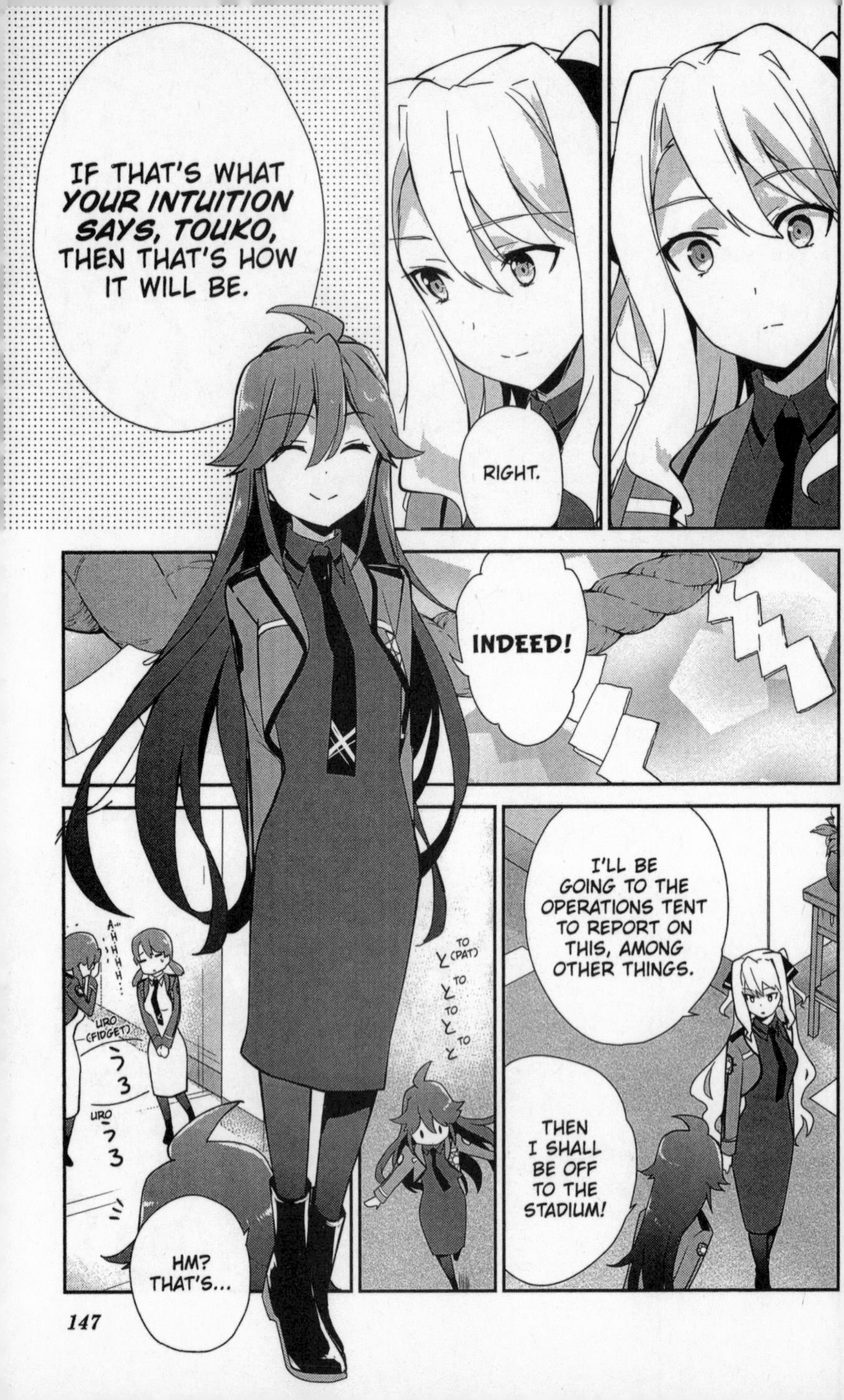
RIGHT.
IF THAT'S WHAT *YOUR INTUITION SAYS, TOUKO,* THEN THAT'S HOW IT WILL BE.
INDEED!
I'LL BE GOING TO THE OPERATIONS TENT TO REPORT ON THIS, AMONG OTHER THINGS.
THEN I SHALL BE OFF TO THE STADIUM!
TO (PAT) TO TO TO
A-H-H-H-H...
URO (FIDGET)
URO
HM? THAT'S...

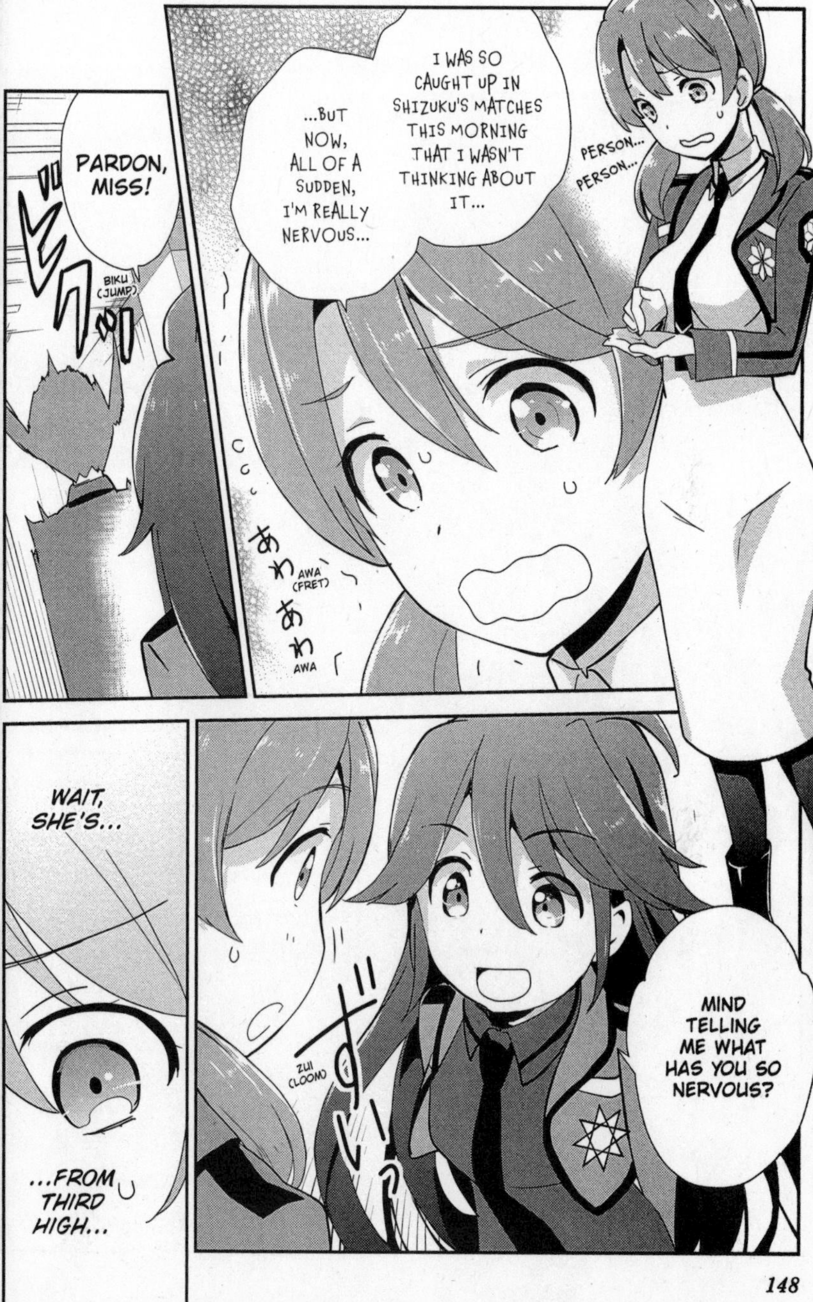
PERSON... PERSON...
I WAS SO CAUGHT UP IN SHIZUKU'S MATCHES THIS MORNING THAT I WASN'T THINKING ABOUT IT...
...BUT NOW, ALL OF A SUDDEN, I'M REALLY NERVOUS...
AWA (FRET)
AWA
PARDON, MISS!
BIKU (JUMP)
MIND TELLING ME WHAT HAS YOU SO NERVOUS?
ZUI (LOOM)
WAIT, SHE'S...
...FROM THIRD HIGH...

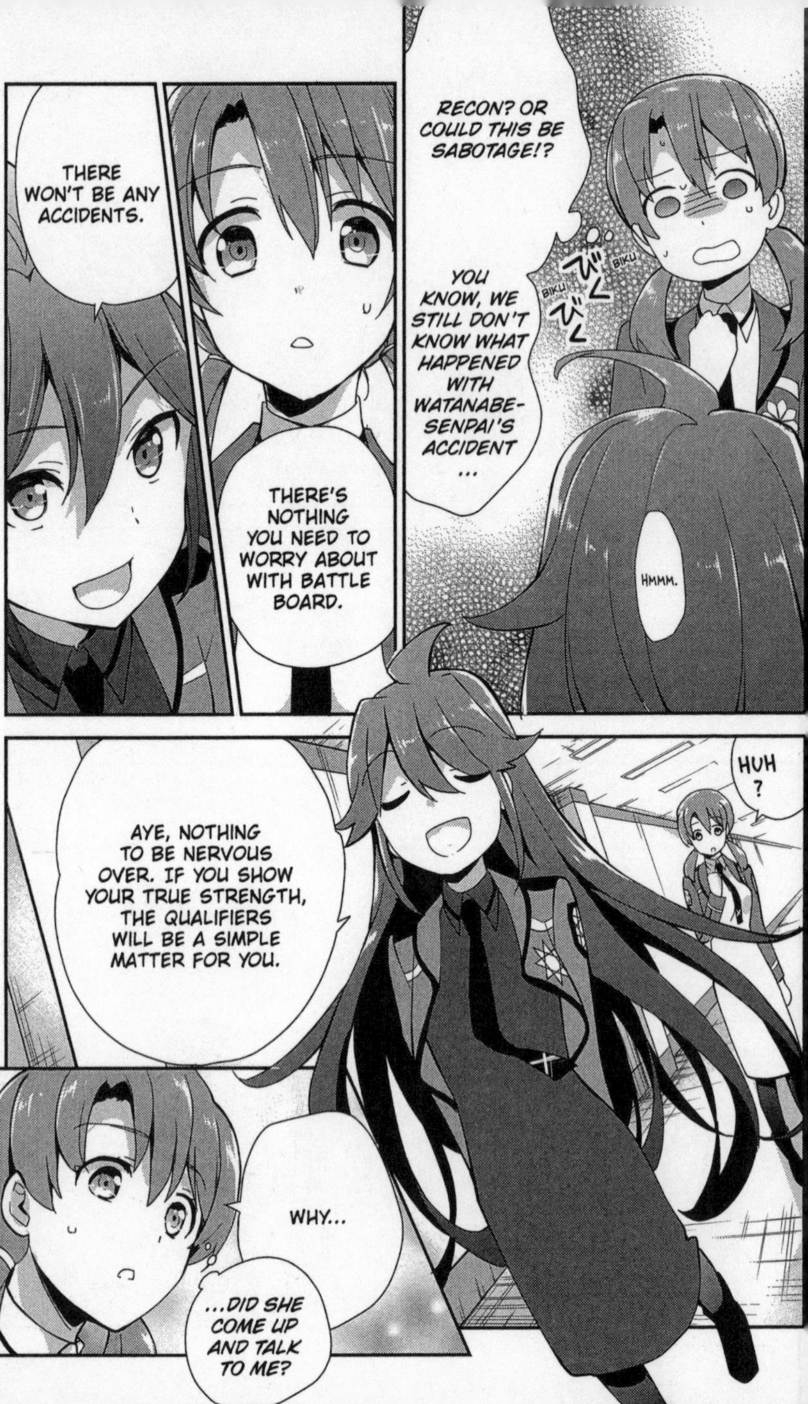
RECON? OR COULD THIS BE SABOTAGE!?
びく BIKU
びく BIKU
YOU KNOW, WE STILL DON'T KNOW WHAT HAPPENED WITH WATANABE-SENPAI'S ACCIDENT ...
HMMM.
THERE'S NOTHING YOU NEED TO WORRY ABOUT WITH BATTLE BOARD.
THERE WON'T BE ANY ACCIDENTS.
HUH?
AYE, NOTHING TO BE NERVOUS OVER. IF YOU SHOW YOUR TRUE STRENGTH, THE QUALIFIERS WILL BE A SIMPLE MATTER FOR YOU.
WHY...
...DID SHE COME UP AND TALK TO ME?

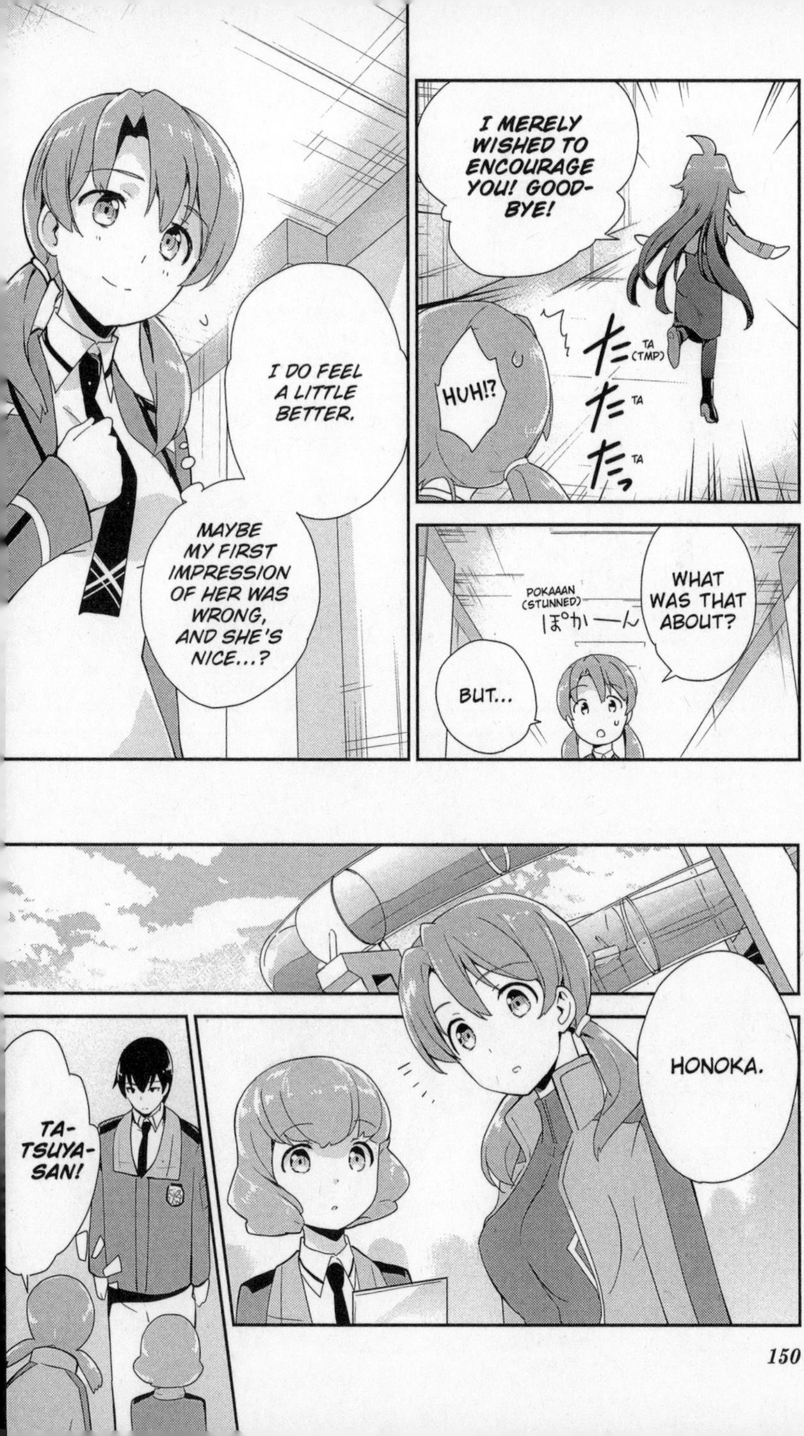
I MERELY WISHED TO ENCOURAGE YOU! GOOD-BYE!
HUH!?
たた TA (TMP)
た TA
たっ TA
WHAT WAS THAT ABOUT?
POKAAAN (STUNNED) ぽかーん
BUT...
I DO FEEL A LITTLE BETTER.
MAYBE MY FIRST IMPRESSION OF HER WAS WRONG, AND SHE'S NICE...?
HONOKA.
TA-TSUYA-SAN!

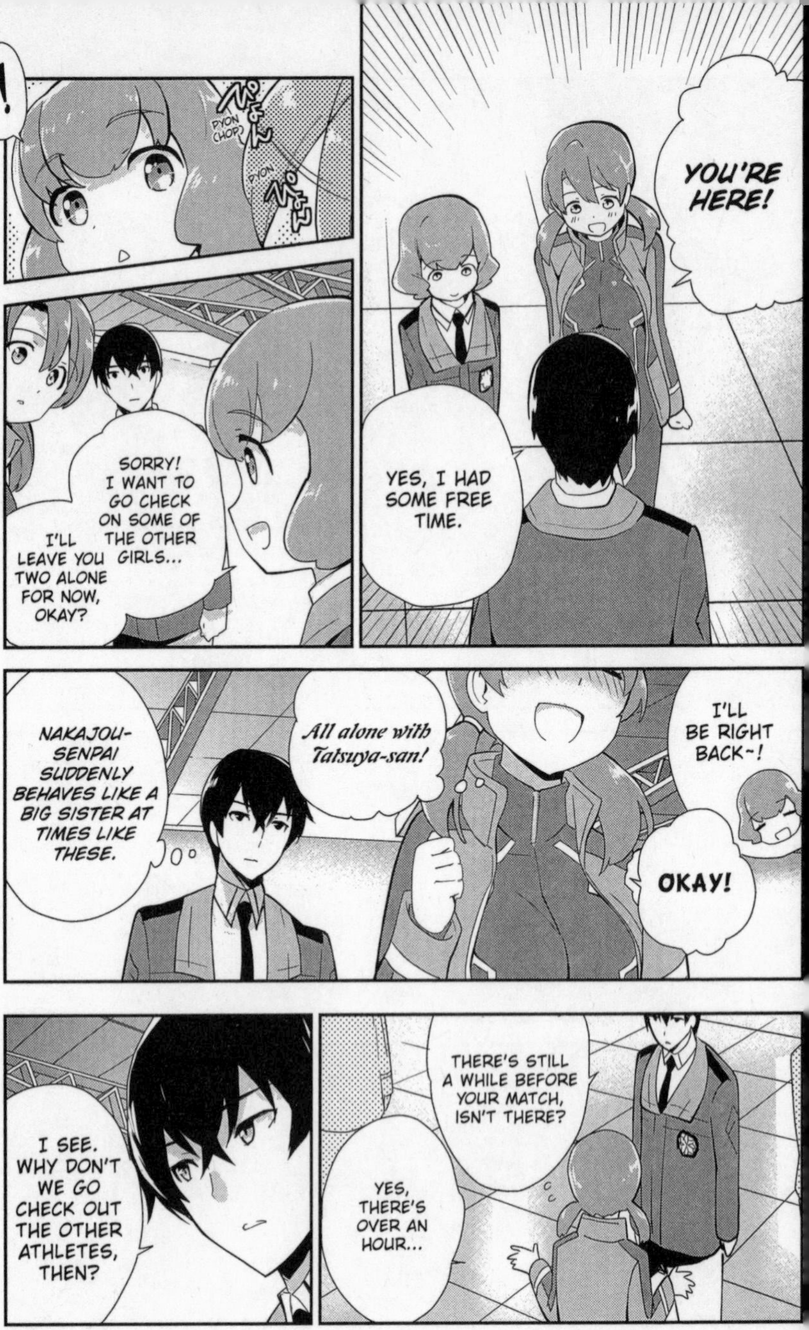
YOU'RE HERE!
YES, I HAD SOME FREE TIME.
!
ぴょん
PYON (HOP)
ぴょん
PYON
SORRY! I WANT TO GO CHECK ON SOME OF THE OTHER GIRLS...
I'LL LEAVE YOU TWO ALONE FOR NOW, OKAY?
I'LL BE RIGHT BACK~!
OKAY!
*All alone with Tatsuya-san!*
*NAKAJOU-SENPAI SUDDENLY BEHAVES LIKE A BIG SISTER AT TIMES LIKE THESE.*
THERE'S STILL A WHILE BEFORE YOUR MATCH, ISN'T THERE?
YES, THERE'S OVER AN HOUR...
I SEE. WHY DON'T WE GO CHECK OUT THE OTHER ATHLETES, THEN?

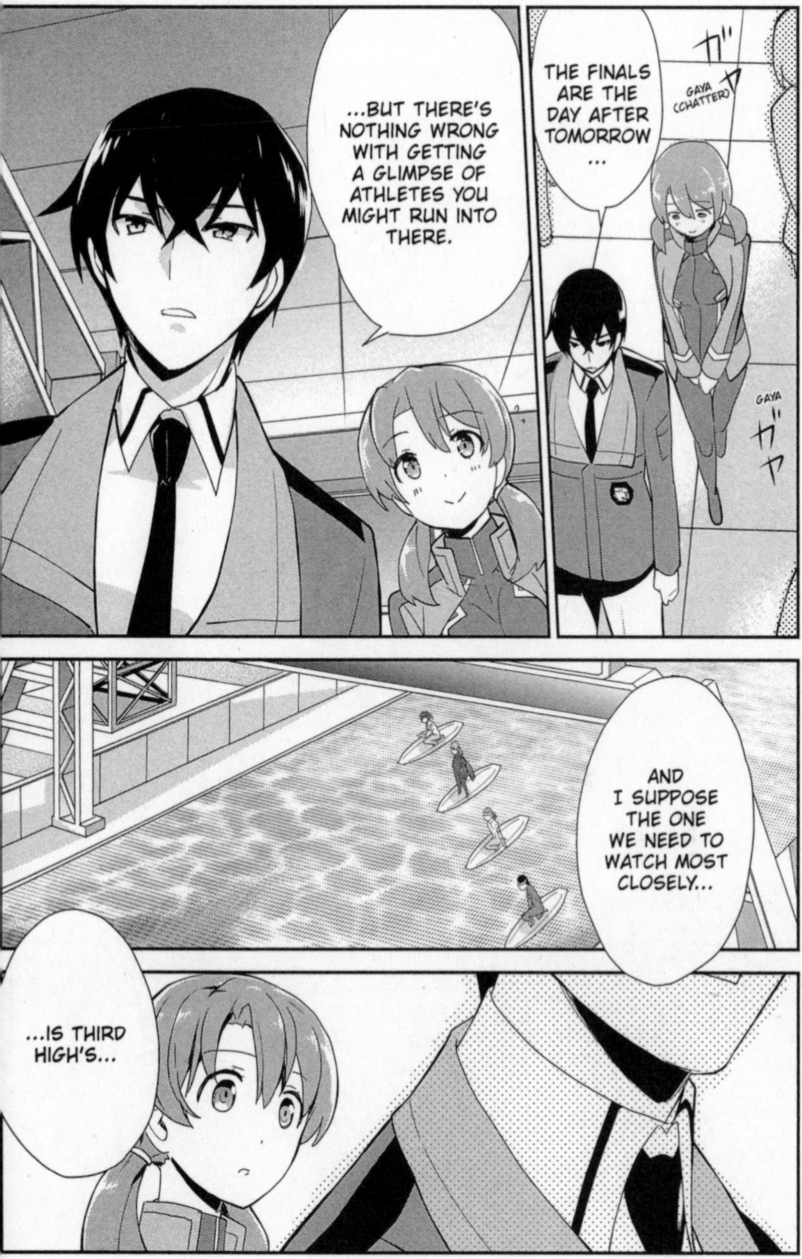
THE FINALS ARE THE DAY AFTER TOMORROW ...
ガヤ
GAYA (CHATTER)
GAYA
ガヤ
...BUT THERE'S NOTHING WRONG WITH GETTING A GLIMPSE OF ATHLETES YOU MIGHT RUN INTO THERE.
AND I SUPPOSE THE ONE WE NEED TO WATCH MOST CLOSELY...
...IS THIRD HIGH'S...

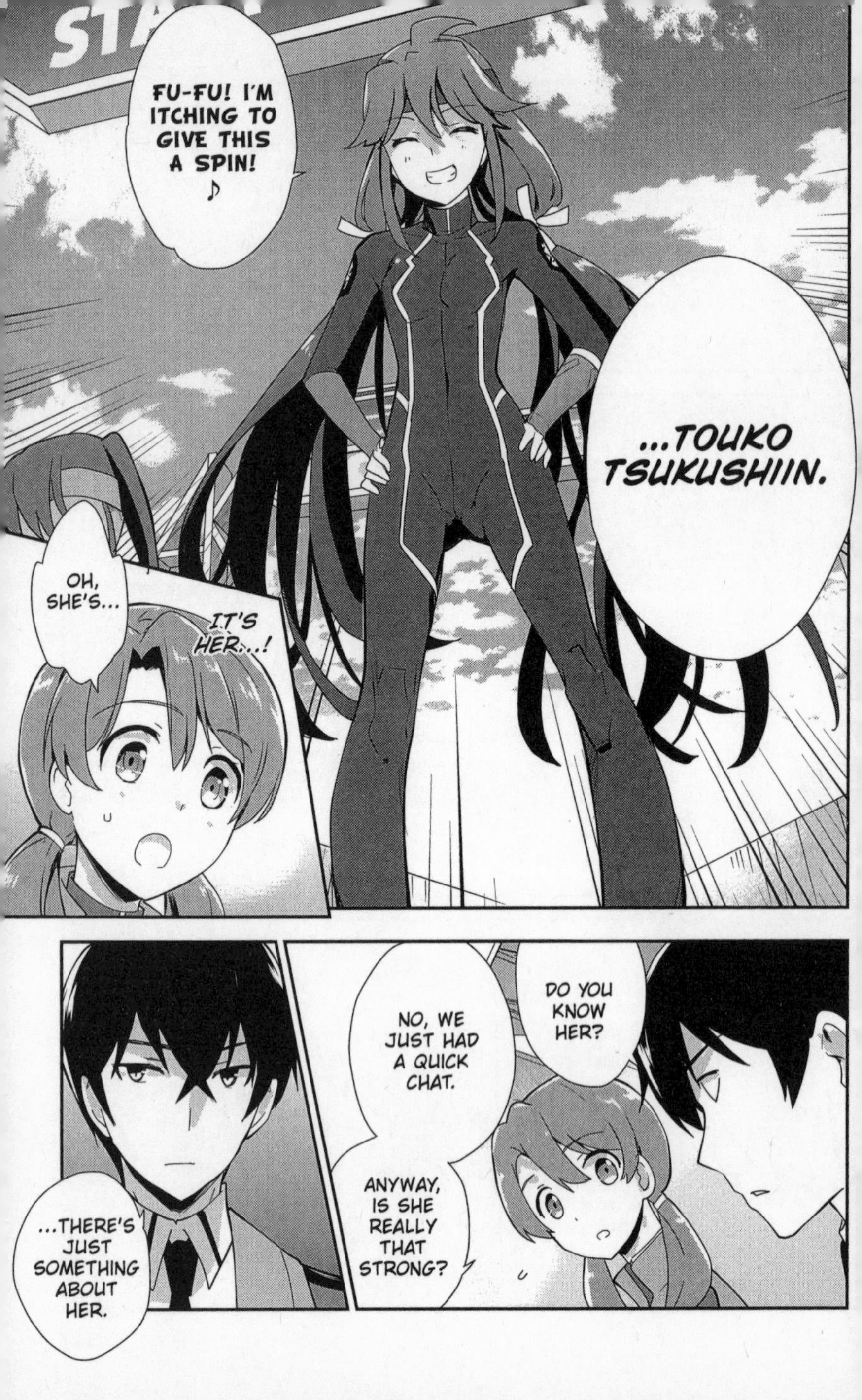
FU-FU! I'M ITCHING TO GIVE THIS A SPIN! ♪
...TOUKO TSUKUSHIIN.
OH, SHE'S...
IT'S HER...!
DO YOU KNOW HER?
NO, WE JUST HAD A QUICK CHAT.
ANYWAY, IS SHE REALLY THAT STRONG?
...THERE'S JUST SOMETHING ABOUT HER.

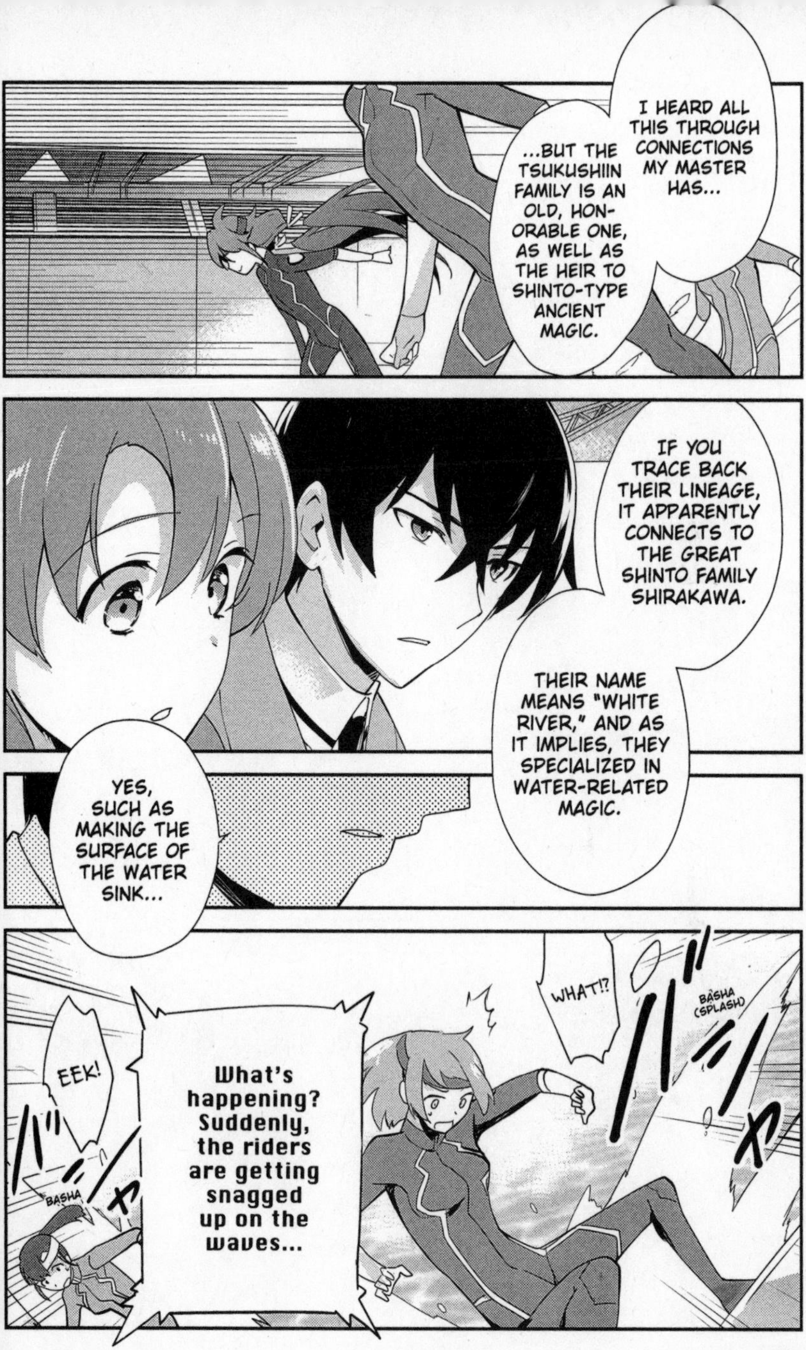
I HEARD ALL THIS THROUGH CONNECTIONS MY MASTER HAS...
...BUT THE TSUKUSHIIN FAMILY IS AN OLD, HON-ORABLE ONE, AS WELL AS THE HEIR TO SHINTO-TYPE ANCIENT MAGIC.
IF YOU TRACE BACK THEIR LINEAGE, IT APPARENTLY CONNECTS TO THE GREAT SHINTO FAMILY SHIRAKAWA.
THEIR NAME MEANS "WHITE RIVER," AND AS IT IMPLIES, THEY SPECIALIZED IN WATER-RELATED MAGIC.
YES, SUCH AS MAKING THE SURFACE OF THE WATER SINK...
WHAT!?
BASHA (SPLASH)
What's happening? Suddenly, the riders are getting snagged up on the waves...
EEK!
BASHA

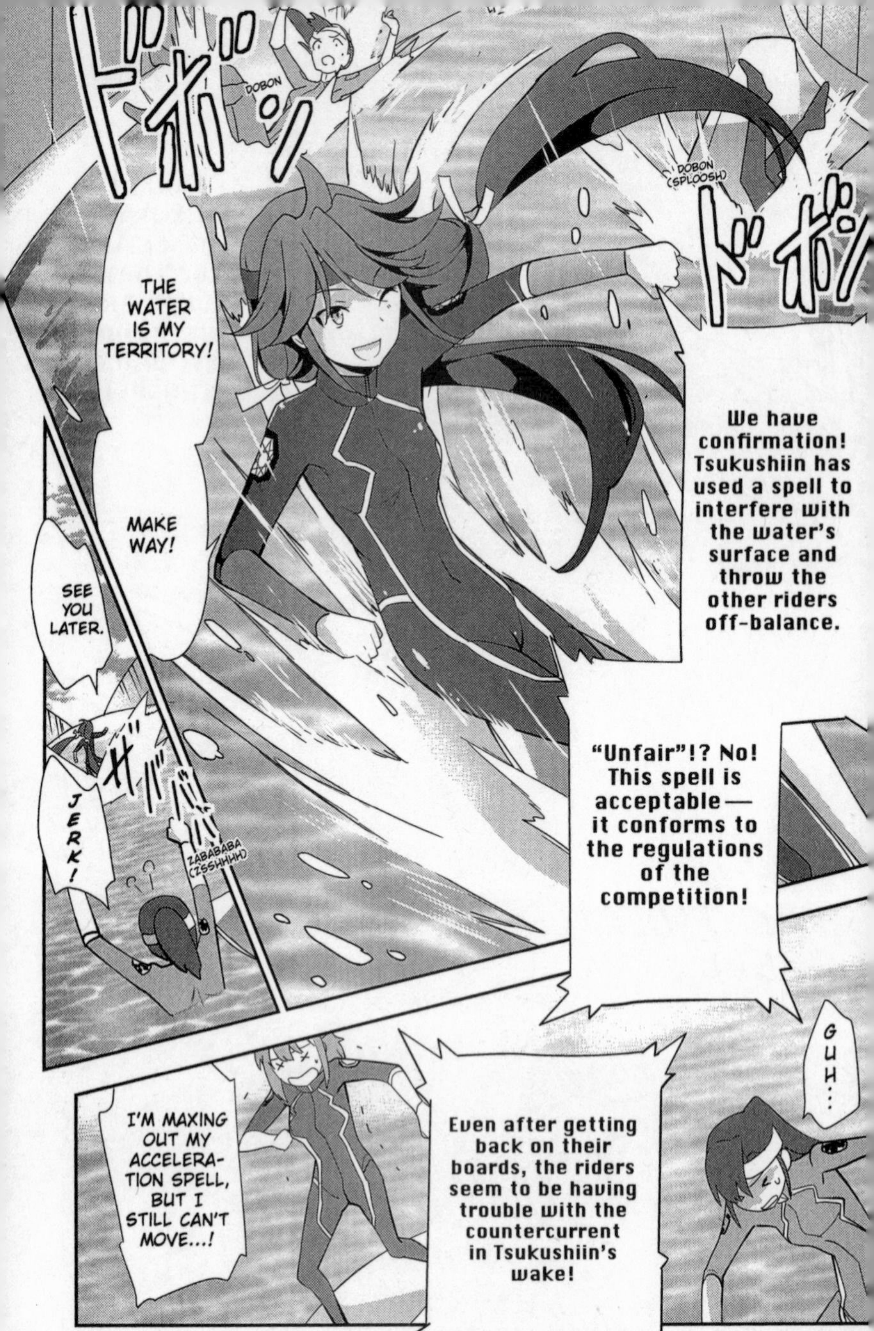
ドボン
DOBON (SPLOOSH)
ドボン
DOBON
THE WATER IS MY TERRITORY!
MAKE WAY!
We have confirmation! Tsukushiin has used a spell to interfere with the water's surface and throw the other riders off-balance.
SEE YOU LATER.
ザババ
ZABABABA (ZSSHHHH)
JERK!
"Unfair"!? No! This spell is acceptable— it conforms to the regulations of the competition!
GUH...
Even after getting back on their boards, the riders seem to be having trouble with the countercurrent in Tsukushiin's wake!
I'M MAXING OUT MY ACCELERATION SPELL, BUT I STILL CAN'T MOVE...!

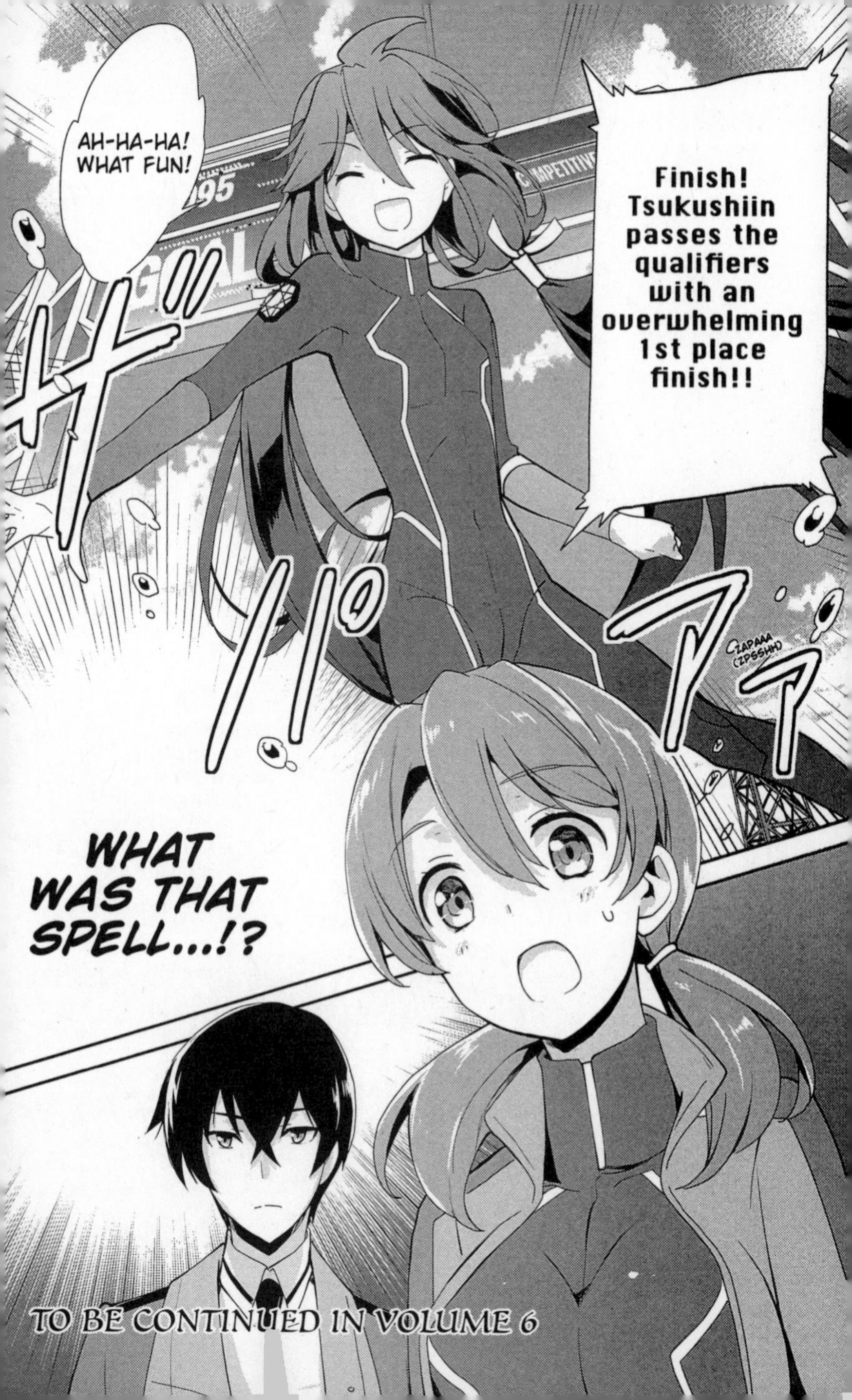
Finish! Tsukushiin passes the qualifiers with an overwhelming 1st place finish!!
AH-HA-HA! WHAT FUN!
GOAL
ZAPAAA (ZPSSHH)
WHAT WAS THAT SPELL...!?
TO BE CONTINUED IN VOLUME 6

THE
HONOR
STUDENT
AT
MAGIC HIGH
SCHOOL

### Activation sequence
The blueprints for magic and the programs used to construct it. Activation sequence data is stored in a compressed format in C.A.D.s. Design waves are sent from the magician to the device, where they're converted into a signal according to the decompressed data and returned to the magician.

### Antinite
A military-grade commodity only produced in lands where ancient alpine civilizations prospered, such as part of the Aztec Empire and the Mayan countries and regions. Extremely valuable due to its limited production quantity and impossible for civilians to acquire.

### Blanche
A national anti-magic political organization with the objective of uprooting discrimination in society based on magical ability. They hold protest activities based on the criticism of the fictional concept of the current system giving special political treatment to magicians. Behind the scenes, they engage in terrorism and other illegal activities and are strictly watched by the public peace agency.

### Blooms, Weeds
Terms displaying the gap between Course 1 students and Course 2 students in First High. The left breast of Course 1 student uniforms is emblazoned with an eight-petaled emblem, but it is absent from the Course 2 uniforms.

### Cabinets
Small, linear vehicles holding either two or four passengers and controlled by a central station. Used for commuting to work and school as a public transportation replacement for trains.

### Cardinal George
Shinkurou Kichijouji's nickname. Given to him for having discovered one of the Cardinal Codes, which only existed in theory beforehand, at the young age of thirteen.

### Cast jamming
A variety of typeless magic that obstructs magic sequences from exerting influence on Eidos. It weakens the process by which magic sequences affect Eidos by scattering large amounts of meaningless psionic waves.

### C.A.D. (Casting Assistant Device)
A device that simplifies the activation of magic. Magical programming is recorded inside. The main types are specialized and all-purpose.

### Crimson Prince
Masaki Ichijou's nickname. Given to him for having fought through a battle "drenched in the blood of enemy and ally alike" during the Sado Invasion of 2092 as a volunteer soldier on the defensive line at the young age of thirteen.

### Égalité
A branch organization of Blanche. They take in young people who hate politics, so they don't reveal that they're directly related to Blanche.

### Eidos (Individual information body)
Originally a term from Greek philosophy. In modern magic, Eidos are the bodies of information that accompany phenomena. They record the existence of those phenomena on the world, so they can also be called the footprints that phenomena leave on the world. The definition of "magic" in modern magic refers to the technology which modifies these phenomena by modifying Eidos.

### Four Leaves Technology (F.L.T.)
A domestic C.A.D. manufacturer. Originally famous for its magic engineering products, rather than finished C.A.D.s, but with the development of its Silver line of models, its fame skyrocketed as a C.A.D. manufacturer.

### Idea (Information body dimension)
Pronounced "ee-dee-ah." Originally a term from Greek philosophy. In modern magic, "Idea" refers to the platform on which Eidos are recorded. Magic's primary form is a technology wherein a magic sequence is output onto this platform, thus rewriting the Eidos recorded within.

### ◉ Loopcast system
Activation sequences made so that a magician can continually execute a spell as many times as their calculation capacity will permit. Normally, one must re-expand activation sequences from the C.A.D. every time one executes the same spell, but the loopcast system makes it possible by automatically duplicating the activation sequence's final state in the magician's magic calculation region.

### ◉ Magician
An abbreviation of "magical technician," referring to anyone with the skill to use magic at a practical level.

### ◉ Magic Association of Japan
A social group of Japanese magicians based in Kyoto. The Kantou branch location is established within Yokohama Bay Hills Tower.

### ◉ Magic calculation region
A mental region for the construction of magic sequences. The substance, so to speak, of magical talent. It exists in a magician's unconscious, and even if a magician is normally aware of using his or her magic calculation region, he or she cannot be aware of the processes being conducted within. The magic calculation region can be called a "black box" for the magician himself.

### ◉ Magic engineer
Refers to engineers who design, develop, and maintain apparatuses that assist, amplify, and strengthen magic. Their reputation in society is slightly worse than that of magicians. However, magic engineers are indispensable for tuning the C.A.D.s, indispensable tools for magicians, so in the industrial world, they're in higher demand than normal magicians. A first-rate magic engineer's earnings surpass even that of first-rate magicians.

### ◉ Magic high school
The nickname for the high schools affiliated with the National Magic University. There are nine established throughout the country. Of them, the first through the third have two hundred students per grade and use the Course 1/Course 2 system.

### ◉ Magic sequence
An information body for the purpose of temporarily altering information attached to phenomena. They are constructed from the Psions possessed by magicians.

### ◉ Nine School Competition
An abbreviation of "National Magic High School Goodwill Magic Competition Tournament." Magic high school students across the country, from First through Ninth High, are gathered to compete with their schools in fierce magic showdowns. There are six events: Speed Shooting, Cloudball, Battle Board, Ice Pillars Break, Mirage Bat, and Monolith Code.

### ◉ Psions
Non-physical particles belonging to the dimension of psychic phenomena. Psions are elements that record information on consciousness and thought products. Eidos—the theoretical basis for modern magic—as well as activation sequences and magic sequences—supporting its main framework—are all bodies of information constructed from Psions. Also referred to as "thought particles."

### ◉ Pushions
Non-physical particles belonging to the dimension of psychic phenomena. Their existence has been proven, but their true form and functions have yet to be elucidated. Magicians are generally only able to "feel" the pushions being activated through magic. Also referred to as "spirit particles."

### ◉ The Ten Master Clans
The strongest group of magicians in Japan. Ten families from a list of twenty-eight are chosen during the Ten Master Clans Selection Conference that happens every four years and are named as the Ten Master Clans. The twenty-eight families are Ichijou, Ichinokura, Isshiki, Futatsugi, Nikaidou, Nihei, Mitsuya, Mikazuki, Yotsuba, Itsuwa, Gotou, Itsumi, Mutsuzuka, Rokkaku, Rokugou, Roppongi, Saegusa, Shippou, Tanabata, Nanase, Yatsushiro, Hassaku, Hachiman, Kudou, Kuki, Kuzumi, Juumonji, and Tooyama.

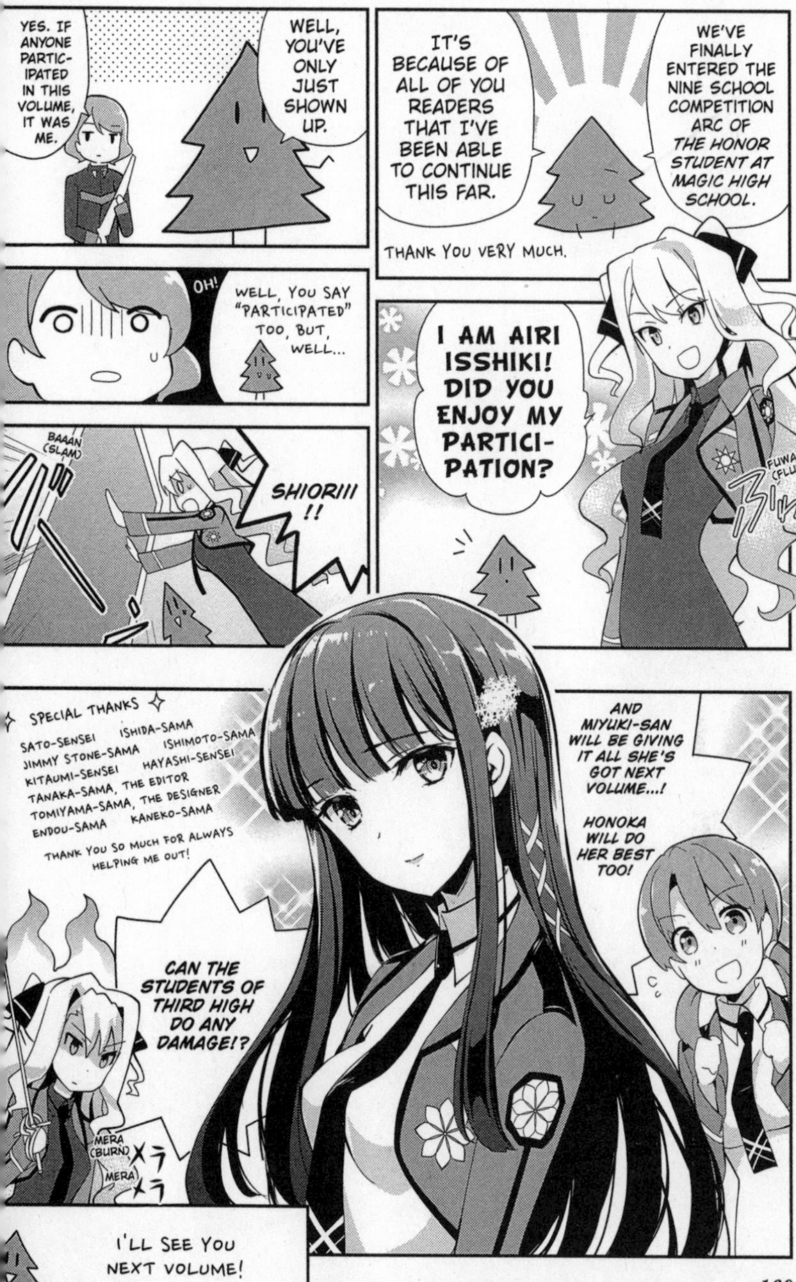
WE'VE FINALLY ENTERED THE NINE SCHOOL COMPETITION ARC OF *THE HONOR STUDENT AT MAGIC HIGH SCHOOL.*
IT'S BECAUSE OF ALL OF YOU READERS THAT I'VE BEEN ABLE TO CONTINUE THIS FAR.
THANK YOU VERY MUCH.
WELL, YOU'VE ONLY JUST SHOWN UP.
YES. IF ANYONE PARTICIPATED IN THIS VOLUME, IT WAS ME.
I AM AIRI ISSHIKI! DID YOU ENJOY MY PARTICIPATION?
FUWASA (FLUFF)
OH!
WELL, YOU SAY "PARTICIPATED" TOO, BUT, WELL...
BAAAN (SLAM)
SHIORIII!!
AND MIYUKI-SAN WILL BE GIVING IT ALL SHE'S GOT NEXT VOLUME...!
HONOKA WILL DO HER BEST TOO!
SPECIAL THANKS
SATO-SENSEI ISHIDA-SAMA
JIMMY STONE-SAMA ISHIMOTO-SAMA
KITAUMI-SENSEI HAYASHI-SENSEI
TANAKA-SAMA, THE EDITOR
TOMIYAMA-SAMA, THE DESIGNER
ENDOU-SAMA KANEKO-SAMA
THANK YOU SO MUCH FOR ALWAYS HELPING ME OUT!
CAN THE STUDENTS OF THIRD HIGH DO ANY DAMAGE!?
MERA (BURN) MERA
I'LL SEE YOU NEXT VOLUME!

# Discover the other side of Magic High School—read the light novel!

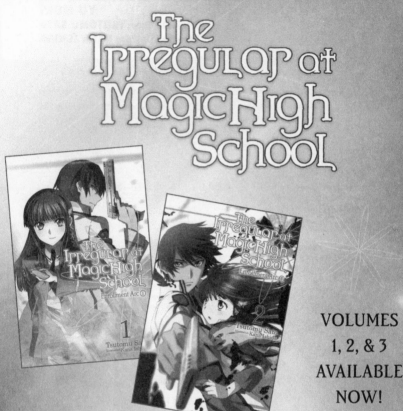

The Irregular at Magic High School

**VOLUMES 1, 2, & 3 AVAILABLE NOW!**

Explore the world from Tatsuya's perspective as he and Miyuki navigate the perils of First High and more! Read about adventures only hinted at in *The Honor Student at Magic High School*, and learn more about all your favorite characters. This is the original story that spawned a franchise!

# THE HONOR ST[
# AT MAGIC HIGH

**Translation: Andrew Prowse**
**Lettering: Phil Christie**

MAHOUKA KOUKOU NO YUUTOUSEI Volume 5
© TSUTOMU SATO / YU MORI 2015
All rights reserved.
Edited by ASCII MEDIA WORKS
First published in Japan in 2015 by KADOKAWA CORPORATION, Tokyo.
English translation rights arranged with KADOKAWA CORPORATION, Tokyo,
through Tuttle-Mori Agency, Inc., Tokyo.

English translation © 2016 by Yen Press, LLC

Yen Press
1290 Avenue of the Americas
New York, NY 10104

Visit us at yenpress.com
facebook.com/yenpress
twitter.com/yenpress
yenpress.tumblr.com
instagram.com/yenpress

First Yen Press Edition: December 2016

Yen Press is an imprint of Yen Press, LLC.
The Yen Press name and logo are trademarks of Yen Press, LLC.

Library of Congress Control Number: 2016932699

ISBNs: 978-0-316-39914-2 (paperback)
       978-0-316-46616-5 (ebook)

10 9 8 7 6 5 4 3 2 1

BVG

Printed in the United States of America